*Foreword by* **Morton T. Kelsey**

# MYTHS
## gods, heroes, and saviors
*Leonard J. Biallas*

Lincoln Christian College

TWENTY-THIRD PUBLICATIONS
**Mystic, Connecticut**

Twenty-Third Publications
P.O. Box 180
Mystic, CT 06355
(203) 536-2611

Library of Congress Catalog Card Number 85-52140
ISBN 0-89622-290-X

Cover photo by Jeff Brass
Cover design by Kathy Michalove
Edited and designed by Andrea Star

Bookstore

6.00

# FOREWORD ———————————————

Most people are fascinated by the world beyond, the world
of meaning, transformation, and religious experience. Myths
give us clues about how we can relate to that world and live in
relationship with our total meaning and destiny. Like our
dreams, they nudge us toward wholeness. Indeed, myths are the
universal dreams of humankind.

Although many books have been written about mythology,
this one is unique in many ways. It is practical and engages us
at once. The author does not study myth for its own sake, but
shows us how the narrative in myths aid us on our journey
through life. It is the only study of mythology I know that takes
up the full cycle of myths: from the creation of the universe to
its final consummation and from the beginning of the human
life cycle to life beyond death.

Leonard Biallas speaks from a Christian perspective, and
yet he uses vast amounts of cross-cultural data to illuminate each
aspect of mythology. The feminine element in mythology is often
neglected by male writers, but this author wonderfully balances
the masculine and feminine elements. He presents so many different types of myths, all of them congenial to the many varieties
of religious temperament.

The book is clearly and simply written, and it presents the
depth and mystery of myth and human life. The author provides excellent material for stimulating new insights into the
Christian drama as well as a true vision of the nature of the
human journey. The material presented will be fascinating to
anyone interested in mythology, including serious students of

*iii*

9 Oct. 86

73605

the subject. It will also be a valuable book for study groups in churches and elsewhere. For teachers wishing to introduce students to the significant issues of life, Professor Biallas offers a gold mine of material that can be used in high schools and colleges. The stimulating questions and quotations at the end of each chapter are provocative, searching, and valuable in themselves.

*Myths: Gods, Heroes, and Saviors* is skillfully written. By leading us through the tragedies and victories of our human journey, the author shows us how myths can help us come to our goal of wholeness on the inner journey. At the same time he shows how most religious ritual reenacts the transforming moments of myth and helps people uncomfortable with the inner way to experience and participate in the renewing power of these stories of the soul. The author also shows that changes take place in our outer lives when we assimilate great myths. These changes can even lead to social transformation as well as personal renewal.

Several years ago my wife and I visited Bali. What struck us most was the cohesiveness and the sense of meaning and peace that pervaded the lives of the people there. These people were living out the magnificent myth of the *Ramayana*. If we of the West were to participate in the same way in our Christian story, we might experience the same transforming power. This book offers many valuable suggestions and insights from other religious traditions on the many ways we might live out the power of the Christian cosmic drama. In addition, mythological narratives do not separate us from other people as so many theological statements do. Understanding our religious mythology makes possible real religious tolerance.

What impresses me most about this book is that it gives us practical guidelines on life's journey from birth through evil and death to eternity and resurrected life. I have known the author well for many years and this book is an authentic description of his own journey as well as a profound guide to the human venture.

Morton Kelsey
Gualala, California
Author of *Myth, History, and Faith*

# PREFACE

Myths are stories from cultures and religious traditions that help us become aware of our true selves. They are the larger story of humankind, bringing enrichment, excitement, and meaning to our individual lives. Expressing the fears and hopes that reverberate within a tradition's collective spirit, they create a world in which persons can live and feel comfortable. They help us comprehend our human limitations and point to the sense of mystery that is conveyed only in religion.

One purpose in writing this book is to help us become aware of the gods, heroes, and saviors in the various religious traditions. These gods, heroes, and saviors are at the very core of our selves. We do not define them; they define us. They are not so much manifested in our behavior as they are the impulse, the motivation, and the energy that links us to the whole web of life. By discovering them within us and consenting to them, we give substance to our own potential divinity.

Because I am convinced that all world religions share a common essence or common source in the human psyche, I also hope to provide a different context in which Christians can understand their own religion and bring a deeper integrity and fresh commitment to their own faith. If we can penetrate into the depths of other religions through their stories rather than through theological discussions, we can give fresh cogency to our own traditions and make them lively in thought, devotion, and action. If we can bring these other religions into a more significant place and permanent role in our lives, we can better understand and appropriate our own mythic symbols.

*v*

This book is for persons of all ages and lifestyles. I hope that by being introduced to a wide range of myths, we will gain an appreciation of the timeliness, as well as the timelessness, of the mythological frame of mind. I hope that by becoming familiar with the myths we will recognize our own story and find some novel approaches to our existential problems. Perhaps by studying the myths and recognizing that they illustrate a variety of patterns of response to perennial human situations, we will allow transformations to occur in our lives. Perhaps a comparison of various stories around the same central theme will help illuminate the breadth, depth, and complexity of human nature and stimulate our sense of mystery. I hope that the study of myths will be liberating, helping us to go beyond the confines of our personality, our family, and our culture to the larger experience of the self in communion with the universe.

I want to show that myths can help us grow into wholeness, where each small self is gradually replaced by a larger self engrossed in religion's mysteries. This larger self is the intuitively known spiritual center of each one's personality. It is the network of our ever-expanding awareness and development of the gods, heroes, and saviors inside of us in relation to the cosmos outside of us. By retelling the myths and heeding their deeper symbols, we can experience the entire gamut of human experience, the many routes to wholeness and personal fulfillment. Myths help us through the personal crises that accompany the process of religious maturity. Though this process is unending, as long as we are bound in space and time, myths provide us the occasion to rejoice here and now in our being and our becoming by enabling us to realize our mysterious potential and anticipate our ultimate reunion with Absolute Reality.

Myths are so powerful that their meaning changes in every crystallization and any method of interpretation we utilize will eventually break down. We can never fully understand these myths in their original context. We have trouble understanding people in our own family; what possible chance do we have then of understanding someone from, say, the 5th century B.C.? For these reasons, my approach to myths is not that of the expert; in fact, it is quite casual. I don't intend to provide any substantive new data. I seek rather to find some new and potentially illuminating slants and insights into our selves through the comparison and juxtaposition of myths. Rather than professing to be a master of some specialist approach to myth, perhaps that of a psychologist, an ethnologist, or a comparative religionist, I prefer to draw insights from different specialists to broaden our understanding of the myths and enrich our perceptions of our selves.

Perhaps a poetic sensitivity or adequate knowledge of the original languages of the many myths in the following chapters would render them even more accessible. These myths come from around the world, however, so I have to rely on translations by others. Rather than worry about a particular translation for each myth, for all translation involves interpretation, I have decided to paraphrase the texts and incorporate various readings when they are significant. Even in translation there are themes in Homer, in Gilgamesh, and in Dante, for example, that can move us greatly. Rather than bringing us to the myths (which would demand that I provide a broad context and exhaustive literary criticism), I want to bring the myths to us (to challenge us to determine their relevancy in our everyday lives).

The various religious myths and classical stories bear a meaning and a permanence that resist definitive interpretation. While it would be cultural narcissism to impose our own problems on the myths of other religious traditions or to abstract them out of their own significance, they can still provide illumination as we relate them to the problems of our own life situations, our information systems, and our value systems. These stories may deal with mystery, but they are also a revelation of the great secrets about the gods, heroes, and saviors that are at the core of our religious selves.

Gods, heroes, and saviors neatly divide the book into three parts. The distinction between them is convenient, not steadfast. Indeed, the same mythical figures may pop up in all three parts, variously as gods, heroes, or saviors, depending on whether they give insight into our divine characteristics and potential, our quest for the full life, or our struggle with the mysteries of evil and death. The structure of the book also reflects our human life cycle: the gods figure most prominently in stories about our past; the heroes in stories about our present task; and the saviors in stories about our future dilemmas.

The first two chapters are introductory and perhaps a bit more abstract than the rest of the book. Chapter One describes how myths can help our self-development and our awareness of our religious selves. We then study (Chapter Two) some possible interpretations of the nature and functions of myth within a religious context, showing how they can bring out the meaning and values of human existence. We focus on the elements of the creation process (Chapter Three) and consider various gods and goddesses — P'an Ku, Nu-kua, Yahweh, and many others — in the context of stories of the formation of the world and of the first humans. We look at many expressions of the Absolute Reality. This Absolute Reality (or God, or Allah, or Supreme Being) is one way of naming that human experience of the numinous, that is, the fascinating, awesome, and mysterious dimension of existence.

Chapter Four illuminates the basic aspects of the unfortunate, yet inevitable, separation of humans from the Absolute Reality. The story of Adam and Eve sets the scene for considering the qualities of what it means to be human. Tricksters, culture heroes, and clowns (Chapter Five) are expressions of human dissatisfaction with their limitations. Maui and Prometheus, for example, are not only quasi-divine helpers in the process of creation, but they provide us with a spirit of play in our all-too-serious world.

Chapter Six serves as a hinge. While still dealing with beginnings, it directs our attention away from the cosmos to the world of heroes. We look at the birth and early childhood of heroes, especially Gotama the Buddha, and we discover how their miraculous births and early confrontations with monsters and evil forces point to their future heroic and savior roles. Prior to his adult task, the hero withdraws for meditation in the vision quest (Chapter Seven). This withdrawal for new power involves an interior struggle, as we see in Jesus' temptations from the devil. The withdrawal is also mirrored in many rites of passage, as well as other rituals such as pilgrimages and the Christian Lent. The pattern of the heroic quest — crisis, struggle, and return — is traced (Chapter Eight) through the adventures of Rama and Odysseus and through Parsifal's search for the Holy Grail. In their long struggles and their desire to provide a boon for their community, they provide models for the life-long career of every adult. Because the heroic quest always seems to be male-oriented, we consider it (Chapter Nine) from another angle. The love story of Psyche and Eros frames our inquiry into the gentle side of heroes and provides the background for a discussion of another task of adulthood, growing from infatuation to love.

In Chapter Ten we begin the final section of the book, on the savior role of the heroes. Ahura Mazda's struggle with Ahriman, the Prince of Darkness, is the starting point for discussions of the mystery of evil, various theodicies (ways of trying to explain why there is evil in the world) and various soteriologies (ways of overcoming evil). Death is the mystery that the saviors confront in Chapter Eleven. Myths of death often describe the quest for immortality (Gilgamesh), the origin of death, the symbolization of eternal death (hell), and also point to ways of overcoming death. The last set of myths (Chapter Twelve) further elaborates the savior's eschatological role in helping us participate in heaven and eternal life. Egyptian and Greek mystery religions hold out hope of immortality, and their versions of the afterlife become embellished in other religions, especially in the apocalyptic Jerusalem and the Paradise of Dante. In the apotheoses of Jesus and Gotama, where they are taken outside the cycle of life and given permanent status of divinity, we find expression of the final goal of the full religious self.

In each chapter we examine one particular myth in detail. We then introduce and analyze variations on that myth's central focus as they appear in other religious traditions. When appropriate and meaningful, we also briefly study rituals which dramatize this central focus. The comments on the myth's possible applications for our religious selves and for the story of our own lives will obviously strike people quite differently. I hope everyone will be able to internalize some of the myth's themes and thus act in a more holistic fashion. Though it may send people in rockets to the moon, our modern world still has much to distill from the stories and concepts of religious traditions that were old before the harnessing of the horse. It is my hope that, after we have studied the myths and appropriated their heritage, we can return to our familiar world, thrilled with the possibilities both manifest and latent within ourselves, with a clearer vision of the human dignity and divine possibilities inherent in each of us.

# CONTENTS

# CHAPTER ONE

# MYTH AND SELF-AWARENESS

Each of us is in continual process. We gradually grow aware of our individuality as we absorb and relate to our ongoing experiences. If we can learn to define ourselves by our imaginative perception and active relationship to the possible — what might be — we open ourselves to a deeper vision of humanity, to something more profound than our own personal notions of our selves. The self is not only what we have or do, but also what we want to be and how we absorb what comes to us, what happens to us.

For those with inquiring minds, the fun and challenge of living, in part at least, is to learn more about who we are and who we can become to overcome the ignorance that has a way of limiting our lives. For many, there are other goals beyond learning skills that will lead to financial security. One of them is how to find and define the self in human terms in such a way that they can enjoy life, even if they don't make much money. Such inquisitive people want to attain a new level of consciousness, to learn insights about the self each of us carries within. They want to disentangle themselves from the masks (of age, sex, occupation) that are not essential for who they are. They want to learn about the real self, not the mere externals, not the role playing many mistake for their true identity. They ask, "What must I be about as I move through life and life moves through me?"

Asking such a question is part of what it means to become fully human, a task that comes with our very breath. They want to learn how to evoke their potential, to develop a unique self in relation to their own experiences, values, and critical judgments, a self not limited to group affiliations or social expectations. Trying to explore their orientations, articulating their own beliefs, reflecting about life in relation to the world, they are both discovering and determining their selves in a quest that never ends.

Becoming our full selves is a lifelong task that calls upon us not to avoid life's difficulties and dangers, but to perceive the meaning in the pattern of events that forms our lives. The supreme achievement of the self is to find an insight that connects together the events, dreams, and relationships that make up our existence. Such an insight cuts through the crust of externals and reveals the underlying unity and inseparability of our individual selves and the universe. It gets us away from the assumption that our roles are our true self and that each of us is free, independent, and totally different from everyone else.

Attaining this insight is never totally completed, never fully reached, because our human potential is too rich and the demands of life upon us are constantly changing and calling forth new responses. We are continually learning to synthesize both our conscious and unconscious personalities, to relate events in everyday life to the core of our being. Still, what it means to be whole seems to be known at the center of our selves, and from this core the process of becoming individuals is begun. The quest for wholeness is thrust upon us by this force within us. In this perspective, wholeness is not so much an ideal that cannot be fully realized; rather, wholeness is being aware of and consenting to the very process of attempting to achieve it.

The quest to find the self is both exhilarating and painful. How are we to go about it? By listening to the stories of other religions, we both invent and discover our own selves. We create our own story. Paying attention to the stories of the religious traditions, we can more easily identify what we have in common with other selves, and also find those elements that are unique to our selves. We live our story within the context of a larger story, which dynamically impels us to become aware of our selves and to act on them. We sense that our own inner self and meaning are somehow connected with the beginning and end of the story of the earth and the universe.

But how do we come to know and share in this larger story? We have to recognize that we live by a constellation of myths which, though they remain largely unconscious, limit our perceptions about hard reality. Only then can we open our selves to and appropriate the larger story of humankind as told through the world's religions.

## The Cultural Self

First of all, we have to become aware of our own myths and their limitations. We all need a cognitive touchstone to provide us with an orientation, with a believable and satisfying map of our lives. All humans require moorings in order to make sense out of things, but because our minds are often unreflective, we are often not aware that they are just moorings. Thus, for example, as North Americans we live unquestioningly within a horizon of our North American culture's images, stories, rituals, and symbols. We do not question the fundamental structures of understanding that our myths provide, even though they are essentially arbitrary. Our attitudes toward reality are conveyed by our parents, our education, our laws, even by our entertainment. In a society as diverse and rapidly changing as ours, attitudes from different and occasionally conflicting myths are promulgated simultaneously. But, even so, they are accepted without question. Until we learn to understand the eyes with which we look at the world and recognize that our perceptions and experiences are culturally bound, we are, in effect, prisoners of our own tradition. Only by recognizing these limitations can we fruitfully begin to explore the elements of the myths of other cultures and religious traditions that will allow us to celebrate the full range of human life.

Before we can come into contact with the core of our larger self, we have to peel back the layers of the American myth. What are the commonly held perceptions and expectations that make people distinctly American? Perhaps its cornerstore is the "scientific mentality," that legacy from the Enlightenment that considers science and technology as the prime indicators of a society's wisdom. In this world view, the machine becomes an instrument of conquest. It determines our work, our happiness, our progress. It determines what is advancement (what is intelligent, rational, and sophisticated) and what is regression (what is primitive, irrational, and innocent). Science and technology are so pervasive and interwoven into our sense of meaning and existence that it rarely occurs to us that such a standard of judgment may not be universal, and that other, non-technological cultures may be more concerned with the goals of life than about the means to them.

Another constellation of images that controls the impulses and lifestyle patterns of Americans are expounded regularly in Fourth of July celebrations, Memorial Day speeches, and presidential inaugural addresses. Resting on the ideals of the Revolution and on emancipation from slavery, freedom is another part of the code or grammar by which Americans orient themselves. Freedom, understood in a distinctively American way, includes the absence of social restraints, absence from the invisible shackles of social conformity and oppressive institutions. Its heroes are Huck Finn rafting down the Mississippi and Thoreau trodding a path to Walden Pond. To be free is to be footloose in a pathless wilderness, unbounded by geography or history, utterly unconstrained by social bonds, looking for the way away from confinement. Its expression today is in seeing the wilderness as a place to escape to, whether as a second home, or on weekends. Authenticity and self-realization are achieved outside of or against society, not through it. Like Horatio Alger, persons are judged on their abilities and hard work.

Freedom also includes another component: the pursuit of unrestrained competition in the business enterprise. Where else but in America can we find four gasoline stations on the same corner: two in use, one boarded up and for sale, the other not yet ready for business. Human life is organized around the laws of supply and demand in the market place; competition makes the world go around.

Americans consider themselves a nation mighty in its youth (though one of the oldest democracies in the world), powerful in its purpose (in spite of the loss in Vietnam), with a manifest destiny to bring its scientific know-how and problem-solving abilities to other cultures. As Ahab pursued the monster, Moby Dick, America perceives itself on a messianic mission to struggle against the common enemies of humankind, such as tyranny, poverty, disease, war.

Americans value time. Time is measurable, quantitative, and like money, it can be saved or wasted. Americans are looking for instant gratification. They prepare instant coffee and take instant photos; they fix microwaved meals at home and frequent fast-food franchises when they go out. Push-button telephones and drive-up banks provide part of the status symbols that trigger desires and help define the good life. Americans are uncomfortable with silence. They don't have the discipline or endurance to wrap their minds around a thought; instead, they prefer to grab, snatch, and make stabs at ideas. They are happier dealing with statistics than with nuances, and exclude from wisdom anything that cannot be placed on a poster or bumper sticker and read at a glance. They think in seven-minute segments — the time in between TV commercials.

To admit that those perceptions and experiences are culturally bound is not to reject them. Rather, it is a way of recognizing that they are not the only possible ways to celebrate human life. It also opens us to the reality of other cultures, to the possibility that we can appropriate images and values that can enrich our own system.

This is true not only of our mythical-political system but also of our religious tradition. The commonly accepted religious assumptions are not questioned by the majority of those living within the system, Again this is not to belittle any religious traditions in America, but rather to acknowledge them for what they are: time-bound, space-bound attempts to bring meaning to their lives, attempts to answer the most basic questions of personal identity that seem to "work."

## The Spiralling Self

Once we become self-consciously aware of the boundaries of our conventionally held cultural (and religious) outlook, we can begin to appreciate the notion of an ever-expanding self. Conscious that our vision of meaning, coherence, and value is partial, provisional, and contradicted by the visions and claims of others, we can be open to new possibilities for the self. With growing intelligence and progressive freedom, we construct other than purely reactive ways of responding and interacting with others. The "I" is no longer synonymous with our bodies. We become wary of the "self." Which self? Today's? Yesterday's? The one a month from now? Gender, race, profession, nationality, age, and status all become relative as the "I" comes to think of itself as something essentially connected to larger realities. The understanding of the self becomes more complex. We begin to recognize that the myths of other cultures and religious traditions can help us determine and evaluate our perceptions and experiences of what is "real."

Becoming aware how thickly we are encrusted in our own myths helps us uncover our presuppositions, biases, limited awareness, and distortion. And then integrating insights from myths of other religious traditions helps us recognize and appropriate the divinity that we have, or are. Both of these processes are necessary for living the full human life. These processes also make change inevitable.

Giving up early dreams, ideals, or goals and taking on others is a continual process of dying and rising, of death and growth. But the process is not the same for all. Some people go through life in one dimension. There is no real excitement for them, and sometimes it is a burden just to get through the day. This is human life at its lowest. Others are aware of the rhythms of life and enter into them. Like the author of the biblical book Qoheleth, they recognize the patterns: a time to weep and a time to laugh, a time to embrace and a time to refrain from embracing, a time to love and a time to hate, a time for war and a time for peace. Life has its ups and downs, but still no central focus or sense of direction. Still others see a cyclic pattern in life with themselves at the center. There is more equilibrium as they experience the ups and downs, but life still seems, at times, to be a vicious circle. There is a certain resignation to the inevitability of it all.

A fourth group has a different perspective altogether. For them, the process of dying and rising has a sense of direction. Each up and down is integrated into a vision of life that is future oriented and increasingly human, rather than fixed and backward looking. The wheel of the self keeps getting bigger and bigger with each revolution. The self experiences both the equilibrium of a still point (the pull at the core) and the ups and downs, joys and sorrows (the pull of everyday life). For them, life is an open-ended spiral rather than a vicious circle. Their self is continually expanding, while always connected to the still point at their core.

This spiralling self dies and rises continually. The familial, economic, political, and religious myths that have thus far made us who we are and what we can be are found to be too small to encompass our experience. As we develop a critical intelligence and cultural sense, we become aware of the relativity of our perceptions and experiences; we perceive contradictions and discrepancies between the way we experience reality and the way others experience it. We bite the bullet and die to our smaller selves. This is difficult, for whatever we learn is not always what we would like it to be, at least from the viewpoint of our former narrower vision. But the spiral goes around and we grow. We take on a consciousness that is cathartic and enriching. We gradually rename reality and totally reorient our entire person to it. We say yes to the new reality, consent to the growth and change in our selves, and act on our new perceptions.

The spiralling self is never completed but always expanding, for there is always a dimension of possibility that awaits its further actualization. There will always be uncloseable gaps of experience, perspective, and emotional structure. If we are serious about growth, we will continually move from a naive acceptance of our own story, to a critical distance from it through questioning, and finally back to a recovery. This includes new insights and wider horizons for the self, which is never quite the same.

For growth to occur, the spiral journey must be undertaken. To refuse to launch out into disequilibrium is to go backwards on the spiral, not back to the still point at the core, but into a narrowing circle of debilitating prejudices. And once we have moved out, we must be careful to return. If we seek to avoid the return (by getting lost in our experiences, for example) we remain cut off from the center, the still point. To attempt to avoid the return, we make it impossible to use the insights we have gained, which may make us able to respond more wisely the next time.

There are spiral journeys daily and also throughout the major stages of life. Young children, upon reaching the age of reason, struggle away from a need-oriented life to move into a larger framework of their immediate family. Adolescents struggle to find a somewhat more stable sense of their selves which they will need later in order to give their selves totally to their love

and their work. Adulthood ordinarily includes growing in mature
intimacy with another person, a dying to one's solitary vision
and a growing into a mutual perspective on life. And in old age,
persons can let go of control, not letting their own agenda inter-
fere, not trying to fashion others in their self-image, but caring
so much for others that they try to guarantee their future, knowing it is a future that they won't share.

Each time the spiralling self repeats the process of dying
and rising, it returns to a larger self, which is always open
to new growth and new potential. There is a dying, because there
is a letting go, a brokenness, a collapse, a wrestling with the
unknown. The old self recognizes its limitations so that it can
break out of them. The old self dies as a precondition to a larger
self, and there is no new consciousness without pain and confusion. There is also a rising, an uplifting of human consciousness to the awareness of its true self, to a self in which compassion, love, and responsibility are paramount. This spiralling
process is a journey from darkness to life, from isolation and
alienation to association and communion. It is a freeing process,
helping the self to move away from its narrow identification with
its body and its ego, from relating to others in terms of its own
drives, from a false sense of separateness from the cosmos as
a whole.

The spiral process of dying and rising is the movement from
crisis to crisis resolution, from unity to variety, from consensus
to conflict, from continuity to change, and back again. It is the
sacrifice of the old and the opening up of the new. It is the taking on of a strength within us, and yet beyond us, a strength
that heals and then opens up new vulnerabilities. The ebb and
flow between healing and wounding, closing and opening, is an
acceptance of my self both as I know it and as it still remains
unknown. The process is a movement from consciousness to consent, that is, becoming aware of my potential and saying yes
to it, somehow related to my ability to transcend my self in relation to the world and to other people. It is the achievement of
a harmony within my self, combining the opposites — light and
dark, good and evil, pleasure and anxiety — into some kind of
higher unity. Opposites are not so much contradictory as complementary. Attraction and repulsion, reason and energy, love
and hate are not so much alternatives as alternations of the single
process of dying and rising.

## The Religious Self

The struggles involved in the spiralling self effect a transformation in consciousness that leads to many types of growth. This growth is intellectual, for we become aware of the human situation as it is in a world not of fantasy, not an escapist world, but a world where we experience both joys and sorrows, where we begin to see our self and our potential more clearly. This growth is also moral, for it helps us change our horizons from selfishness and self-satisfaction to awareness of social injustices and community values. It is psychological, for it makes us aware of those human attributes and qualities that we often fail to recognize and develop and occasionally seek to repress. Most of all, this growth is religious. The meaning of religious practices is manifested in giving up attachment to personal limitations, idiosyncracies, hopes, and fears, and no longer resisting the self-annihilation that is a prerequisite to the realization of one's potential.

When the spiralling self recognizes that its core is both immanent (within the self) and transcendent (outside the self), it is becoming a religious self. There is a paradox in becoming a religious self, for one's identity consists in committing itself to something beyond the self, though already within the self. The religious self is not so much the self that is becoming divine as it is, rather, the self that is becoming aware of the divinity it already has within. The religious self is grasped by this divine within and makes a permanent self-surrender to it without conditions, qualifications, or reservations. It says yes to the divine within and relates that divine core to the universe outside its self. From then on, the ups and downs in life are stages in overcoming the false division we have set up in our selves between the present and the future, between our selves and something else that stands apart from us. They are stages in the gradual self-realization that we are already one with the universe and, therefore, have nothing outside of our selves to be gained. The divine core of the self is a pivot for the spiral, a reference point that continually pulls us back as it also pushes us out toward ever fuller self-realization.

The core within us — whether called the infinite spirit, or God, or the Absolute Reality, whether referred to as a god, a hero, a savior — is not evident to us without conscious effort.

Only gradually, in the course of a lifetime of development, living, and contemplation, can we become fully aware of and relate to this core. This divine core has been in plain sight from the beginning, and yet, for this very reason, it is hard to see. The dynamics of relating the force at the core of our being to our external circumstances is the essence of adult religious development. Discovering and becoming our full selves is the goal of religious wholeness.

The gods, heroes, and saviors in the myths of the great religious traditions of the world remind us of that divine core. By listening to and responding to their myths and rituals, we embark on the religious quest of discovering who we are and of developing the fullness of our human potential. We participate in a graced moment, a peak experience that is the source of new strength. It is a liberating experience, so much more powerful than the feeling that life is the mere succession of moments, of one thing after another, where we are helpless in the face of onrushing events.

The religious self is the complex of experiences, images, expectations, and operations by which we act out our divinity. The religious self thrives on the divine core, which gives meaning to its activities, the inner reference point that gives sparkle to humdrum existence and order to random events. The myths of gods, heroes, and saviors symbolize this still point of the religious self in both personal and impersonal ways. In Christianity, for example, it finds expression in the Christ and the kingdom of God; in Judaism, the expected Messiah and the messianic age; in Buddhism, the Buddha and Nirvana. The core may be the cosmic consciousness of the universe, or the forces of Yin and Yang contained within a circle, a certain at-one-ness in the midst of the 10,000 things of everyday existence. The numinous, in both East and West, is at the center of life, issuing a call to personality. The more we concentrate on this core of mysterious potential, the more our religious self stands forth in its true completeness and meaning, and the more we relate harmoniously to everything outside us. The religious self is distinct from the gods, heroes, and saviors within, yet more and more identifying with them so that there appears to be just one self, one God.

While the gods, heroes, and saviors may be a useful shorthand for envisioning and calling up needed qualities and strengths

within us, we must not reduce them to our own image and
likeness. Whenever we examine myths for clues to the nature
of human beings, we are really looking in our own mirrors. The
numinous is not in the mirror, and it remains free of all our
human pretensions. In fact, as we study the stories of the different
religious traditions, we must acknowledge that every definition
and description of the divine image is called into question by
other myths. Conflicting traditions are always reminders of the
essential mystery of the divine.

Even though the myths of gods, heroes, and saviors often
contain human projections, they still portray the possibility for
wholeness of the religious self. Wholeness is alternatively active
and receptive, flowing with life in a give and take, a holding
and a releasing according to the moment. The wholeness of the
religious self may be variously tender or firm, flexible or strong,
ambiguous or precise. Wholeness provides new insight for hand-
ling changed circumstances and clarity for transcending impasses.
Participating in the mythic deeds of the gods, heroes, and saviors,
the religious self experiences not merely a momentary feeling
of ecstasy, but a total transformation of life.

The religious self acts on its wholeness. The harmonious
relationship with the numinous translates into a harmonious relationship with the world. The religious self acts not so much to
alter events to suit its own wants or to utilize its power to reach
the top but rather to bring about a convergence of other selves.
Intellectual cognition and awareness combine with existential
commitment in building relationships with and between others.
Socially responsive and responsible, the religious self enhances
community identity by binding people together and motivating
them to live according to higher standards. Deriving its strength
from its core, it can be socially subversive, living in tension with
whatever injustice it encounters, even bearing the pain and potential despair of seeing ethical causes and movements of compassion exploded or subverted by less universalizing interests. Selfishness and altruism both disappear as the religious self acts freely
for the common good, bringing closer the reconciliation of the
one and the many, the reunion of all with the Absolute Reality.

From the perspective of the religious self, we can no longer
perceive myths as instruments which imprison us in our own
culture. Nor can we claim any longer that our own myths and
religious traditions are real while all other myths and religious

traditions are false. All myths are existentially true to the extent that they are effective in aiding us to become fully human. We can no longer dismiss the faiths and feelings of others as heretical or ignorant, for we recognize in them elements of our essential humanity. We can now begin the voyage into other people's hearts, encounter the sentiments and ideas that animate them at their deepest level, and appropriate insights from their traditions. Without taking over their myths in an eclectic fashion — for this would be living someone else's story — we can look at their religious traditions and study their stories to help crystallize our own world view. More, we can strengthen our foundation for practical action from a richer, broader, more fully human perspective.

The symbols in religious traditions other than our own may be relative, but they are also representative of something absolute. In them we find patterns and images which are constant in a transcultural way. Studying these common structures in the various religions, we find what it means for the religious self to be whole in a way that is not possible if we restrict ourselves to just one tradition. Some gods may strike us negatively; some heroes may lack the elements of transcendent freedom and creativity necessary for a complete sense of selfhood; some saviors may deliver their people from something we don't perceive as a problem. Still the mythical figures do represent the leading tip of conscious evolution, and their stories do allow us to participate vicariously in their lives. Each human, in consort with the gods, heroes, and saviors, can share in the one and same reality. As the Buddha expresses it, "Look within, thou art the Buddha"; and Krishna, "By understanding the self all this universe is known"; and Jesus, "I and the Father are one." We incarnate the gods, heroes, and saviors today. More than that, we *are* the gods, heroes, and saviors.

# Review Questions

1.  What is the supreme achievement of the self?

2.  What are the layers, the constellations of images, that constitute the American myth?

3.  Describe the spiralling self in terms of the continual process of dying and rising.

4.  What is the difference between the cultural self and the religious self?

5.  How can a study of myths of gods, heroes, and saviors help us in the process of becoming whole?

## Discussion Starters

1.  "If one desires to understand the spirit and inner life of a people, one must look at its art, literature, philosophy, dances, and music, where the spirit of the whole people is reflected."

2.  "The self, the place where we live, is a place of illusion, so by opening our eyes we do not necessarily see what confronts us. The psyche. . .constantly seeks consolation, either through imagined inflation of self or through fictions of a theological nature." (Irish Murdoch)

3.  "To the young, the discrepancy between what could be and what is, is overwhelming; perhaps it is the greatest single fact of their existence." (Charles Reich)

4.  "If we take man as he is, we make him worse; if we take him as he ought to be, we help him become it." (Goethe)

5.  Thanksgiving and Independence Day are two ritual celebrations of the American myth. What truths do these rituals affirm?

6.  "The main emotion of the adult American who has had all the advantages of wealth, education, and culture is disappointment." (John Cheever)

7.  We are part of the American myth. If you could claim as yours the myth of any other culture, anywhere in the world, which would you choose? Explain what it would mean to you. What would it add to your own myth?

8.  Centuries from now, when people look back at the myths of the 20th century, what do you think they will say about us? How will they characterize us?

# MYTH AND RELIGION

Myth is a word that is forced to carry excessive weight. Myths function both to limit and to expand preconceived ideas. The American myth, for example, provides images and ideals that set Americans apart from other peoples. But myths also play a broadening role, especially in religious myths that bring us into contact with the gods, heroes, and saviors that are latent at the core of our selves. In this book we give our attention and emphasis to this second role, and we emphasize the capacity of myths to help persons expand their selves and achieve wholeness.

Myths are stories that give significance to historical events, revealing the mysteries of archetypes, the constants of human experience. As sacred stories structuring the meaning and values of human existence, they strengthen and complement the doctrines of religious traditions.

## The Myth of Myth

Perhaps the biggest obstacle to a proper understanding and appreciation of myth is its misuse in the everyday speech and writing of many people. For example, when they mention the "myth of male chauvinism" or the "myth of racial equality" or the "myth of the Loch Ness monster," they refer to something that is false or needs clarification. Even when myth refers to stories, it implies that these stories are not true; and lacking truth, they are no longer to be taken seriously. Living as we do in a scientific Western world view (perhaps we should say scientific Western myth), we tend to consider the stories in myths as anachronistic, surviving only in an environment that is somehow protected from the impact of historical change and understanding.

From the scientific perspective, the only truth are those which can be verified by empirical methods: What is true is what is testable and predictable. Myths here are illusions or even lies, primitive and mistaken ways of relating to the world that are destined to be replaced by science.

To many, myths have a pejorative connotation, such as when they say, "We have to distinguish the myth from the reality." Dictionaries foster this sense when they define myth as a fictitious story, an unscientific account, or an imaginary person or thing spoken of as existing. Some tend to reduce myth to a kind of rationalization for human behavior. But by and large, the battle against this downgrading of myth in the name of science has been won.

It is generally recognized that when people reduce their beliefs and hopes to empirical certainties or philosophical proofs, they impoverish and delude themselves. It is not so much that they have reduced human life to a story without a point or a journey without a goal. It is rather that they have fabricated other myths of economics, or politics, or technology. Far from avoiding myth, they create demeaning ones; and in limiting truth in this way, they have to find some other way to describe those meaningful elements of life that cannot be reduced to their model, elements like grief, or happiness, or friendship.

Another popular usage of myth, which also detracts from its power today, considers it as a primitive, fumbling effort to explain the world, a naive philosophy that may have been true "once upon a time." Myth was necessary for those primitive people living thousands of years ago. It was necessary for them, for it provided a way of projecting their fears and hopes onto the mysterious gods. It provided them with a vehicle for moral truths, for sentimentally describing nature, perhaps even for controlling nature by magic or sacrifice. It was all very odd, very queer, not rooted in real life.

To reduce myth to some kind of sociological function in this way is to say, in effect, that myths are other people's view of life with which we disagree. It denies that other people who may have been more primitive from the point of view of the scientific myth really knew what it meant to be fully human or how to relate to each other in a civilized way.

This approach to myth is also generally considered to be invalid. Now we recognize that these earlier groups had powerful ways of relating individuals to the group. Far from the alienation and lack of social cohesion that many experience today, primitive people asserted that the group had a special power that emanated to each individual who participated in the stories. The sacred beliefs and practices evoked in the myths united the believers into a single community. The myths narrated the fundamental unity of the group and actually created it. Telling myths created a group self-consciousness, a common story in which all who participated knew who they were.

A third misleading usage of myth regards it as the product of poetical fantasy, a type of literature not really different from legends, folk tales, or even fables. It is contended that like these other literary forms, myths furnish entertainment, awe, nostalgia, or amusement by evoking a make-believe world. Also, they may contain some moral truths, but these are presented in allegorical form so that they might be easier understood, digested, and accepted. Like legends, folk tales, and fables, myths are never to be taken too seriously, provide no breathless air of authority, and are best suited as plots for movies.

In this view it is generally recognized that myths are much more than these other forms of literature. Legends and folk tales, for example, are imaginative treatment of events that are believed to be historical at least to some degree. The neatness and finality with which an awkward situation is resolved or any enemy confounded brings much satisfaction to their hearers. Legends and folk tales are didactic, cleverly illustrating proper political or ethical behavior by evoking a world of magic. They are national in their presentation of human character; for example, Odysseus is the embodiment of Greek ideals of manly courage, sagacity, and endurance; Sigurd, the personification of the Norse Code of heroism; King Arthur, of Norman-English chivalry.

Myths, as we are using them, do include not only stories about gods, heroes, and saviors, but also those historical events of religious significance in a tradition, such as the account of Israel's delivery from oppressive slavery in Egypt, or Muhammed's Night of Power and Excellence, or the narratives of Jesus' resurrection. But generally they do not depend upon or revolve around a historical basis because their concern is with basic human dilemmas that transcend place and time.

Much of the value of myths lies in their open-ended meanings, their way of illuminating a wide range of experiences, telling us much about ourselves, whoever we are and whatever our circumstances. Myths are the revelation of mysteries rather than clever illustrations or didactic entertainment. Their preoccupation is with more profound problems, such as creation, the origin of evil, or the destiny of humankind. Myths are cosmic and universal rather than national and immediate. They offer reflections on the constants of human experience, both personal and social.

## Myth and the Religious Self

Myths help humans in their quest for the religious self. They are a complex of images, metaphors, and rituals that provide humans with a map for charting their course through the baffling regions they encounter in their lives. An integral part of religion, they proclaim a central reality and then build a structure of values around and in relation to it. Their stories point to the inner meaning of the universe and of human life. Appealing to the imagination, they provide a comprehensive view of reality. They serve to reveal or explain the mysteries of life, death, and the universe, though their images at once reveal and conceal, are implicit rather than explicit, and suggest rather than state. Myths are religious, for their narratives deal with the Absolute Reality at the core of the self, the essence of the self, which is both transcendent (true for all times and places) and immanent (true here and now). Myths convey concrete notions about how this Absolute Reality at the core is to be approached.

Insofar as myths are sacred stories that traditionally have structured the meaning and value of human existence, they are part of the language of religion. Myths show how the experience of the sacred is given form within an individual's life and the life of the community. They outline a picture of a larger reality beyond our own limited personal experience. Adumbrating an entire universe of sacred and secular, they provide a perspective on human origin and destiny, the limits of human power, and the extension of human hopes and desires. They circumscribe all of human experience, providing stories of the values that give significance to people's lives and lift them out of the humdrum of daily existence.

Like all symbols, myths function on levels of the human psyche other than the rational. They fulfill deep psychic and spiritual needs by providing the images, symbols, and rituals that enable people to cope with limiting situations, such as suffering, evil, or death, and to pass through important transitions, such as birth, puberty, adulthood, and old age. They narrate the human dilemma, the discordance between our fundamental reality (symbolized as the divine image at our core) and our actual mode of being (symbolized as sinful, guilty, and alienated from or unaware of that core). Myths let us divine (rather than define) how to resolve this dilemma by relating the aspects of our existence to that religious core.

Myths provide "soul"; they get beyond "merely making a living." The stories they narrate are classics because their message and significance are permanent. Myths are texts that never belong to the past but always to the present; they are always contemporary, for in them humans, precisely because they are humans, keep rediscovering themselves. Their themes of love, truth, courage, mercy, compassion are valid for all generations and transcend any concrete, material expression of them. Their themes cannot be analyzed by empirical methods but demand to be illustrated in stories.

Myths are not the same as doctrines, though they both are ways of bringing insight to religious experience. Doctrines basically use philosophical language as their form of expression. Myths exist alongside and in interaction with the more abstract ideas of the doctrinal dimension. They are generally located in and derive their authority from the sacred books, the scriptures, of the world's major religious traditions. These scriptures include, for example, the Hebrew Scriptures for Jews and the Bible for Christians, the *Qur'an* for Muslims, the *Lotus Sutra* for many in the Buddhist tradition, the *Vedas* and perhaps the *Bhagavad-Gita*

for Hindus. These scriptures are generally older than the doctrines that often take centuries to develop. Myths are told not
to distort these doctrines but to strengthen them and root them
in the religious tradition. This does not mean that myths are
necessarily the source of the religious doctrines; indeed, these
doctrines often derive from other sources.

Myths and doctrines both have an element of compelling
authority, both have an equal claim to be believed, for they are
both attempts to provide people a way of experiencing and interpreting the mystery of human existence. Still, neither doctrines
nor myths are to be equated with the experience of the Absolute
Reality. This would lead to a dysfunction, and perhaps to a loss
of faith.

Myths are not the enemy of doctrines but their complement.
The stories in myths help provide some understanding of the
more abstract content of doctrines. They can enhance traditional
interpretations and illumine perennial theological problems. They
can liberate doctrines from the strait-jackets that were fastened
on them by all the cultural, intellectual, and political circumstances they encountered when they were formulated. By attend-
ing to the images, symbols, and metaphors in myths, people can
come to a greater appreciation of the content of the doctrines
of their own religious tradition and they can relate more con-
structively to the myths and doctrines in other religious cultures.

The use of the term "myth" in relation to religious phe-
nomena is quite neutral regarding the story told in the myth;
indeed, the actual story may not be factual. Myths may be false.
Still, the truths that myths deal with are "infinitely true"; that
is, they tell a special kind of story that describes the basic
mysteries of life and provides a way to respond to them. Myths
are not just pictures of images that might be meaningful to
religious believers but remain meaningless to the outsiders.
Rather, they are dramas placed in the familiar world of space
and time that attempt to reveal, through particular details,
universal truths. There is a sort of convergence at the level of
truth in the great religious traditions. It makes no sense to say
that one religious myth is "better" or "truer" than the other.
They are not antithetical. We cannot say, for example, that the
truths in the myths of Buddha must be contrasted with the truths
about Jesus in the gospels, or that the truths in Taoism must
be opposed to the message of the prophets in the Jewish Scriptures.

The Hindu *Vedas* expresses it this way: "Truth is one; the sages call it by many names."

Myths are responses to the real world that seek, in their various conditioned ways, to reveal to religious believers an unconditioned reality. Beyond the variety of languages and expressions, there is a common meaning; beyond the disparity of religions, there is a common revelation. To refuse to recognize this truth, we fall into the trap that a Buddhist parable warns us against: We mistake the finger pointing at the moon for the moon itself. To recognize this truth, we shift our sight from the pointing finger to the moon itself. We then transcend any particular mythic (or doctrinal) expression and experience the reality at the very core of our humanity.

## Approaches to Myth

There have been skirmishes on the nature and function of myth in many academic areas in the past century. Linguistics, psychology, cultural anthropology, and structural analysis are just a few of the fields that claim myths as their special province and their particular possession. They have charted the relationship of myths to rituals, struggled over the origin of myths, traced the diffusion of myths from one culture or religious tradition to another, and developed typologies of myth (cosmogonic, heroic, utopian, etc.). While admitting valuable insights from all these fields, I feel that it would take us too far afield to rehearse all their arguments here.

Myths won't go into one packet; they cannot be coerced or owned by one academic area. They are too rich to allow for only one method of interpretation. They never allow of a single meaning, once and for all. Valuable insights into how myths interact with and challenge the human personality to strive for wholeness may be drawn from any number of methods of interpretation. Freud's classical tri-layered picture of the personality (the id, ego, and superego), and Levi-Strauss' model of binary oppositions, for example, are neat, elegant, and attractive. Important, too, are the phenomenologists who provide insights by studying the variants of particular myths, and also literary critics who explore the symbolic language of myths from still different perspectives.

Throughout this book I will be utilizing the insights of many persons, most of whom build on the thoughts of three persons. I would now like to introduce the major thrust of each of these three — Mircea Eliade, Joseph Campbell, and C.G. Jung — who have had such an influence on scholarship in myth studies. I pick them because they attend specifically to the religious and communal dimensions of myth. They have opened up perspectives that beckon us further to become conscious of and to consent to the mysteries of our existence. They concur that the underlying thrust of myths is somehow connected with deep impulses in our psyche and that the ultimate function of myths concerns the achievement of personal wholeness.

This wholeness is not fully understood or achieved except in a context of the community. Myths, they insist, are not just about *me;* they are about *us.* Myths tell the members of the religious tradition who they are and where they are going. The insights of these three men on the religious and communal dimensions of myth have helped many persons develop an attitude toward myth that makes their past sensible, their present meaningful, and their future possible.

## Mircea Eliade: Sacred Beginnings

A champagne bottle is used to whack the prow of a ship to launch it into the waters for its maiden voyage. Politicians and local entrepreneurs appear at the ribbon-cutting ceremony for a new business. Hospital and school administrators have their picture taken with the first overturned shovel of dirt from the construction site of a new wing. All of us delight in celebrating our birthdays and in making New Year's resolutions. People delightfully celebrate religious rituals of beginnings, too. The Jews, for example, commemorate their deliverance from slavery each year at Passover time; at Easter, Christians rejoice in the resurrection of Jesus.

The human desire to commemorate our beginnings is at the basis of Eliade's writings on myth. The pattern of the eternal return to the beginnings, to the sacred, primordial time is found throughout *Sacred and Profane, Patterns in Comparative Religion, From Primitives to Zen, History of Religious Ideas,* and his many other works. For him, the fundamental characteristic of religion, expressed in myths and rituals, is the "nostalgia for paradise," the desire to live as much as possible in the sacred, ideal world of the beginning.

In retelling myths, humans relive their deepest symbols and re-create the realities (the gods, heroes, saviors) at the core of their religious self. They recall the fabled time of the beginnings when they are released from the terror of history into a secure and meaningful world. They overcome that tyranny of time, which affects everyone to the extent that they allow themselves to be governed by deadlines, clocks, and schedules, or to live in the shadow of time and change. In narrating myths and celebrating rituals, they exercise a way of healing, of overcoming time, the devourer. They annihilate chronological time and come into contact with sacred reality. For example, for the Jews, Yahweh is liberating his people now (not just at Passover); for the Christians, Jesus is risen today (not just at the first Easter). Because myths (and rituals) are not mere commemorations but true experiences of the sacred beginnings, Eliade asserts that they are the most precious human possession. They are sacred, exemplary, and significant.

First, myths are sacred. For Eliade, the sacred is not another world alongside the "real world" of everyday existence. The sacred world is a real world of events and things that can be re-experienced within the everyday world. The symbols and images of myths provide the framework for uncovering this real world. Persons in religious traditions want to participate in this sacred reality, to be saturated with its power. They want to find ways of discerning evidence of this sacred in their consciousness. They open themselves up to this sacred world when they recount and appropriate the primordial deeds of the gods in forming, establishing, or creating the cosmos.

At the sacred time of the beginnings, the supernatural beings brought a reality into existence, whether the whole of reality (the cosmos itself) or a fragment of it (such as an island, a species of plant, a particular kind of human behavior, an institution). This is the sacred time of the primordial events, a time qualitatively different from profane time, from the continuous and irreversible time of everyday existence that persons desire to re-enter and re-experience. The sacred beings brought order out of chaos at the beginning. In opening themselves up to this sacred world, persons hope to put some order into the chaos of their own environment, so as not to be overwhelmed by it. Repeating and participating in the myths of the beginnings, they then attempt to articulate their behavior, their understanding of the world, and their value systems in terms of a sacred time and a sacred space.

Second, myths are exemplary. The primordial happenings recounted in myths are the exemplary models for all behavior in the profane world. Although people want to shape the profane world according to their needs, they want to bring themselves into conformity with the sacred world. By encouraging pre-existent models, myths thus promote social cohesion. To treat religious myths and rituals as efforts to gain control over new dimensions of the environment would be to consider religion as magic. They are rather the elements of religion that bring humans and their world into harmony with the objectively real world (which they cannot control). This harmony comes gradually through the constant repetition that lends importance and significance to the stories and dramatic action.

What happens on earth, in history, is unreal and illusory, while what happens in myth is real and substantial. To the extent that persons coordinate their earthly activities with the deeds narrated in the myths, they participate more fully in reality. Through regular repetition, they recall and imitate the exemplary pattern of their gods, which thus constitutes their world view and lifestyle and organizes and shapes their environment.

Third, myths are significant. They convey the models or paradigms of meaningful human actions. Myths address the whole person, not the intelligence or the imagination only; and they put persons in touch not only with themselves, but with the entire cosmos. They speak to the similarity of existential situations in which humans find themselves: similarities of social relationships (of male and female, of parent and child), of physical environment (storms, sunshine, drought), and of individual experience (of birth, growth, maturity, old age, death). Myths of the different religious traditions have much in common, for they all treat those common problems and struggles (of goodness vs. evil, of life vs. death, of unity vs. diversity) that make life meaningful. Far from alienating persons in different religious traditions, myths can unite them by revealing the very substance of human existence and the meaning of human destiny in recounting the deeds of the gods.

Eliade's understanding of myth is very beneficial for us, but it is not beyond all criticism. For example, his notion that myths are always accounts of beginnings is a bit narrow. Perhaps stories about origins may be the prototypes for other myths, but they are not the only type. Not all myths should be interpreted as accounts of how time-bound things came out of something timeless and eternal, out of something that was ''in the beginning.'' Myths of heroes' quests, myths of saviors, and utopian visions of the end of the world are obvious examples of myths that cannot be reduced to this pattern.

Secondly, his division of the world into sacred and profane, into real and unreal, seems to discount all those moments of time that are not a repetition of a mythical beginning. By separating the world into sacred and profane, there is a tendency to empty the profane sphere of significance and worth. Actually, the reaction should be quite the opposite. When events of the immediate, ordinary world are related to sacred time, they should be viewed with renewed fascination, for they become significant and noteworthy in their own right. All time is now sacred, either as ecstatic moments when we are called outside the realm of everyday experience or as moments when we stand more deeply within that experience, reaffirming and revitalizing it. Sacred and profane time interpenetrate each other; they are not rival modes. If we understand this, we can stifle the temptation to find new universals by means of which we order the world and the temptation to regard the empirical world as the ''real'' world (since it is experienced daily).

## Joseph Campbell: The Monomyth

When Joseph Campbell was asked if he considered himself a guru for students of myth, he replied that he was not directing anybody and that his idea of a top scholar in myth studies was Eliade. Campbell suggested that he and Eliade stand back to back, one facing a popular community, and the other the academic community. Despite Campbell's reluctance to admit his own scholarship, his contributions to the study of myths, including *The Hero With a Thousand Faces,* the four volumes of *The Masks of God,* the lavishly illustrated *The Mythic Image,* and *The Way of Animal Powers,* have secured his place among this century's top mythologists.

Campbell describes myths in many ways. They are symbols that evoke and direct psychological energy. Vivid stories or legends, they are but one part of a larger fabric that expresses a culture's attitude toward life, death, and the universe. Myths are not fantasies or misstatements; rather, they are veiled explanations of the truth. They are the secret opening through which the inexhaustible energies of the cosmos pour into human cultural manifestation. Myths are public dreams that move and shape societies. Conversely, one's own dreams are the little myths of the private gods, antigods, and guardian powers that are moving and shaping each person. Even though they are localized in religious traditions, myths express an intentionality that goes beyond that limited context and a meaning that pushes toward universality.

Unlike Eliade who finds the significance of myths in relation to the past, Campbell finds it in relation to the present. Eliade considers myths as repetitious returns to the sacred time of the beginnings; Campbell attends to the divine energies that myths manifest in our lives at the present moment. The central significance of myths for our present existence is made clear in the four functions that Campbell assigns to myths.

The first function of myth, the spiritual or mystical, is the most distinctive, eliciting and supporting a sense of awe, gratitude, and even rapture in relation to the mystery both of the universe and of human existence. Myths help persons experience and appreciate, if not understand, the numinous power outside human control. They provide the possibility of release for human emotions, ranging from demonic dread to mystical rapture, vis-a-vis what is strange and "other," fascinating and terrifying.

Myths address fundamental realities and basic mysteries of human existence: What are we? Why are we here? What are our responsibilities as humans? Why aren't the unjust punished? Why do innocent children suffer? Why are there earthquakes, hurricanes, devastating floods, cancer, and other calamities? How can we achieve composure knowing that we shall die? What happens when we die? Though the myths of the various religious traditions address these and similar questions in a different fashion, they do indeed address them.

The second function of myth, the cosmic or cosmological, provides an image or model of the universe that supports and is supported by this sense of the numinous. Genetically built into humans is an organizing mode of perception by which they can interpret the world with a sense of order. Based on this order, myths offer a comprehensive, understandable image of the world that is roughly in accord with the best scientific knowledge available. With symbols and images that correspond to the actual experience and mentality of each culture, myths tell humans what their universe looks like and where they belong in it.

Myths present an image of the universe as an organized, sanctified arrangement rather than its opposite, chaos, where disorder, confusion, and absence of structure are rampant. Mythic images shape and validate the environment, perhaps by setting boundaries between the sacred and the unsacred (perhaps places, or animals, or activities), boundaries of time (perhaps festivals corresponding to lunar and solar cycles), or boundaries between the spheres of sky, land, and sea. Even though the details of myths may alter as circumstances change over time, they help people know what to expect, so that they can feel comfortable in their orientation to their surroundings and can act with familiarity in specific circumstances. Myths comfort people in the fictions and fantasies they invent. These people have no difficulty living as if there were such a thing as a minute or a second (rather than just the tick-tock of a clock), as if there were a mathematical zero or an actual infinity, as if a utopia were politically achievable.

The third function of myth, the social or sociological, serves to support the current social order and help integrate the individual organically within the group (for example, the caste system in India, making life bearable for the impoverished). Myths establish links between the individual and the group. They serve to develop conformity and to mold the young, perhaps through stories as in the recounting of American ideals of freedom, conquering the wilderness, sharing the gifts of a new land (at Thanksgiving time), or through organizations such as the Boy Scouts with initiation rites promoting the virtuous life of honor, respect, and obedience.

Myths provide social orientation and direction by instilling the culture's values and by providing persons with routines in times of crisis. In America, all citizens are commonly taught that the United States is the world's natural moral leader, and they are encouraged to defend such principles as freedom of speech, tolerance of diversity, and equality of all before the law. Again, the customs and gestures that prevail at funerals, while varying widely from one religious tradition to another and even within the same tradition, do help the bereaved at their time of loss. The habitual, socially acceptable activities (the wake, the grieving, sharing food after the funeral) all help build up a sense of group solidarity through communal expression of sorrow.

If it seems that the social function of myth suggests that some necessity of conformity is vital for society — "We've always done it this way," or "Where do you draw the line if we allow some changes?" — it is more than offset by the final function, which calls for creative individuality.

The fourth function, the psychological, initiates persons into the order of realities of their own individual psyche, guiding them toward their own spiritual enrichment and realization. Campbell states that this is the most important of myth's functions. It guides individuals, stage by stage, through the inevitable crises of a useful life: from the childhood condition of dependency, through the traumas of adolescence, and the trials of adulthood, to the deathbed.

Myths help children through the fears that arise from their smallness and dependence by alluding to the hidden power they have within, not quite yet ripened or revealed. Mythic fantasies keep children from being overwhelmed by a world of large and mysteriously powerful adults. Adolescent boys and girls are eased through crises by supernatural helpers who encourage them to trust their intuition, and take the risk, to challenge elders when they are no longer worthy of respect.

Adults find in myths the insight that people who misuse their potential lose it, but those who use their power and creativity both generously and wisely are richly rewarded. Those who spend their lives for the sake of others achieve the complete realization of their religious selves.

Finally, those in old age find in myths the vehicle for communicating their wisdom to the younger generations. Moments of fullness and moments of happiness are not something in the distant future awaiting us after death; rather, these moments are possible in everyday experience to be realized here and now.

Myths make possible the experience of such moments of wholeness, of complete realization of the religious self, by enabling persons to participate in the greater drama concerning the journey of the human race. Through sharing the adventures of the gods, heroes, and saviors, they discover this precious secret: The god is not just Yahweh or Brahma; the hero is not just Perseus or Parsifal; the savior is not just Ahura Mazda or Jesus.

These and other mythical figures are just the local faces or the temporal manifestations of the numinous. The true gods, heroes, and saviors, by contrast, are at the heart of the self; indeed, they are the self. By developing this spiritual awareness, persons help to heal the split between their subjective psyche and their objective world, between their ego and their religious self. Problems and dis-ease of emptiness and meaninglessness are dissolved as persons become aware of and consent to this larger self, this divinity within.

Campbell's four functions of myth, and the psychological function in particular, are developed within the framework of his monomyth. This monomyth is his attempt to synthesize different myths from around the world into a single unified whole, a kind of multiplicity within a unity. Campbell adumbrates a universal pattern of departure, initiation, and return by linking together the heroes of various cultures and traditions who set out to answer the call of adventure, the call of life itself. Impelled by some crisis, the hero leaves the protective but unchallenging milieu of home and sets out feeling that he will be incomplete unless he does so. The hero has embarked on a quest for separate identity as a person of exceptional courage and wisdom. After crossing the threshold of the unknown, the hero has to perform some task, perhaps slaying a monster, rescuing someone, gathering up a hoarded treasure, or fetching the water of life from a well at the world's end. Vulnerable and facing the possibility of failure, the hero generally achieves the task. Occasionally, the hero is reluctant to return to his everyday world, but most often the hero does return, transformed. In the homecoming he shares the fruits of his labor, his boon or reward for the task, with the community.

Implicit in the departure, initiation, and return of the mono-mythic hero is a kind of spiritual death and transformation that is valid for humans as well. What the hero ultimately finds is his own self, his identity. Every person lives, in symbolic fashion, through the same stages in the process of maturing into the religious self. Myths thus portray a universal condition, outside of time and applicable to all humans. By participating in the myths, and, in particular, the monomyth, humans embark on a life cycle greater than their own and follow a model on the path to psychological and religious maturity.

Campbell's reconstruction of the monomyth is criticized by scholars. In tracing it through several cultures and religious traditions, Campbell is very selective and focuses on those features that are the same in all the variants. He randomly skips centuries and cultural provinces to dwell on the myths that fit his overarching pattern well. His desire to synthesize world mythology, to find a unity in human cultural history, is most intriguing, especially since so many extraordinary features fall into place. But the connection is only suspected and not susceptible of proof. Whether this criticism is valid or not, Campbell's monomyth paradigm may help us understand ourselves better and provide insights into the nature of the religious self.

The other criticism routinely leveled at Campbell concerns his hypothesis that mythology is a function of genetics or biology. It may be intriguing to suggest that myths are a product of the human imagination moved by the energies of the nervous system operating against each other, but this, too, is no more than a suggestion. It is gratuitous to argue that myths are similar because humans have the same biological needs and the same kind of unconscious processes no matter what situations they find themselves in. Scholars would prefer to approach mythic similarity in terms of diffusion from one culture to another. Whatever the cause of the similarity, there is still much we can learn about our own mythic structure and our religious self by studying the mythic themes common to the world's religious traditions.

## C.G. Jung: Individuation and Wholeness

The language I used in Chapter One to explain the spiritual journey from the empirical self (the center of our consciousness) to the religious self (at the core of our unconsciousness) is based on the insights of Jung. His commentaries on the reality of myths (as well as dreams and fairy tales), which greatly influenced both Eliade and Campbell, are spread throughout the more than twenty volumes of his *Collected Works*. Representative of his approach to the interpretation of myths are *Aion* and *Mysterium Conjunctionis;* a short book he edited near the end of his life, *Man and His Symbols,* is probably more easily accessible.

Jung was fascinated that the same stories arose in India, the Middle East, Europe, the Americas, as well as in China and Japan. So many of the same symbols and mythological motifs are found in different parts of the world. In spite of differences in culture and consciousness, there is something universal in human experience. Similar, if not identical, reactions to the same basic human situations are found in people throughout history and in all parts of the globe. For him, this was the clue that their proper soil and seeding place is not in any geographical location but in humans themselves. Myths are indestructible and they have a startling likeness to one another around the planet. The same themes seem to emerge, he felt, as though something in the psyche of a race had ripened and produced a fruit that corresponded, not in its form but in its substance, with the fruit of all other races.

Jung contended that myths give expression to certain unconscious processes that produce dream images that apparently have no relation whatsoever to conscious experience but are similar in all persons. He was convinced that within every person exists the "collective unconscious," the seedbed of images linking each person to the psychic life of human beings everywhere. Different from the personal unconscious that contains all the repressed, forgotten, subliminally perceived experiences of each individual's life, the collective unconscious consists of the elements characteristic of the human species. It contains the whole spiritual heritage of humanity's evolution, born anew in the brain structure of every individual. Biologically inherited, these images do not exist passively, but have their own energy and operate on the emotions, drives, and interests of human beings. They influence how humans behave and react to others.

Jung referred to these images that regulate the forces of the psyche as "archetypes." The archetypes are analogous to the instincts, but operate in the psyche instead of the body. They are inherited primordial images that emerge from the unconscious to bring the human psyche some insight and awareness into the constantly repeated experiences of humanity. As universal and timeless patterns or dramas of human experience, they are manifested in the individual's psyche in ways that are drawn from and peculiar to that person's total experience.

Archetypes are not the same as prototypes. Prototypes are acts or events that happened at a certain time in history and continue to be effective throughout history. They are formative insofar as they change people's lives and continue to influence subsequent generations. Really, though, they are relevant only for the culture or tradition in which they first occurred. When they are repeated, it is because they were effective at one time, and people within that culture hope they will be so again. Archetypes, on the other hand, have universal application. It is their timelessness that people value. Archetypes show the truth of the moment as having the same structure and meaning as an absolute and eternal truth.

Nor are the archetypes the same thing as stereotypes, which are outer forces or patterns of activity. Stereotypes refer to the roles that a society or culture expects persons to perform. They are unvarying forms or patterns, fixed or conventional notions or concepts, allowing for little individuality, freedom, or critical judgment. As for archetypes, though, they are powerful and invisible forces that shape behavior and influence emotions. They are the inner forces personified by the gods, heroes, and saviors in myths, which do make individuality, freedom, and wholeness possible.

Since many archetypes repeatedly appear in the cycle of human life, we will have occasion to look at many of them in the course of this study of myths. Perhaps the most basic archetype is the *self*, which, as we have already seen, is the center of the total personality, which no longer coincides with the ego but with a point midway between the conscious and the unconscious. A psychological construct that served to express an unknowable essence that could not be grasped or defined, this self was called the ''god within us'' by Jung.

A second archetype, the *hero*, exemplifies the course of action needed to achieve the task of creating the self. This is spelled out at length in Campbell's monomyth of the hero who sets out on the journey or quest for a successful life. Two other essential archetypes, the *anima* and the *animus*, are the contrasexual part of the psyche, the image of the other sex that each of us carries within. Developing this unknown side of the self is another of the tasks for each person, female or male, in the process of coming to maturity.

One last archetype, the *shadow*, is a composite of personal characteristics and potentialities the individual is unaware of. It usually contains inferior characteristics and weaknesses that the ego's self-esteem will not permit it to recognize. This archetype is relevant in any discussion of evil. As with any of the archetypes, it can be interpreted either in a negative or positive fashion, depending on the context in which the ego experiences it.

The archetypes lead the way in each person's spiritual development, playing an important role in the journey toward wholeness. When a person knows which gods, heroes, and saviors are dominant forces within, he or she can acquire self-knowledge about the strength of certain instincts, about priorities and abilities, and about the possibilities of finding personal meaning through choices that others might not encourage. The archetypes in myths are worthy of our attention because they help bring meaning to the facts of ordinary life. Transpersonal and trans-cultural, they speak directly to the perennial mysteries of life — birth, fear, hope, love, suffering, death — as they are experienced by each person. The archetypes in myths provide structures of consciousness through which the entire human situation can be appropriated. They can give new depth and meaning to each human life, insofar as we become conscious of them and con-sent to their action in us.

The spiritual development of the individual, as it is achieved through recognizing and appropriating the archetypes, leads to the reconciliation of the different, polarized aspects of the per-sonality. To this process of reconciliation, Jung gave the name *individuation,* which for him is the future goal toward which humans strive, for the most part, unconsciously. Myths help make this striving conscious. They are the doorways to wonder, the passageways to the experience of the numinous. Arising out of permanent and universal elements of our human spirit, myths transmit signals to our psyches from the collective unconscious. They provide the clues for potential development, for the self's possibilities with respect to the future. When they become alive and enable individuals to make continual contact with their inner selves, myths have great power to vivify persons and bring them to wholeness.

Awareness of and consent to the archetypal elements in myths thus help persons appropriate the elements of the collec-tive unconscious. These elements are constellated in polar, binary groups — Eros and Thanatos, good and evil, man and woman, love and hate, order and chaos, Yin and Yang — which serve to distort the totality. Though the totality of human life consists of both sides, we lean toward one pole or the other. We are either male or female, young or old. We, therefore, need myths which help us attend to both poles without neglecting either one. Through the archetypes, the myths rehearse for us our limitations, our undeveloped human elements. Through them we enlarge our vision and embrace the totality of what it is to be human. We discover our self enhanced, enriched, supported, and magnified. Through stories and rituals of birth, initiation, marriage, burial, and so forth, myths incorporate our individual life-crises and life-deeds into a larger whole. This is a healing process moving toward that wholeness in which we recognize that we are one with the universe.

Criticism of Jung's thought, as with Campbell's, centers around the hypothetical nature of his concepts. They are not clearly defined, nor are they based on hard empirical evidence. He presents the archetypes and the collective unconscious as universals in such a way as to make them immune from psychological or sociological analysis. His suggestion that certain behavior is appropriate and necessary for all individuals if they are to achieve individuation is derived from non-scientific generalizations. Just to give one example, his archetype of the *animus* seems to have resulted from forcing a mirror image where there is none, from deducing its presence in women solely as a conclusion from his hypothesis that the *anima* is an essential feminine component in the masculine psyche.

Admittedly, there are risks involved in utilizing someone else's concepts, especially if we remove them from their original context (in Jung's case, analytical psychology) and start from different assumptions. Still, Jung's system is very useful as a way of teasing the fragments of life into a vision of wholeness. His language of individuation, collective unconscious, and archetypes has been a welcome tool for understanding and interpreting myths and for describing the development of the spiralling, religious self. His insistence that it is impossible to achieve an authentic personal identity if we are forced to discard the encounter with the numinous as unscientific nonsense is a powerful stimulus to self-development.

## The Value of Myths

Myths from different cultures and different times in human history have provided different points of view and different stories about the meaning and outcome of life. Since humans all share basic experiences, myths often contain the same or similar motifs, modified and elaborated. They confront us in the telling, and we can learn something about ourselves in listening to them. The whole pattern of our lives and thoughts is symbolized in a few recurring themes. Myths are the food that feed our sense of identity, often leading us to exlaim, ''Aha, that's my story too.'' By evoking the gods, heroes, and saviors that exist as perpetually incarnate in ourselves, myths help us see our purpose from the vantage of the religious self, the full and eternal significance of our humanity appears. We are acting out not mere piddling affairs of everyday life, but the great archetypal situations. Myths enable us to see our identity and our destiny in relation to the unseen world — God, Dharma, Tao, Nirvana — and give us an added impulse, a sparkle to our faith, our feelings, and our dignity.

Even though myths contain similar motifs, their interpretation cannot be reduced to illustrating some simple truism. There is no way of interpreting myths that solves all the problems they raise, and no two interpretations leave all the same problems unsolved. Myths bear a meaning and a permanence that resist definitive interpretation. The three approaches to the interpretation of myth that we have glanced at in this chapter are all similar in approach, but their differences do shed new insights on each other. Eliade's approach is more retrospective; Campbell's is more oriented to the present; and Jung's is more teleological. Taken together, they help us understand better the gods in our past, the heroes in our present, and the saviors in our future.

These three approaches to myth, taken from so many other possible approaches, stress more than others that when we enter the realm of myth, we are already in the ''eternal now,'' as much as we will ever be in some imagined heaven later on. Myths, according to their interpretations, help us live fully in the present time, making grand connections with our future and our past. They help us ''overcome time'' by linking us with the past and orienting us to the future. They tell us not what did take place, but rather they point to those universal events that always do and will take place. Myths tell us of those events that can focus our impressions of human life, rather than leaving them loose and disorganized. They transform life from a wearying succession of isolated events into a passion for meaning.

Though myths of different religious traditions and cultures deal with the perennial themes of shared human experience, they offer different paradigms and idiosyncratic metaphors. The religious traditions offer their own integrated system for understanding all the parts of reality as a whole. And that is precisely the attraction of studying the myths of the various religious traditions. To the extent myths are dissimilar, they introduce us to something new, unexpected, unpredictable. To the extent they are similar, they help us find points of contact with our own myths. They are dissimilar enough that we can never complain of boredom; they are similar enough that we can find the overarching patterns.

The viability of the myths of other religions depends on their applicability to peculiar conditions of history and environment rather than on the extent that we find them useful or entertaining. These stories merit our understanding as well as our admiration, for they can tell us truths about ourselves as well. The joy and fun in studying these myths is not in taking them literally, for this would turn them into obstacles of meaning rather than conveyors of it. Taken literally, the myths would describe a world removed from and irrelevant to our own.

If we study them precisely as myths, we let their power become conscious. They can stretch our minds and imagination, opening up new paths for further exploration of the nature of the religious self. Myths have the power to transform us when we appreciate them for what they are, rather than getting bogged down in details about their source, their variants, their translations, their claim to be taken literally. They can move us beyond our limited horizons of experience by their power of disclosure. Studying them in their variations and in their various interpretations, we can integrate our life experiences into a totality and can respond to the pull of the religious self at our core.

# Review Questions

1. Describe some ways the word "myth" is misused and misunderstood in everyday speech today.

2. How do myths help humans on their quest for the religious self?

3. In what ways do myths differ from religious doctrines?

4. What does Eliade mean when he suggests that the fundamental characteristic of religion is the "nostalgia for Paradise?"

5. What does Eliade mean when he suggests that myths are sacred, exemplary, and significant?

6. Explain the four functions that Campbell assigns to myths.

7. What does Jung mean by the "collective unconscious?" What are archetypes?

8. What does Jung mean by the process of individuation?

# Discussion Starters

1. "The occupational hazard of mythologists is a Faustian drive to round up all the myths of the world in a single place and sprinkle scientific salt on their tales." (Wendy O'Flaherty)

2. "Myths are maps, and myth is a symbolism, and for this reason myths are not to be taken literally. It is rather that when the dust falls from before our eyes, human beings are themselves the gods and demons, acting out, not the piddling business of worldly life, but the great archetypal situations and dramas of the myths. The gods are the archetypes, but they exist as perpetually incarnate in ourselves." (Alan Watts)

3. "In dealing with symbols and myths from far away, we are really conversing with ourselves — with a part of ourselves, however, which is as unfamiliar to our conscious being as the interior of the earth to the students of geology. Hence the mythical traditions provide us with a sort of map for exploring and ascertaining the contents of our own inner being to which we consciously feel only scantily related." (Heinrich Zimmer)

4. "Myths permit us to examine our place in the world by comparing it to a shared idea. Myths are shared fantasies that form the tie that binds the individual to other members of his group. Such myths help to ward off feelings of isolation, guilt, anxiety, and purposelessness." (Bruno Bettelheim)

5.  "Poetry is a kind of speech which cannot be translated except at the cost of serious distortions; whereas the mythical value of the myth is preserved even through the worst translation." (Claude Levi-Strauss)

6.  "Theoretically everything a man can do can be programmed into a machine and the machine will do it — everything except this: man's capacity for religion and poetry." (Andrey Voznesensky)

7.  "The destiny of the world is determined less by the battles that are won than by the stories it loves and believes in."

8.  "Those who are the heart of their different religions are all closer to one another than those who are at the fringes." (C. S. Lewis)

9.  "Everything is a myth: youth, profit, class struggle, patriotism, freedom, the university, sociology, enzymes, vacation, the automobile, pollution, history, science." (Jacques Ellul)

# CHAPTER THREE

# CREATION

Creation myths are the most universal kind of myth. They portray human attempts to discover or provide some cosmic order and meaning. In story form they give an explanation of how the world and the first humans came into existence, and they reveal how humankind has sought to come to terms with the mystery of the environment and with the experience of powers that lie outside human control, whether benevolent and life-enhancing or malevolent and life-destroying. In the myths of creation of the cosmos, religious traditions express their under-standing of the ultimate meaning of the world and of human existence. They tell of the role of gods and goddesses in creating and sometimes even dying through sacrificial dismemberment to make the entire world holy. They describe how the world (oceans, land, mountains) came to be. And they separate the world into different realms (most often a tripartite division of heaven, earth, and underworld).

In myths of creation of the first humans, the religious traditions tell us why humans suffer and die, how they set up and maintain social cohesion and balance, and how they might overcome the separation from the Absolute Reality which has been present from the beginning. The myths tell us about this Absolute Reality — the impersonal and personal aspects, the interventions in human history, the basically unknowable essence. The Absolute Reality may appear in its feminine aspect in those mother goddesses who are life-giving, nurturing, protective, and working to transform humans. They tell of the masculine aspect in the creator gods who give meaning to chaos, and call humans to exercise responsibility in using their creative capacities to reshape the world. The Chinese tradition, which is probably unfamiliar to most of us, can serve to introduce us to many of the themes that are common in creation myths throughout the world.

## China

Though the Chinese have one of the largest bodies of world literature, they have no single clearly defined myth of the origin of our universe. There is a vague ascription of infinite creative power to Shang Ti, the Great Ruler of the Universe, and there are impersonal Taoist cosmologies found in the *I Ching,* and the writings of Lao Tzu and Chuang-Tzu. But the stories that have best captured the imagination of the Chinese involve P'an Ku, a god in human form who labored on creation until he died and the various parts of his body were dispersed to become the natural elements of the universe.

In the beginning neither earth nor heaven existed. Nothing had taken shape; all was confusion and Chaos. Chaos was like a giant hen's egg. In time, after countless years, P'an Ku emerged from this egg. The parts of the egg separated, with the heavy elements forming the earth, and the light, pure elements forming the sky. From this separation arose the two principles, Yang and Yin, light and dark, sky and earth. P'an Ku slowly came into being and grew each day. He stood with his feet on earth while the sky rested on his head. Day after day he stood, for 18,000 years. As he did, the distance between earth and sky increased by ten feet daily. P'an Ku grew by the same rate, so that his body always filled the space between the two. They could not come together again.

P'an Ku continued to grow until the time when he could be sure that earth and sky were fixed and firm in their places.

His body was a link between heaven and earth as well as a column that kept them apart. His task achieved, P'an Ku lay down; and in resting, he died. In his death, he gave his body to enrich and beautify the universe. His head became the mountains, his breath the winds and clouds, his voice the thunder, and his beard the constellations. His arms and legs became the four quarters of the earth; his blood the rivers; his skin and hair the herbs and trees; his teeth, bones, and marrow the metals, rocks, and precious stones. His sweat became the rain; his eyes the sun and moon; his flesh the soil of the fields; the hairs on his body and eyelids became flowers and trees; his semen pearls. And so out of Chaos P'an Ku brought heaven in all its glory and earth with all its splendors.

The first humans are also described as originating with P'an Ku. They had been the insects that crept all over his body. Another myth provides a different version of their origin from P'an Ku. Once the plants and animals had sprung up, P'an Ku was dissatisfied because there was no reasoning being who could develop and make use of other living creatures. He therefore set out modeling men and women in clay. As soon as this clay dried, he impregnated it with Yin and Yang and they became humans. Each day he made a large supply, which he then baked in the sun. One day dark clouds appeared, so he heaped up his drying figures and carried them inside on an iron fork, for he feared to waste his day's work. But the storm burst before he got them all to safety and some were damaged. That is why there are crippled and defective people on earth today.

Still another myth describes the creation of the first humans, this time by the goddess Nu-kua. The earth seemed dull for the gods who roamed it; they wanted more humans who could dance and make sounds of joy to bring delight to their ears and eyes. Nu-kua, whose body was that of a dragon but whose head was of human form, set out to model humans out of yellow earth. To quicken this tedious process, she dipped a rope in the muddy clay and trailed it behind her, letting drops fall off. From the specimens that she had fully modeled came the noble and the rich, while those who dripped from the muddy rope were the humble and the poor.

Many blessings were given to the humans by the gods. Nu-kua worried what would happen when the sons and daughters of her creation grew old and died. They wouldn't live forever. She decided to teach them the ways of marriage. Now they could create their own sons and daughters, who would continue to populate the earth and rule over the beasts. Again, she intervened when a fierce battle between Fire and Water raged over the earth. She quelled the fires and floods, tamed the wandering beasts, took stones from river streams to patch up the holes in the sky, and thus restored peace. Her husband, Fu-hsi, also brought men and women blessings. He gave them the lute for music and taught them how to weave ropes and make nets for fishing. His also was the priceless gift of fire, and the gift of the eight Trigrams of the *I Ching* so they could record their past and divine their future.

In these Chinese myths we see their concern for establishing and maintaining order. We find the beginnings of a complex bureaucracy, which becomes later an organized imperial bureaucracy with departments controlling every aspect and activity of the world, whether good or evil, whether approved or disapproved. Creation for them is the act of reducing chaos to order, of regulating heaven and earth under the rule of a Great Law to which everything in the universe is subject. Nature is divided into the forces of Yang and Yin. All finite things are produced from the Yin, or female principle of nature, which combines with the Yang, or male principle of nature, to form the eternal Tao. The universe is in constant and perfect flux — moving and resting, penetrating and receiving — the basic ingredients for creation and continued existence. Everything is the result of the spontaneous action of nature. To avoid chaos in one's life, each person's proper activity is to recognize this great Law of the universe and to avoid any craftiness that would defile the original innocence or purity.

## Cosmogonic Themes

Obviously, not all religious traditions tell of creation in the same way, and they reveal significant features that distinguish one tradition from the other. Still, they do share certain common patterns in the search for the ultimate meaning of the world and human existence. In telling of their origins, religious traditions formulate a definition of themselves and their world, just as we might do today in our theological or scientific speculations. Creation myths provide insight into the beliefs, customs, and institutions of different cultures. By finding the resemblances, we discover structures of the human mind that remain constant over barriers of time and space, the structures that are fundamental to all human beings.

Creation myths express in symbolic, paradoxical stories both the mystery of human life and the limitations imposed on it. They deal with transformation, with the dynamic process of life that is ever growing, ever moving on toward its mysterious conclusion. They ask the universal questions, the ones that humans confront in times of crisis: What is the origin, if any, of everything? What is the order or nature of the universe, if any? What is the purpose of everything? Why are we born to die? Can we transcend death in an afterlife? Is there an ''eternal plan'' that helps us to find meaning in our mortality? Why isn't life fair? Why are humans estranged and alienated from each other?

Creation myths advocate moral beliefs and social structures, reflect human psychology and wisdom, and embody religious paradoxes in everyday symbols. They are human attempts to find order and meaning in relation to the mystery of the universe. The language is symbolic, for humans need symbols to express their emotions, to convey the deepest human relationships; and thus, they are even more essential to describe human interaction with the transcendent world. Mythic language is symbolic because ordinary language is incapable of describing encounters between divinity and humanity or of expressing the relationship between time and eternity. There really is no other human way than through symbols to order the relationships of the human and the divine, the finite and the infinite.

Order is generally perceived through relationships. Thus humans are related with the soil, the seed, the crops, the seasons, usually in a position of domination or stewardship. They are related to the gods. Comprised of earthly and divine elements, humans have the potential to maintain or to disrupt the divine order imposed on the world. Since the creation myths show the human mind wrestling with the same basic tensions, these relationships are often binary: life and death, male and female, cold and warmth, gods and demons, matter and spirit, Yin and Yang, fire and water, war and peace, work and leisure, freedom and necessity.

In the attempt to find some order amidst the chaos of the universe, most religious traditions have two major parts to their creation myths: the formation of the world itself (called the cosmogonic myth), and the formation of the first humans. We saw both of these elements in the Chinese creation myths. Now I would like to point out certain recurring themes in both these types of creation myths, a kind of a catalog of creation themes throughout the world.

In cosmogonic myths, the creator (also referred to by other titles such as the Absolute Reality, the One, the Numinous) brings about the creation of the world either through a sacrificial process, following a destructive model, since it portrays death as a necessary prerequisite to life on earth, or through a voluntary, spontaneous process.

We have seen that the Chinese god, P'an Ku, creates through sacrificial dismemberment with various parts of his body becoming the elements of the world. By bestowing the gift of his being itself, P'an Ku "made holy" (that is the meaning of the word "sacrifice") the whole world. The absolute died to become part of the relative, dynamic, changing world. Quetzalcoatl in the Aztec myths, Ymir the frost giant in the *Eddas,* and Tiamat the Babylonian mother goddess split in half by Marduk are all gods who are sacrificed for the creation of the world. Life is created from their corpses or from parts of their bodies. Such myths are widespread. In Egypt, for example, the eyes of a god become the sun and moon. In India, from Purusha, the sacrificed primordial giant, some of the gods are born. The four castes come from his mouth, arms, thighs, and feet; the sky from his head; the air from his navel; and the four quarters from his ears. Although the mysterious one is dissolved into the flux of the universe and is lost in the dynamic change and flow of temporal reality, it is essential to recognize, as the religious traditions themselves do, that all of the earth, or at least some parts of the world, have within them the divine, or "holy," element.

More common than these sacrificial myths of creation are the various types of voluntary creation. World-parent myths, in which intercourse between male and female deities produces the created world, are quite common. In the Hopi Indian creation myth the god Sky Father and the goddess Earth Mother lie close together, and with the rain as fertilizing agent, they produce as children all the natural forces and creatures of the world.

There are many variations on this intercourse theme. Sometimes an Earth Mother goddess gives birth spontaneously and independently, without need of a mate. Or, if the sole god is a male, he may sometimes imagine a mate into being or use some aspect of himself as the feminine "other." Thus, the Aranda people of Australia tell of the god giving birth to the universe through his armpit. In the Hindu *Upanishads,* there is a kind of divine masturbation where the god has union with his clenched hand, pours the semen in his mouth and, having fertilized it by his words and ideas, spits it forth as creation.

Another type of voluntary creation portrays the god-creator as a kind of administrator who brings about order out of evil chaos. He puts light here, dark there; solids here, liquids there; day here, night there. This disordered chaos might take the form of a terrifying monster that has to be sufficiently controlled (a dragon or snake performs this role in Babylonian, Celtic, and Huron and Mandan Indian myths). The chaos may be a primeval abyss or an infinite watery deep (as in India, Scandinavia, Egypt) or "nothing" itself (as in the Jewish cosmogonic myth in Genesis 1) out of which the god has the cosmos emerge.

Perhaps some other form of activity on the part of the god or goddess brings about the cosmogony. Creation may be thought or dreamed (as the gods brood over the waters in Polynesia). Creation may occur through naming. By giving a name to a tree or animal or mountain, for example, the creator determines both the function of the being as well as its nature. Creation may occur through sound or a divine fiat (as in the Mayan *Popol Vuh,* or as with the sound *om* in the Hindu epics).

The two most common types of primordial material out of which the world is gradually shaped, are earth and water. In Hesiod's *Theogony,* for example, the world — sky and mountains, rivers and oceans — are all generated from dry land, Gaia, Mother Earth. Again, in the creation story of Adam and Eve in Genesis 2-3, Yahweh produces the earth before any shrubs or plants or rain. Myths that assume a sailor's view of the world as primarily water include the Peruvian god Viracocha's creation from sea-foam and a Hindu epic describing creation emerging from an ocean of milk. The Babylonian *Enuma Elish* portrays the primordial world generated from the divine waters of Apsu and Tiamat. Some myths, (especially among some American Indian tribes) are of the earth-diver type, in which a divine being, usually an animal, dives into the chaotic water to bring up mud to form the first particles of earth.

In those cosmogonic myths that involve no creator and where the primal transformation is more spontaneous than voluntary, the primordial stuff is most often the cosmic egg. Similar to the Chinese myth of P'an Ku, all created reality in the cosmos is hatched in the splitting apart of this egg. This occurs in traditions throughout the world, for example, in Egypt, Japan, Peru, and Polynesia. One Hindu cosmogony is representative: The world egg opens to form the heavens from its upper part and earth from its lower. Brahma emerges from this egg and by incantation produces eight celestial elephants who stand at the quarters and four midpoints to hold the earth and sky apart.

The Chinese myth contains many other elements that are common in the world's cosmogonic myths:

1. P'an Ku is an *Axis Mundi,* a world pole, separating the Earth and Sky. In most myths that contain such a pillar — such as Yggdrasil, the Norse Ash Tree, or the Navaho Giant Reed, or the Jewish Tower of Babel and Jacob's Ladder, or the African Vines or Spider's Rope — it serves as a connection between the divine and the human, between the Absolute and the Relative.

2. Etiological elements (stories which describe why or how something came to be) also abound. Thus, we read how the mountains and rivers of China were formed, how the rainbow got in the sky (in the Genesis story of Noah or the Sioux myth of the flowers taking to the sky each autumn), how the fawn got its spots or the squirrel its black tail.

3. The Flood theme — as in the Chinese story of Fire struggling with Water — is very common. In the Hindu epics, the flood is due to a water monster and only one person, Manu, is saved (by the god Vishnu disguised as a fish). In Greece two gods survive in a box that comes to rest on Mount Parnassus after the flood. The Jewish story of Noah and his family and the earlier Babylonian epic of Gilgamesh where Utnapishtim and his wife are the ones to survive also describe a universal flood.

Such flood stories may explain the origin of the oceans or suggest periodic creations and destructions of the world, but they also symbolize a religious tradition's hope for a new beginning.

Recognizing that evil has entered the world as a result of the primordial separation from the divine origin, these traditions express their hopes to purify or cleanse the cosmos, to start over again with a period of peace and bliss.

4. As part of their attempt to order their world, traditions will include spatial references to different worlds. In China it is simply the earth and the sky. More common is the separation into three worlds (this world, the upper world, the lower world) as among Babylonians and Jews, though occasionally there will be four or more (the four underworlds of the Navaho, the four wombs of the Zuni).

5. There will also be indications of time. In China, the various stages of creation took 18,000 years. In the Hindu epics, each cycle of creation, before Shiva destroys it again, continues for forty-three million years. Among the Jews, it was the seven-day cycle, and among the Aztecs a 52-year cycle.

6. Helpers in creation (Nu-kua and Fu-hsi) are almost universal. They occur both in the cosmogony and in the stories of formation of the first humans. These helpers, called tricksters or culture heroes, are so prevalent that we will devote an entire chapter to them. Here, it is sufficient to note that they often represent the element of uncertainty or arbitrariness. They are each religious tradition's way of admitting that there will always be disorder, chance, or fate in their lives, no matter how much they try to order or rationalize the world in their myths of creation.

## Human Creation

The Chinese myth of P'an Ku, after describing the creation of the universe, continues with the formation of the first humans. This myth contains several elements common to various religious traditions. It is instructive to look at what the people in these religious traditions are saying about their relationships to their gods, to each other, and to the cosmos itself.

The earth (dirt, humus, clay, dust) from which the first Chinese humans are created is probably the most universal element and the one we know from the Jewish myth in Genesis. Often this primordial clay is mixed with various substances, perhaps blood (as we find among some North American Indians). Usually the religious traditions take some element that is essential or all-pervasive in their daily existence to be the original material. Thus, those subsisting in a cold northern climate would never describe their original substance as corn (such as we find in Mexico and the Indians of the American Southwest), nor would those from a warm climate delegate the same role to frost (as the Norse do). Common, too, are myths where the first humans are created from the corpse or parts of the primeval god's body: Humans emerge from the tears of a god in Egypt, from the sweat of a giant god in Scandinavia, and from the blood and bones of the Babylonian Tiamat. Deriving their origin in some way from the divine being, the people tell us in their myths that they somehow participate in and have a share in the divine life.

The etiologies in the Chinese myths describe the origin of people who were defective and cripples, humble and poor. Myths describing why there is pain, suffering, and death are very commonly suggestive of a whole spectrum of poignant dilemmas and limitations associated with being human. They express both the mystery of human life and its limitations. Thus, in describing that people have to work by the sweat of their brows, the Jews express the anxieties and cut-throat competition they connect with the human lot. The Blackfeet and Arapahoe Indians describe how death comes as the result of an innocent game — throwing buffalo chips into a river to see if they would float. In an African and Indonesian myth, the first couple could choose either the kind of death of the moon (which periodically renews itself) or of the banana (which puts forth shoots to take its place). Their choice was difficult. If they decided to remain childless (moon-death), they could avoid death for themselves, but they would also be very lonely and have to do all their work themselves and have nothing to strive for. So they ask the creator god for the gift of children, well aware of the consequences of their choice (banana-death).

Not all etiologies in the creation myths of the first humans concern suffering and death in the world. The Senegalese explain why people tell lies: They can get along better with each other this way. American Indian myths describe why women must not hunt: If they did, they would upset the social cohesion and balance of the group. The Hindu *Upanishads* tell why humans are afraid to be alone, why they laugh, and why they enjoy sex: In each case, they are imitating the activity of the gods. In Jamaica, they give an account why there are various shades of brown in different human cultures: Mother Earth did not have enough time to bake all the humans (who were made from dough) before she had to remove them from the oven to escape the wrath of Father Sky. The Genesis myth of the Tower of Babel narrates why people belong to different cultures and speak in different languages.

We recall that the gifts bestowed on the Chinese by the gods included the lute for singing, the rope for fishing, and the Trigrams for writing and interpreting the *I Ching*. Myths of similar gifts from the gods are almost as common as stories of the human substance and etiologies in creation myths. The American Indians tell stories of the gift of corn (Pueblo), the peace pipe (Sioux), and how to build hogans (Navaho). From Egypt and other parts of Africa, it is the gift of how to brew beer (a very civilizing element!). Often it is the gift of sexuality and procreation — again a human action that somehow participates in and continues the divine activity. The Japanese tell, for example, of the pair Izanami and Izanagi, who are at first unaware of the social convention that the man should always do the bidding. They fall in love, but as the female Izanami has taken the initiative, their child is hideously deformed. Asking advice from the gods, they are told to repeat their whole courting ritual, this time with the male speaking first. Doing as they are told, they have beautiful children. As part of their creation story, the Japanese are thus taught that the woman is not to upset the order of the world by thinking that she can act as a man.

In the Chinese myth, we are told that the humans were created because there were not as yet any ''reasoning animals.'' The implication is that humans are somehow different, somewhere in between the gods and the animals. This same theme is brought out in other traditions where humans are seen either to evolve or to devolve. Among the Zuni, the first humans slowly proceed over several generations through four wombs of the earth before they are ready to come to the surface and face the Sun God. In Genesis, too, there is an evolving human awareness as the first man and woman become aware of the knowledge of good and evil. The Delaware Indians in the beginning live under a lake, in darkness, grubbing roots and vegetables for sustenance. Their culture hero, pursuing a deer, follows it to a hole that permits escape from their miserable underworld. He returns to his people with the deer meat. Partaking of it, they are awakened, recognize the goodness of Mother Earth, and leave the underworld to rejoice, populate the earth, and worship the maternal spirit of the woods. The Greeks, on the other hand, describe human development in terms of weakening rather than growth. In Hesiod's *Theogony,* the humans pass through the five ages of gold, silver, bronze, heroes, and iron, in each stage ending further and further from the gods. Prometheus's gift of fire may be a boon to human intelligence, but one of its effects is the gods' gift of Pandora to humans by which the gods hope to make them weaker. In her curiosity, her exercise of human freedom, Pandora opens the urn that lets loose all sorts of evils in the world: lies, treachery, deceit, diseases, natural calamities, and plagues.

Two small elements from the Chinese myth suggest still another theme common to many creation myths — the separation of humans from the gods, each other, and the world. Because the first Chinese were created to dance and give joy to the gods, they are clearly subordinate to the gods. Also, instilled in them are the forces of the Yin and the Yang, the polarities that again serve to alienate or separate. Perhaps this separation of humans and gods is due to a simple withdrawal as, for example, the African god who moved to a remote place in the sky because humans allowed smoke to blow in his face when they did their cooking and then wiped their hands on him as if he were a towel. Or perhaps an African trickster will cut down the ropes and vines that carried humans back and forth to the divine world, or a North American Indian trickster will shoot down the arrows that formed a ladder up to the hole in the sky. Myths of hermaphrodites also symbolize the human separation from each other, as do myths of brotherly strife. In Genesis, the enmity between Cain and Abel, the struggle between Jacob and Esau, and the Tower of Babel stories all point to the separation of humans from each other. Separation of humans from the gods and from each other is a reality that myths address; in fact, it is one of the major reasons why traditions tell their creation stories. While they recognize the separation, they still long for a reunion, and they develop other myths that allow them to experience the joyous thrill of overcoming this separation, often with the god's help.

## The Absolute Reality

Creation myths are filled with fantasy, excitement, and astute insights into character and motivation. The pleasures we experience in hearing or reading them, however, should not distract us from their main purpose. They provide insight into the age-old wisdom of our ancestors as they pondered the beginnings of the universe and the roles mortals play in it. In these myths we encounter their attempts to grapple with the mystery of the universe and to put some order into the chaos they experience all around them. The various images and themes they regularly narrate are recognizably human, but so different from our own characteristic modes of thought that they can serve to force us to enlarge our views of what it means to be human.

Each religious tradition has its own perspectives on the mystery of the universe. They provide us with a rich diversity of presentations regarding the Absolute Reality, as well as how humans, nature, and the cosmos are related to that Absolute Reality. This Absolute Reality, awesome and fascinating, has been encountered and named in many different ways by religious traditions, for example, God, the Creator, the Beginning, the Wholly Other, the One, the Sacred, the Unknown. To name it is to evoke the realm of mystery: unanswered questions, unexplained events, uncertainty about the future, confusion about how to live. To relate to it is to resolve many of the tensions of life and to open the self to other values and realities that transcend our human limitations. This mystery is the unknowable source of all life, and all human language about it is relative. It is revealed and known in human experience but not definable in human categories. It is a power outside and beyond the human experience, a force they cannot understand or control, but also a force that has an influence in their lives and a force they feel somehow related to. It touches and transforms human lives, yet words are always powerless to exhaust its depth. All talk about this Absolute Reality is necessarily metaphorical, and all definitions necessarily provisional.

The Absolute Reality may be described as both numinous and mystical. It is numinous because it is radically different from the familiar world, something outside the limits of the ordinary, filling the mind with wonder and astonishment. It is mystical because it is an active, calm, effortless power that is everyhere. It is numinous because it is beyond time and human beings; it is mystical because it is somehow active within us. It is numinous because it is a personal deity, addressed as God, Yahweh, Allah, Brahma, Krishna, Mother Kali, and by a host of other names; it is mystical because it is more a process than a divine being, more an experience than a relationship, whether as Nirvana, or Brahma, or the Tao. Finally, it is numinous because salvation must flow from it as a grace or an intervention; it is mystical because salvation may be attained through human effort, as through meditation or Yoga, which takes persons beyond this impermanent life.

Though the mystical tradition is present in the Western world, the Judaeo-Christian tradition has tended to emphasize the numinous side of the Absolute Reality. Without denying that the Creator God is present and manifest in all of human experience, the Western tradition visually locates the sacred outside the created world. Those persons who are intent on developing the religious self, whose view of reality is open-ended and expansive, will attempt to accommodate both numinous and mystical, theistic and non-theistic, personal and impersonal, conceptions of this one, ultimate, holy, Absolute Reality.

Impersonal forms of the Absolute Reality are present in the Western traditions (the Greek Fate which keeps humans in their places and controls their lives and the Aztec ritual power which is generated from human sacrifices to keep the universe moving), yet by and large, these are found in the religions of the East. Their mystical Absolute Reality is not a being, but a force. It is a power within, rather than a revered personal reality that responds to worship or prayer, that knows what is going on in the world, that guides the path of history. The Eastern religious traditions, rather than accepting the world as a variety of disconnected happenings or forms, order all the categories of nature into one grand scheme, one fundamental pattern.

Thus, Absolute Reality may be the Yin and Yang, those impersonal factors that blend into each other, not as antagonists but as alternating aspects of all reality, providing a pattern of growth and decline, where everything is balanced by its opposite. It may be the Tao, eternal and unchangeable, not outside the universe, but in all and through all, the nameless principle behind all the happenings of the world. It may be Nirvana — pure consciousness, pure bliss, eternal, unchanging, unbounded — the loss of the individual self in Brahman, the divine life force behind the universe.

The divine force is also portrayed in Eastern thought in a more personal and dramatic way, as the great gods Shiva and

Vishnu and as the divine female Kali, replete with power, terror, and love. Also, in a later form of Buddhism, the personal Amitabha Buddha, out of infinite compassion for all of humanity, invites all to set out on the Path of Enlightenment to arrive eventually in the Pure Land. Still, this personal facet of the Absolute Reality is more common outside the Eastern religions and is referred to most often as the creator God.

The personal Absolute Reality is referred to most often as the creator God. This creator God is one, but it is perceived under many different aspects. It may be transcendent as, for example, the god of Genesis 1 or the African Ashanti god, Nyame, who sits on his golden stool in the heavens with his queen consort goddess at his side. It may be immanent, such as the god of Genesis 2-3 who interacts with humans, or the Peruvian god Viracocha, the wise elder, whose power over creation is the power to name it, or the many gods of the American Indians (Wakan Tanka, Orenda, Manito), the object of reverence and worship, present in the world at this moment. It may be either masculine (a god, Sky Father, the single all-powerful god, often found in more pastorally oriented religions) or feminine (a goddess, a world mother, such as Tiamat, or Cybele, or Mother Earth, as found in more agriculturally oriented traditions).

The relationship of this personal creator God to humans varies greatly in the religious traditions. Perhaps the god or goddess is crusty and cantankerous, jealous of prerogatives, insistent on ritual which must be carried out perfectly. On the other hand, the god or goddess may be absentminded, where rituals serve not so much to placate as to remind the divinity of human dependence on it. Perhaps the god or goddess is one who wants to keep humans in their place, as powerless playthings subject to divine whims, or one who sets the universe in motion but then apparently loses interest.

In the Judaeo-Christian myth of Genesis 1, the creator is transcendent, outside and above creation, working at his own pace, unhindered by what he creates. He has total control over creation, manifested in his power of separation of light from dark, of the waters above and below the earth, and of the dry land from the sea, and in his adornment of each of these realms. He makes the world "good," and creates humans in his "image and likeness," insisting that humans participate in the divine power, both through procreation and through domination of the earth.

The Judaeo-Christian god, far from losing interest in humans, is portrayed in anthropomorphic terms as a god of pure unbounded love who intervenes in history in pursuit of humans with whom he is emotionally involved. This god is all powerful, insofar as nothing exists except through his creation and sustenance. He knows everything past, present, and future; thus everything in the universe may be called the expression of "God's will." He is perfectly good, but nonetheless allows evil in the world, due to human freedom and to the laws of nature. Never fickle or capricious, he is completely consistent, merciful and compassionate, friendly, attentive, and caring.

The Absolute Reality is anthropomorphized in different traditions to dramatize properly its various relations to the created world. But this is not the only reason. By portraying it as a personal god, religious traditions are symbolically and poetically saying that the Absolute Reality is in some incomprehensible way what the total perfection of human life, consciousness, and free choice would be like if they were infinite, eternal, and perfectly good. Further, they are professing that there is a dignity in each human, something not relative to others: the divine nature, the "image and likeness" of the god or goddess that is in the heart of each person. At this point the numinous and mystical emerge.

## Divine Image and Likeness

Religious traditions make people aware of their human endowment as created in the image and likeness of the Absolute Reality. Humans have potential for becoming divine, for reunion with the Absolute Reality — that is the fulfillment of human destiny. The development of the human person is a journey toward its likeness with the Absolute Reality, varying according to particular understandings and symbolic formulations of the gods and goddesses. A study of the gods and goddesses thus plays a great role in bringing our human consciousness to understand both our unique personhood and the nature of our own divinity within. This study is a profound exercise of the imagination, creating a multitude of forms to express something mysterious at the heart of human experience. It is the most awesome act available to humankind.

Becoming aware of the endless variations of the gods and goddesses in creation myths helps us to see the variety of idealized roles and values that are part of the human potential. It makes it possible for us to discover more about the archetypal patterns of the human psyche. Males can learn more about themselves not only from the image and likeness of the gods within, but also of the goddesses. Likewise, images of the male gods are as pertinent to the self-understanding of women as a full appropriation of how the goddesses inform their being as women. We need the dialectic of both male and female in our images of divinity so as not to deprive ourselves of an important experiential foundation of the process of spiritual transformation and development. From the gods and goddesses we learn about our roles and potential to comfort, nurture, inspire, feel, relate, bring order from chaos, search for meaning and purpose. Gods and goddesses of many different styles of thought, feeling, and behavior are within all of us, male and female. By becoming aware of them, and not endorsing any one as the only possible embodiment of the fullness of our potential, we can affirm and develop our own spiritual and religious styles.

## Mother Goddesses

The Chinese goddess Nu-kua created the first humans, taught them the ways of marriage, and restored peace after the cosmic battle of Fire and Water. In the historic Western traditions, goddesses are omitted or little emphasized. There is the tendency to center on the masculine godhead rather than the divine motherhood. It is true that Catholics sometimes suggest that Mary continues in the line of ancient mother goddesses and the Judaic tradition used to have strong goddess themes, but by and large, such goddess symbolism has been purged. The extent to which such de-emphasis can be linked to the repression of women or with patriarchalism is not the issue here. Rather, I suggest that those religious traditions that do recognize the mother goddess have retained an important dimension of the revelation of Absolute Reality in a way that other traditions have neglected.

There is an astonishing variety of themes, symbols, rituals, and attitudes focused on mother goddesses if we look throughout the world. Religions throughout history have recognized that the Absolute Reality is both male and female, sometimes by showing the god with male and female attributes, sometimes by splitting the image of god into female and male divinities. In either case, this represents their primary intuition that the male alone cannot represent the fullness of god.

Goddesses are neither a simple phenomenon nor do they appear with equal intensity, application, or significance in all cultures. In their earliest form, the goddesses are associated with the development of agriculture. In Babylon, Egypt, and India, for example, there was an equation between the divine feminine principle, the fertility of the earth, and the pregnancy of women. As Astarte, Isis, Hathor, the mother goddess was the feminine life force, deeply connected to nature and fertility, responsible both for creating life and for destroying it. She was regarded as immortal, changeless, and omnipotent. Patriarchal cultures later made her a subservient consort and appropriated her attributes and power to the male deity. She was demoted and split up into sharply distinct goddesses, all far less than her original self. Her femininity was attacked. The Babylonian Tiamat was the monster of Chaos; the Greek Pandora's curiosity unleashed every woe upon humankind; and the Hebrew Eve was cut down to mere woman, dominated by man, a villainess of a story of the origin of human misfortunes, especially death.

It is not this disenthroned or demoted goddess that I suggest may serve as a model or ideal for humans in their quest for the full self. The goddess within is rather the goddess in her earliest manifestation, the mother of all life, the one with life-giving powers. The mother goddess is the creator, the universe itself giving birth to all forms of life, who gives birth to other creatures from herself. She is the life-giver, the nurturer and provider, the one who transforms grass into bread, who makes milk out of blood. Her life-giving powers are not limited to physical birth, for she is also the mistress of inspiration, nurturing love and creativity in people, bringing the healing arts of civilization.

To her devotees, the life-giving and nurturing mother goddess displays a protective function, defending them in their vulnerability and insecurity from natural disasters and uncontrollable events or from hazards associated with particular occupations (such as protecting fishermen from storms). She is a refuge from disasters: famines, plagues, floods, or blights. She protects her devotees from those enemies who threaten the fragile fabric of human communities.

The mother goddess in her earliest manifestations is both feminine and masculine. She represents a unity that encompasses duality, the mother of kindness and cruelty, of both life and death. Paradoxically, the motherly, nurturing, protective goddess is also the agent of terror, destruction, and death. The goddess is thus ambivalent, fraught with paradox, combining love and anger, trust and terror, forgiveness and vengeance. For example, the Hindu goddess Kali though addressed as "ma" (mother) by her devotees, displays fury in combatting demons, stands on the corpse of Shiva, and receives animal sacrifices to quench her thirst for blood. Warfare and blood are part of her maternal function. Also, the Greek mother goddess, Demeter, the sorrowful mother of Persephone, weeps for the sorrows of the human race for those months each year while her daughter is held in the underworld and nothing will grow on earth.

Because of her cyclical disappearances and reappearances, she is associated with both protection and desertion, creation and destruction, feast and famine, vision and lunacy, life and death. What she gives, she also takes away. The nurturing goddess is also the devouring one. She provokes profound ambivalence. Her cruelty is no less salient than her benevolence. Creation and destruction are two phases of the one ever-recurring inescapable pattern. Perhaps the greatest gift of the goddess is teaching us that good and evil, life and death, are inextricably intertwined.

Thus, the fertility goddess is also the goddess of the underworld, of the realm of death. To die is to return to the receptive, generative mother, to enter the earth as a womb, rather than tomb. In the world of the mother goddess, death is the prelude to rebirth. But if there is a return, it is not a return of the same self. To the extent that we recognize and consent to the goddesses within ourselves, we are continually dying and being reborn. But this rebirth is a new life, not a return to the old; it is a metamorphosis, a transformed consciousness. Ultimately, to say yes to the mother goddess within us is to say yes to our transformation, to our rebirth into the spiralling and religious self. Saying yes to the goddess, we say yes to the attempt to recapture the primal experience of the reunion of the mother and child. We enshrine this reunion, this return to the beginning, with a sense of meaning and sustenance available for all humans, old and young alike.

## The Male God

The roles and ideals that humans can appropriate from the male gods are complementary to those life-giving, nurturing, and transforming powers we can appropriate from the goddesses. We recall that in the Chinese creation myth, P'an Ku fixed the sky and earth in their places in order to bring some sense and order out of confusion and chaos; and secondly, we remember that Fu-hsi gave them the Trigrams of the *I Ching* to help them divine their future. The gods thus help humans with two goals we all face: They give meaning where before only shadows reigned; and they shape and structure a vision to deal with a confusing and troublesome future.

In the very telling of their myths, especially their creation myths, people in religious traditions are imitating the gods. Through their myths they give order and structure to their world and perhaps bring meaning and purpose to existence that otherwise appears meaningless. In telling the stories, they determine a relationship between themselves, their gods, and their world — harmonious relationships within the totality of the environment. They provide themselves with an appreciation and understanding of areas outside human control that affect their well being and destiny. They establish norms, patterns, and limits in relation to the chaos, confusion, conflict, and destruction present in everyday life.

The search for intelligibility is universal. People of all ages experience the feeling of an alien world and the fundamental need to identify the forces of nature so as to bring order into them. The world often appears chaotic, full of random forces that intrude upon the more reliable patterns of life. In the same manner that the gods establish certain laws of nature, we fight against pure chance, against the possibility that behind the strange events of life, there is just random senselessness. The creation myths are stories in which the world is brought into its present order out of a chaotic condition. Those who told the myths possessed imagination, a capacity for intuitive identification, and some deductive powers.

Today we might use more complicated and sophisticated techniques to identify the powers of nature, and we might use philosophical and psychological analyses to bring this order out of confusion. Either way, we have to create a language to deal with the paradoxes of everyday life, and in so doing we explain our world, feel at home with it, and identify intimately with its ways. We celebrate the wondrous forces that created the world; we recognize our particular mission as a people; and we perceive our essential relation to the divine forces.

Categorizing nature and the world may provide meanings for dealing with the world and surviving in it, but it does not change anything. But if humans are created in the image and likeness of the gods, then they are also empowered to identify and evoke the creative capacities necessary for reshaping the world. Humans must maximize their creative potential and facilitate its expression. The creative process consists of a series of thoughts, acts, and functions that result in something, a product, with attributes of both newness and positive value. This creative product — not in the sense of some high artistic or intellectual achievement, but rather the development of one's potential for growth into the religious self — may seem to be in discrepancy with those who live by standard rules and conventions. Still, proper creativity is the exercise of this potential out of a sense of strong positive feelings of concern for other human beings. Though they sometimes oppose and seriously criticize the dominant values of the society in which they live and tend to produce an experience of discomfort and pressures of resistance, their motives are to create a "better world."

Creative persons developing the religious self have a positive relationship to the cosmos. They recognize that they are a part of nature, that they are responsible stewards of nature opposed to exploitation and destruction, and that there is a mutual history and common destiny of human life with all of nature. The realities of the gods, the self, and the world go hand in hand, and all must be understood in light of each other. That is, when creative persons look at the world, they see it holistically. They experience a radical participation with the cosmos, rather than a detailed, objective, scientific non-involvement.

Creative, responsible stewardship presupposes both a holistic vision of the cosmos and a commitment to its well being. In his sacrifice, P'an Ku invested himself in his creation and, thus, made it share in his divinity. In our era of global connectedness and personal creativity, humans who are striving to imitate the gods also must have a comprehensive vision of creation and give themselves for the benefit of the cosmos. They have to be in touch with the earth — they must be "humble" — in order to engage effectively in helping determine the destiny of the world.

This vision and commitment are paramount in regard to two grave questions: the ecological crisis and the threat of nuclear holocaust. To be in touch with creation and with creativity demands that they help formulate attitudes of behavior toward the environment that would assure a livable world for future generations. Also, it calls for developing attitudes about violence and war and the possibility of nuclear war that will effectively avert this overwhelming and literally final possibility for the entire planet.

In the final analysis, the success of becoming fully human is intimately related to a perspective that is eschatological, that is, a perspective focused on ultimate human meaning and purpose, a perspective that envisions reality informed by hope. It moves from a closed world to an infinite universe, serving as a stimulus to action on earth to hasten the metamorphosis of creation toward its final perfection. A determinedly optimistic vision, it is not a disincentive to action or flight from the world; on the contrary, it is a stimulus to greater action. It considers the destiny of each person as inseparable from that of all humankind and of the universe and calls for living this earthly life to the full and for sharing permanently in the eternal life of the Absolute Reality. Acting in the image and likeness of the gods thus entails living in community, alive to the needs of others, working to create communities in which justice (that is, order) reigns rather than injustice (that is, chaos). This final and definitive destiny is even now being shaped and fixed day by day by those who are conscious of and consenting to the development of the religious self.

# Review Questions

1.   What is the purpose of the Chinese creation myth?

2.   What do you suppose religious myths of "sacrificial dismemberment" of the creator god are trying to say?

3.   Why do you think humans are so often portrayed as being created from the very earth itself?

4.  The word "God" is sometimes a handicap to a discussion of the central religious issues to which the word refers. Why do you think we have used the term "Absolute Reality" throughout the book?

5.  Why do you suppose that Christianity has no notion of a mother goddess? Or does it?

6.  Which roles and ideals to you think humans can take on in the "image and likeness" of the creator or gods?

## Discussion Starters

1.  Compose a myth that accounts for the origin of the world and the first human beings; describe a perfect world that existed in the beginning; show how this world was lost through some blunder, mistake, or disagreement; and describe some ways that this perfect world might be regained. Would your world have freedom? Death? Happiness? Why or why not?

2.  "Humans are always trying to manufacture God, or a sense of God, and therefore ignore the one that is actually given because there is no credit to be gained in accepting a gift." (Alan Watts)

3.  "God is an invisible being who sits on a throne somewhere up there, watching us, testing us, punishing us if we're bad and rewarding us if we're good. He is the eternally vigilant lawgiver who is no respector of persons, making heavy demands of obedience on all of mankind, threatening them with eternal damnation should they not keep his laws and walk in his ways."

4.  Campbell suggests that "the Western concept of God is one of relationship while the Oriental one is one of identity. The Oriental idea is to acknowledge the divinity within during one's lifetime; the Western notion is to strive for a paradise after death." To what extent to you agree/disagree?

5.  "God, it seems to me, is a verb, not a noun." (Buckminster Fuller)

6.  "We cannot, in fact, think or speak about God without objectifying him. That means that, strictly speaking, we cannot talk about God. We can only talk to him."

7.  It is often claimed that "Mary is the Catholic symbol which reveals that the ultimate is androgynous, that in God there is both male and female." What justification can you suggest for this statement?

8.  If you could meet and talk with one of the gods or goddesses in the various religious traditions, which one would you choose? Why? What would you like to ask him? Her?

# THE SEPARATION

We have seen briefly one of the roles that humans play in creation myths, stewards of the world. Now we will look more closely at the relationship of humans to the Absolute Reality and at what it means to be human. Myths of creation, though telling about people who lived thousands, indeed millions, of years ago, are primarily stories of people today and of every age. In trying to account for the separation from the Absolute Reality in providing a mythic anthropology of what it means to be human, creation myths express in concrete images the dimensions of human responsibility for the condition of the cosmos. Perennial human problems — the experience of the dualism of good and evil, the difficulties that arise from trying to be totally independent and self-sufficient, and the dilemmas that accompany growth into conscious awareness of freedom — are made to flow into the past until they are anchored in the beginning.

It is important to recall that the first humans in creation myths are archetypes, not prototypes. If they were prototypes, their actions "in the beginning" would have happened in time, would have affected people's lives, and would continue to be formative throughout subsequent generations. As archetypes,

63

however, the first humans may or may not have existed in time; it is the timelessness of their story that compels us. What happens to them has universal application. What happens to them happens to all, but not because it happens to them first. There is no causal connection nor any implication that things might have turned out somewhat differently if they had acted otherwise. By "first" we mean "always." The human beings in creation myths are real and relevant not because they are first (prototypes), but because they represent what is essentially human (archetypes).

After pointing out a few common misinterpretations in the creation myth of Adam and Eve, we will look at many facets of the truth of this myth. Humans live in a world of dualism, made from finite dust and divine breath. Their desire to experience all things and to have a knowledge and control which exceeds the limits of their nature leads them to human pride and self-sufficiency. The cunning serpent shoves humans toward growth and freedom, but also toward the anguish and suffering that the exercise of freedom often entails.

The Genesis myth narrates what it means to be human and offers the choice of accepting or rejecting the responsibilities of being divine representatives and stewards in the world and the choice of building or destroying human relationships in mutuality and equality. Christians have long considered the fall of Adam and Eve to be a "happy fault," for now God becomes human in Jesus, the second Adam, to enable all humans to see their true nature once more, their participation in divine life.

## Adam and Eve

The creation myth of Adam and Eve, found in Genesis 2-3, is perhaps the best known story in the Jewish and Christian scriptures. From the particular Jewish focus of seeing all of life in the context of Yahweh's saving activity in history, it is found at the beginning of the epic which includes stories about Abraham's call, Jacob's struggle with Yahweh, Joseph's stewardship in Egypt, Moses' leadership in the Exodus and the making of the Sinai Covenant, and the final wanderings in the wilderness before arriving in the Promised Land. The Yahwist creation myth in Genesis 2-3 is the centerpiece of a larger creation story, setting the ground for stories of human alienation (Cain and

Abel), the need for purification (Noah and the Flood), and the inability of nations to communicate with one another (the Tower of Babel).

The myth of Adam and Eve is the story of fundamental human questions. It tells us of the loss of human unity with the Divine One, the origin of our separate and individual personalities, and the origin of evil as a consequence of free will. It ranges from the state of innocence to the state of responsibility, from human sorrow at alienation to human joy at affirming singularity and relatedness, and from what humans are to what we are called to become. It reassures humans regarding their future in the face of personal frustration, the hostility of the environment, and the dubious accomplishments of science and technology. The mythic account of Adam and Eve is a masterpiece of symbolic compression, developing the paradoxical interaction between human freedom and divine power, the equality of woman and man, and the mystery of human frailty and human greatness. Included are many etiological elements, descriptions of the causes of such human elements as mortality, sexual desire, pain in childbearing, frustration in having to work for a living, and the use of clothing.

In the beginning there is harmony in the Garden of Eden. Like a potter shaping his clay, Yahweh fashions the first human from the earth. Through a Hebrew pun on the word *adam,* which means "earthy" (or "human" — from *humus,* earth) we call this first human, "Adam." Into Adam, Yahweh breathes his spirit. Everything reinforces the harmony: the beautiful garden with its delightful working conditions, the river branching from the garden into four streams, the human's free reign over the vegetation of the earth, except for the Tree of Knowledge, which he is forbidden to eat under penalty of death. Animals are created subject to the human, whose domination is proclaimed by his power to assign names to all other creatures. After a search, Yahweh surprises Adam with a fitting companion, leading him to exclaim triumphantly, "Now this, at last, bone from my bones, flesh from my flesh! This shall be called woman, for from man was this taken." She will subsequently be called "Eve," that is, mother of all living persons. The first couple's lack of shame at their nakedness underscores their goodness and sexual openness. There is an intimacy and trust between Yahweh and his human creation: The tone throughout is happy.

But then the element of discord enters. The cunning serpent sensually entices them to eat of the tree of the knowledge of good and evil. "The moment you eat of it your eyes will be opened and you will be like gods who know what is good and what is bad." Since the tree is good for food, pleasing to the eyes and desirable for gaining wisdom, the woman breaks the divine taboo and the man follows suit. With this knowledge they discover their nakedness, become conscious of a sense of shame and fear, and hide from Yahweh. Realizing they are hiding, Yahweh's suspicions are aroused, and he demands to know where they are. The man replies that he is afraid and is hiding because he is naked. When Yahweh asks who told him he was naked, the question is met with a silence, a grudging confession of guilt. The jig is up now, and the man passes the buck: "The woman you gave me for a companion, she gave me fruit from the tree and I ate it." The woman tries to pass the blame on the serpent. The original harmony has been shattered by the couple's acts.

Yahweh's punishment follows. The serpent is cursed and condemned to crawl on the ground, a perpetual enemy of the man and woman. The woman has to labor in childbirth and be subordinate to the man. Man must, henceforth, toil by the sweat of his brow. No longer can he just wander through the garden and pick what food he needs; now he shall live only by toil and sweat and great effort. But the most severe punishment is the separation. They are separated first of all from the Tree of Life and thus doomed to mortality: "Dust you are, to dust you shall return." The supreme paradox is that the knowledge that was supposed to make them like the immortal gods ends in revealing to themselves their hapless mortality. Secondly, they are separated from the presence of Yahweh. Since knowledge of good and evil, combined with eternal life, would make them gods indeed, Yahweh must expel them from his presence and sets up a flaming sword and grotesque figure to bar their access to the Tree of Life.

## Misinterpretations

The Adam and Eve myth is the result of skillful creative imagination: It has symbols, etiologies, suspense, paradoxes, and excitement. Because of its powerful mythical character, this creation myth has fascinated people for thousands of years and has been subject to innumerable interpretations. Various elements of the story are so common that they are part of our everyday language and thinking. We have superimposed layers of meaning that make us read things into the story that aren't there. We presume, for example, that the serpent is equivalent to Satan, but the idea of Satan as a principle of evil is of much later origin. We look in vain for the apple Adam and Eve ate. Actually, the word for "apple" and for "evil" is the same (*malum*) in the Latin Vulgate translation. Accretions, beliefs, and prejudices obstruct us from hearing the real story. Paradise (that is, a Persian "garden") is, geographically speaking, nowhere. The first man is described as a gardener, though we know that the first humans were nomadic wanderers and could not have been agricultural or urban. The curses reflect a social and cultural milieu that corresponds to that of the Ancient Near East in the first two millennia B.C.

One major erroneous interpretation concerns woman, claiming that she is created inferior to man and is the cause of misery in the world. This is actually preserved in the Christian Scriptures: "A woman must be a learner, listening quietly and with due submission. I do not permit a woman to be a teacher, nor must woman domineer over man; she should be quiet. For Adam was created first, and Eve afterwards; and it was not Adam who was deceived; it was the woman who, yielding to deception, fell into sin. Yet she will be saved through motherhood." (cf. 1 Tim 2:11-15) Actually, the myth presents a striking contrast between the woman as man's partner and equal and the condition of woman as it was in the ancient world: the property of man, the most valuable of his domestic animals. In a sense, the creation of woman is the climax toward which the whole preceding narrative tends. We would not be too far wrong if we agreed with those who say, perhaps facetiously, that "God created man, then he knew he could do better, so he created woman."

The purpose of the story is not to reinforce male superiority, though it does reflect the thinking of a patriarchal society. Another charge, that Eve is the first temptress, that she uses wicked persuasion, guile, and tears to prevail on Adam, unable to rest until she gets him banished, is also without foundation. Eve has to share this accusation with Pandora, who was curious to know what was stored in a large box standing near her, lifted the lid, and before she could replace it, all sorts of evils and disease flew out and covered land and sea. To insist that through woman evil came is tantamount to putting the blame on Yahweh, for he was responsible for the tree, the serpent, and as Adam says, "for the woman you put here with me."

Another misinterpretation, often attributed to Augustine, is that the myth concerns an original sin of sexuality. According to the argument, since the serpent has always been a fertility and phallic symbol in the Near East (some would add: since the words "snake," "sneaky," and "naked" are so similar not only in English, but also in Hebrew), and since it is a serpent that convinces the woman to eat and who, in turn, convinces the man, and since the first consequence of their act is the knowledge of shame at their nakedness, it follows that their act of breaking the divine prohibition is a sexually motivated act of self-assertion. It is as if all pleasure, anything which is "pleasing to the eye and tempting to contemplate," is sinful. Sex, or at least sexual awakening, the argument goes, cost humans paradise. But this interpretation overlooks the fact that their sexual union is natural and expected, since they were originally one (androgynous). Besides, woman is created expressly as a suitable partner for man, a playmate. We can presume that the first sin is more than the budding realization of their sexuality and shyness about their bodies.

A third misconception is that all humans are born in sin and guilt. People speak with passionate intensity and seem to take bitter delight in quoting passages from Paul's letter to the Romans to the effect that "No one is righteous, no not one. . . . All the world is guilty before God. . .for all have sinned and come short." This has induced many to wallow in guilt with warped minds that foster unnatural repressions and self-hatred. Untold harm has been caused by an unbalanced emphasis on sin and guilt. The original sin is not sin in the personal sense; it is a state of existence. It relates more properly to a cosmic condition that has reflections in each person than to the personal culpability of the individual. What has been known as original sin does not mean that all are born guilty. Sin is universal, but it is not necessary. Although all humans undergo the original separation from the Absolute Reality, sin and guilt are not part of human nature. The essence of the first sin is that humans have lost the face-to-face vision of God and become subject to the power of evil. But the Fall does not change the essential goodness of their nature. It is precisely because all humans have a dignity in the presence of God that they are capable of tragedy. "God created humans in his own image" (Genesis 1). Humans still retain that image, even if they are capable of transgressions from the beginning. The essence, the fullness of human nature — the religious self — is not something that has been irrevocably forfeited; rather, it is something that we fail to attain.

A corollary to this misconception is that sin is something we inherit from the environment. That is, humans are disposed to evil when given the chance. Even before we are old enough to exercise freedom, we are unavoidably caught up in the sphere of evil, an area of darkness that holds us from meeting with God. Hopelessly enmeshed in a sinful world, we are dragged down by living in civilized society. From birth, people are gradually assimilated into an injurious sinful environment with resulting evil consequences. As we grow, our participation in sinful humanity grows too.

If this argument were valid, then all psychological and social influences would be inevitably harmful. The only sensible alternatives would be to turn away from the world or to pursue a path of idealism in which individual self-authentication and the "salvation" of the world become matters of human achievement. These are the very antithesis of what the myth calls humans to do.

## The Tree of Knowledge

If these are all misinterpretations, then indeed what is the truth of the myth? This truth is so powerful that we will approach it from several different perspectives. The myth tells us about 1) *separation* — humans live in a world of dualisms of good and evil; 2) *knowledge* — the desire to experience all things leads humans to pride and self-sufficiency; 3) *freedom entails suffering* — the possibility of creativity, love, and truth also implies the possibility of indifference, hatred, and lies; 4) *human nature* — with divine help we can overcome the separation in our essential relationships to nature, society, and God. The truth of the Adam and Eve myth, in all its dimensions, is summed up in the one taboo that God gives them: not to eat from the tree in the center of the garden, the tree of the knowledge of good and evil.

Separation of good and evil entails a dualism. The moment that Adam and Eve eat of the tree of good and evil, their eyes are opened; indeed, they become aware of good and evil. Though the cunning serpent assures Eve that they will certainly not die if they eat from it, they become aware of the polarity of life and death. Thus they realize they will have to die, and can no longer eat from the Tree of Life. They have fallen into a way of perceiving the world through dualisms, through separation. They become aware of a distinction between subjects and objects, between themselves and God, and they are ashamed.

The primordial couple attains the knowledge of opposites. This polarity takes over their central focus, and they lose all notion of a unifying holy One. Thus, they "miss the mark." This is their "fall," as they tumble into a situation where all of reality becomes limited, conditioned, and relative. Since they have lost touch with the Absolute Reality, they are confused and overwhelmed by the relative, becoming attached to the temporal and created world. They, and all humans, are alienated from their essential goodness. Expelled from the garden, their lives will, henceforth, be a search for the reunion with the One, with others, and with the world. It will be an attempt to overcome the polarities.

Many other religious traditions tell of this basic dualistic structure of the world with a myth of separation. the *fact* of the separation is constant, though *how* it is done will vary. (*Why* it is done is discussed in the chapter on evil.)

Among the African people of Zambia, the separation is also pictured as an expulsion from a paradise garden of harmony, but this comes only after the divine Being has first retreated from the world. In the beginning the creator Nyambi and his goddess wife, Nasilele, live on earth in harmony with all their creatures. One creature, Kamonu, a human, is different from the others and kills animals. Nyambi begins to fear Kamonu and gives him a taboo: "Man, you're acting badly. These animals are your brothers. Don't kill them." Nyambi expels Kamonu to another land, but he later returns and Nyambi allows him to remain and cultivate a garden. Kamonu's dog dies, his pot breaks, and finally his child dies, so he goes to Nyambi to ask for some relief. Nyambi is worried that Kamonu knows the road to where the gods are, so he tries to flee. He goes to an island, but Kamonu makes a raft; he goes to a mountain, but Kamonu climbs up to him. How can Nyambi escape humans?

He finally seeks advice from a diviner who says that his separation depends on Spider. Spider finds a place for Nyambi and his court in the sky and spins a thread for Nyambi to climb up from earth to the sky. Spider's eyes are put out so that he will not be able to make his way there again. Responsible for the separation, Kamonu tries unsuccessfully to breach it. His friends help him build a high tower to Nyambi, but the weight of the trees they use is so great that the tower collapses. Humans are thus separated from their god, and the split is irrevocable.

From now on, when the sun appears every morning, Kamonu greets it and proclaims that their god has come; and at the time of the new moon, the people greet the return of Nasilele, Nyambi's wife.

Two variations stress a similar separation. Among the Bantu people in northern Mozambique, the god Mulungu does not so much fear humans as Nyambi did, but rather claims that by learning to control their environment, to hunt and kill successfully, and to make fires, humans have violated the sacred harmony of the world. Instead of banishing humans from earth, Mulungu calls Spider and has him spin a rope for Mulungu and his court to climb up to the sky. Thus the cruelty of humans drives the gods off the face of the earth.

Among the Krachi people of Togo, the god Wulbari lives close together with humans in the beginning. Wulbari lies atop Mother Earth, Asase Ya, with the humans between them. The humans have very little space to live in, being so close to the gods. In time, they annoy Wulbari in many ways: An old woman keeps knocking him with her mashing tool; smoke from the cooking fires keeps getting in his eyes; men use him as a sort of towel, wiping their dirty fingers on him; and an old woman, to make a particularly delicious soup, cuts off a bit of him at each mealtime. Annoyed and pained, Wulbari goes higher into the sky where people can admire him but not reach him.

Myths of creation account for the primary separation of gods from humans, whether out of fear, or annoyance, or banishment. Adam and Eve are driven from Yahweh's presence for breaking a taboo. By their disobedience, the original union and harmony are destroyed, and the lines of communication are no longer direct. Perhaps because of fear ("The man has become like one of us, with his knowledge of good and evil"), Yahweh exiles the pair. And to guarantee that they won't re-enter to eat of the Tree of Life, he places an angel with a flaming sword at the entrance to the garden. A story that is tragic and ironic: Humans are told to control all of creation, but when they exercise their freedom, it is seen as a threat. It is a cosmic game where human initiative is foiled by a divine countermove. From now on their relation to God is not based on innocence, but on shame, fear, and withdrawal.

Eating of the Tree of Knowledge brings dualism not only in their relation to God, but also in a second relationship, to the world. Humans now live with both curses and blessings. We now have knowledge that life is a composite: matter and spirit; earth and heaven; mortal and divine; the Yin and the Yang. Some things are pleasant, some are painful. There are gentle animals, but also monsters and beasts of prey. Dogs and cats are tame and pleasant to behold, but some animals are ferocious and death-dealing. There are gardens, parks, and oases, but also wastelands, barren deserts, and frozen tundras. There are roses, but also thorns; mansions, but also prisons; gentle rainfalls, but also torrential downpours. Spring and summer become autumn and winter; sunrise becomes sunset. Plants and trees are a delight, but their soil must be tilled, and their fruits gathered and harvested. Children are a blessing, but childbearing and, sometimes, childrearing are a pain.

There is a third dualism too: Not only are humans alienated from God and from the world, we are also out of harmony with each other. (A fourth broken relationship, insofar as the individual self sees the dichotomy between what is and what can be, permeates the entire thrust of the religious self.) Instead of human communication and dialogue, we often yield to alienation and hostility. Instead of being "suitable partners" for each other, we are fragmented. Toward each other we are hard of heart, insensitive to human values, lacking in gratitude and compassion. This is the social reality of sin, of separation; we live with untruth, lawlessness, injustice, and oppression.

Nowhere is this dualism more oppressive than in the separation of male and female. The very life of man and woman was to be united sharing in procreation, in mutuality, in partnership, but this is not the way it has worked out. From the beginning of the fall into duality, males and females have had oppositional roles and ways of viewing the world. Aware of their nakedness, the first humans choose to stress just one pole of their sexuality, either the male or the female dimension. The search for wholeness from then on consists in trying to reunite the two halves of humanity into one totality. Only the union of these two principles, though in different proportions, constitutes the full human person. Each of us is only half human, seeking for the other half in order to restore the lost totality, the lost original harmonious relationship.

## Battle of the Tapestries

The ancient Greeks told the myth of Arachne ("Spider," "Spider-Woman") and her contest with the goddess Athene. Arachne has wonderful talent as a spinner and weaver, and her skill makes her famous. Her head turned giddy by admiration, she boasts openly that she can indeed weave a better tapestry than Athene herself. She rashly challenges Athene to a contest, convinced that she will carry off the prize. Athene disguises herself as an old woman and tries to dissuade the vain girl, giving her advice to back down and confine her challenge to other mortals. The old woman suggests that Athene is gracious and will pardon her arrogance. Arachne, however, rejects the advice not to try to better the goddess. She boldly insists that Athene is even afraid to compete with her because she hasn't answered the challenge. At such rashness Athene assumes her divine shape and takes up Arachne's offer. Arachne trembles a bit, but maintains her defiant attitude, rushing to her fate in blind passion.

Two looms are set up. Athene depicts gods and goddesses in scenes of victory over humans — subtle warnings of what may befall Arachne. In her tapestry, Athene portrays different results of human rashness: Mortals are turned into mountains after assuming the name of the high gods; a Pygmy queen is turned into a crane; Antigone who competed with Hera is turned into a stork; and some girls are changed into the steps of the temple where they are walked over. In all four cases, instead of the humans "becoming divine," they are "lowered to dust" (to a lower level than they were). Meanwhile, Arachne is busy with her tapestry, which she designs mostly with stories of how the gods have deceived mortals. Zeus takes the shape of a shower of gold, a flame, and a snake to deceive women. Poseidon and Apollo trick women by appearing as animals and taking on other disguises.

When Arachne is finished, no one can find a flaw in the work. This makes Athene furious. In a rage she tears at the tapestry that shows the crimes of the gods and starts to pommel Arachne who, no longer able to bear the punishment, tries to hang herself. At this pitiful sight, Athene is moved to compassion and lifts her up to keep her from strangling. She proclaims that Arachne, foolish as she is, may go on living; but just to keep her mindful of what it means to "defy the gods," she will have to hang all the rest of her days, she and her offspring. Athene then sprinkles poison on her. Her hair falls off, her nose and ears disappear, her head becomes shrunken, and her body withers, all except her large belly. From it spring long fingers that seem to cling to the sides like legs. And from her belly she still keeps on spinning and spinning, never forgetting the skill she used to have.

Arachne's downfall to the animal level, the spider, is the result of her pride and defiant struggle against her inevitable fate of submission to the Greek pantheon. It depicts her desire for self-sufficiency and total control as the cause of her alienation from the goddess Athene. Turning inward and becoming her own center, she becomes only a skeleton of her former self. This Greek myth gives us another insight into the basic truth of the Adam and Eve myth of breaking the taboo and eating of the tree of knowledge of good and evil. Till now we have considered one element of that basic truth, namely, the dualistic character of the world (the separation into *good and evil*); let us now take a closer look at the knowledge of good and evil.

## Knowledge of Good and Evil

Knowledge here is the lust for unqualified command and for the desire to experience everything. The Tree of Knowledge represents all knowledge, or a kind of self-sufficient knowledge. It does not refer to academic knowledge, nor scientific experimentations, or mere intellectual curiosity, nor merely knowing right from wrong. Knowledge of good and evil in our earlier discussion was a disjunctive; here it is a conjunctive. It refers to everything that is encompassed by good and evil.

What could this possibly be for Adam and Eve? They were formed out of the dust of the earth and the breath of God. Dust for some people refers to something that collects under the bed, but it does have a symbolic meaning. It points to the finiteness of human existence. We are contingent, dependent, and mortal. Dust means we are dependent on others; we are afflicted by evil, suffering, and death. But wait. Humans also share the divine breath. The creator has blown the divine breath into Adam's nostrils. Humans may be made of dust or clay, but they are also exalted by the breath of God. Each breath a human takes is the affirmation of the presence of God to human life. Breath is something special: Like blood, it is a sign of life itself. Humans have divine life within them; they partake of the holy, just as all things beautiful partake of beauty. Humans are formed from dust and breath. The eternal and Absolute Reality is connected to humans in their very relative, changing world.

From their state of nothingness (dust) humans are lifted to divine life (breath of God). Yet, evidently they feel there is some kind of incompleteness, a kind of flaw, due to this dualism of dust and spirit. By eating from the Tree of Knowledge, they attempt to make up this deficiency by taking what they do not rightfully possess. The essence of the serpent's trick is to persuade them to reach for what they can never obtain, though it should be "good for food, pleasing to the eyes, and desirable for gaining wisdom." They want a knowledge and a control that exceeds the limits of their nature. They want full possession of mental and physical powers. In their desire to be self-sufficient, to "be like the gods who know good and evil," to assume a godlike stance and authority, they go too far. With their lust for unqualified command, their will-to-power, they overreach the limits of human creatureliness. Ignoring the dust, they want too much spirit, assuming that they can gradually transcend their finite limitations, thus disturbing the harmony of creation. Reaching for the divine spirit, for mystery, they are forced to settle for dust, for finiteness.

The serpent's deception ("You shall be as gods") is not in sowing the dream of divinization, but in suggesting that humans pursue their divinity in isolation from God. Somehow we humans "know" that we can make it alone. Even though there is evil in life, we are somehow convinced that in spite of it, and even to some degree through it, we can grow without limit toward godlikeness. In the Hindu and Buddhist traditions, this is not knowledge, but ignorance. Humans are alienated, they say, because they are wrapped in a veil of ignorance (Avidya) which hides reality from them. Humans have a false belief in the independent reality of the "I." They experience the separated self — the Atman separated from Brahman — as supremely real. They are, thus, living in an illusion (Maya), cut off from Absolute Reality and from their own more abundant life within it. In both traditions, the Jewish-Christian and the Hindu-Buddhist, the separation is due to the desire for self-sufficiency. In one tradition it is the desire to transcend the self; in the other it is the clinging to the idea that there is a self to transcend.

In the Adam and Eve myth, the common denominator of humans is their infinite quest in their finite beings. In the process of overreaching human limitations and trying to be divine, we become less than human. The desire to get beyond the dust is a basic motivation in life, but it runs afoul and loses its course when it is pursued in isolation from divine reality. By our refusal to be radically helped, we humans would rather hide (in shame) from God. Our ambitions are beyond our reach, and we fall short of our dreams. Created from dust, we grasp for the divine breath, and end up in dust.

The deliberate eating of the Tree of Knowledge, the desire to be self-sufficient, is sometimes called the "sin of pride" or the "sin of concupiscence." Seeking one's own glory or wishing to make one's own life rather than receiving it from God is megalomania. Using others for concentrating all our energy into our own self-enhancement and self-aggrandizement, finding light and love in narcissistic reference to our selves alone are the intoxication of pride. Fleeing our dust side and trying to extend our freedom beyond human limitations we fall "up to" pride. The lawless and selfish desire by which we lose our selves in finite things is concupiscence.

Actually, this could just as easily be called the "sin of sloth" or the "sin of despair." Some persons have to face the temptation not so much to pride or the will to power, but rather to lack of self-esteem or willingness to remain weak. By disposition and temperament they are not aggressive. Satisfied with the self as it is, they are tempted to settle for the dust half, either deluded by its apparent accomplishments or dashed by its accidental failures. Some flee from their freedom (their divine breath side) and try to bury themselves in day-to-day activities, in the immediate needs around them, and thus fall "down to" dust. Rather than striving for the divine side, through independence, self-assertion, domination, they are content with subordination, laziness, or weakness. This is a complementary form of the broken relationship with the divine breath, another way of settling for dust.

Adam and Eve grab for the fruit of total knowledge and Arachne challenges the goddess in a weaving contest. In both myths they reach too far and have to settle for less. They are archetypes, and what happens to them also happens to us. When we strive to "be like the gods," we run the risk of losing our human dignity. Our eyes are opened, and we are suddenly aware of our selves outside the divine unity: We know vulnerability, emptiness, and shame. Like Adam and Eve who "saw they were naked," we are self-exposed in our own nothingness and seek to cover it. No longer clothed in divine breath, but only in dust, we hide from the divine presence. Overstepping our human boundaries, our human glory is crowned, not with glory and honor, but with fig leaves, thorns, and thistles.

Gone, too, is our harmony with each other: Self-justification leads to social sin. We are tangled in a web of structures of oppression, enmeshed in the warp and woof of racism, sexism, and other "isms" of self-justification and self-pride. Finally, in settling for dust we are surely doomed to die. Death is the termination of our struggles. Grabbing for the fruit of the Tree of Knowledge, we are banished from the Tree of Life. In settling for dust, we shall return to dust.

## The Serpent as Benefactor

This second glimpse of the truth of the Adam and Eve myth — that the desire for total knowledge ends up in our settling for less, for dust — may seem a bit negative. Perhaps a third approach, through a consideration of the serpent, will be more positive. The serpent tells Adam and Eve: "The moment that you eat of the tree, your eyes will be opened, and you will be like gods who know what is good and what is evil." The biblical serpent — known throughout the ancient Near East for its subtlety, wisdom, and secret power of regeneration — vastly enriches life, qualitatively and quantitatively. By offering humans the fruit of the Tree of Knowledge, the snake frees infant-humans from their garden-crib and opens to them the chance to acquire a far more spacious life than they have known in the garden. To the extent that people prefer life with freedom and anguish to a static existence with no growth possible, the snake is a human benefactor. The snake is a carrier of evolution, the forward thrust of purpose away from the regressive pull of the status quo to a world of responsibility.

Some people spend untold amounts of energy resisting risks, trying desperately to stay innocent and secure in the garden. They try to refuse to eat the fruit of knowledge; they hold on to dependence, avoid making responsible decisions, grasp at comforting dreams, and find substitutes for the difficult task of choosing what to know and to do. Their "sin" is the refusal to evolve, the refusal to assume their fundamental human responsibilities for nature and for history. The serpent's word to them is that life is not like that; every child ventures out into the street and thus becomes involved with the fruit of good and evil. Some parents try to be overprotective, to keep the knowledge of good and evil away from their children as long as possible. But good and evil are at the center of life. The dawning of human consciousness and of the need to exercise our freedom cannot be avoided if we are ever to grow up.

The snake brings us to the realization that we cannot hide from time. We discover that all the potential for happiness we felt in our childhood is not often realized in adulthood. Building sand castles is not the same as maintaining a home; playing war is not the same as putting a bullet through someone's head. The fall, the loss of innocence, is facing the facts of life, seeing the reality behind the mystery, and the mystery behind the reality. It is being drawn into the "web" of experience of good and evil, where it is constant with our humanity to work, to experience pain, to fear some creatures, to know human conflict, and to recognize our mortality.

The snake makes humans conscious of the opposites existing at the center of life. Without its influence there is only inertia, no challenge given, and no achievement demanded. Like an older sibling or wise uncle, the serpent has been around long enough to know that to exercise freedom and to take risks is the only way to maturity, the only way to break out of idyllic innocent childhood. The serpent is similar to the noble Titan, Prometheus, who elevates humanity by suggesting that a certain knowledge and power have been unjustly withheld from humans because of divine jealousy and fear of potential human exaltation. With his gift of fire to humans — the spiritual gifts of reason and consciousness — we are more than able to hold our own in the world.

One promise of the serpent is fulfilled — their eyes are opened — but the second promise — sharing the knowledge of the gods — translates into awareness of their mutual nakedness. New emotions overcome them and they go into hiding. They are now aware of their separateness, their individuality. This happens to all of us when we first become aware that we are different, unique, that people are looking at us. We all have our Adam-and-Eve moment, our moment of evolving self-awareness. Eating the fruit of the knowledge of good and evil is thus the emergence of consciousness, an evolutionary advance, an act of growth. This initial act of freedom is the dawning recognition that spiritual and moral growth come by both joy and pain. By our ''loss of innocence'' we begin to know what it is to face opposite pulls and to choose between them. Indeed, there can be no movement toward the full religious self except in a world where conflict and choice are possible.

Perhaps some may argue that it is not correct to talk of evolution in human awareness as a growth into freedom. In fact, they will say, it is rather a devolution into increased guilt, vulnerability, knowledge of mortality and finitude. The consequence of eating the forbidden fruit is the corruption of human knowledge and power. There is fratricide (Cain slays Abel) and there is the inability of humans to communicate across cultures (the Tower of Babel). Environmental rape and scientific manipulation, threats to human survival through pollution and the nuclear arms race, even subjection to the laws and institutions of civilized society are rather the continuing legacy we inherit from Adam and Eve. They will further argue that to talk of evolution is to presume that civilized people today are better than primitives and thus there should be visible signs of progress from savage beginnings to the heights of civilized refinement. The vastly greater tendency to madness, divorce, and suicide today should make us abandon the idea of evolutionary progress, of a gradual uplift of humanity along a scale of increased sophistication. Finally, they will argue, growth through evolution presumes that there is a kind of ladder of humanity. This goes against our democratic grain because it implies that there is a hierarchy of persons, that there are different qualities of being and life, of understanding and consciousness.

These arguments, far from making a case against the snake
as human benefactor and carrier of evolution, actually strengthen
it. It is precisely because of the snake's urging that humans
achieve the knowledge of good and evil, come to recognize that
there are both good and evil in them and every situation, and
can now know the difference between the two. That is why horror
comes from the intellectually advanced as well as the primitive.
Destruction knows no time or place; it is as much at home in
universities as in remote villages. The effort to climb the evolutionary ladder to achieve the full religious self will not be taken
by everybody, and not everyone who undertakes it will climb
with equal speed or energy. The snake points to the burden and
glory of human life. Wholeness stands at the center of a choice-
ful life, just as the tree stands at the center of the garden. By
freely choosing to be like the gods, knowing good and evil, Adam
and Eve — and all of us — are bound to have struggles and rever-
sals, along with rejoicings and success.

The free choice of Adam and Eve is their beginning of
growth in self-awareness, of their spiritual evolution into their
religious selves. It brings the recognition — to them and to us
that "life is suffering." We shouldn't expect that life will be easy,
that growth should come naturally. It is rather by fighting life's
battles, by facing and solving the problems it poses, that we come
alive and expand our selves. Some will come to religious maturity
through action, through discovering inner values; but all will
do it in anguish and moral struggle. If we harbor the illusion
that we can simply achieve wholeness top-speed, we will assuredly
slip back. No matter what heights we achieve, we must be
prepared to face the depths.

Within us a perennial struggle is going on: on one side,
resistance to change and revitalization; on the other, the thrust
toward wholeness. On one side, the thrust toward light and the
good; on the other, the thrust toward darkness and the bad. Jung
expresses it this way: "When Yang has reached its greatest
strength, the dark power of Yin is born within the depths; night
begins at midday when Yang breaks up, to change into Yin."
Freedom struggles between two irreconcilable pulls: the desire
for satisfaction and security in the status quo against the ruth-
less passion for creating the new and destroying the old. In this
sense, "original sin" is not the unhappy residue of a past event,
but the present opposition between our history and the dynamism

of our ultimate future; that is, the dichotomy between who we are now and who we can become. We are grateful to the snake for urging us to become aware of our real condition, to become involved in the process that carries with it an awareness of guilt and responsibility, of suffering and freedom.

## The Full Human Self

Adam and Eve are the archetypal humans. The essence of their story is so rich that we have had to approach it from different angles. We have seen so far that human separation from Absolute Reality is the severest dualism in our lives; that human pride and self-sufficiency create monstrous new problems; and that human freedom precipitates growth through suffering. There is still another way to become conscious of their story and consent to the Adam and Eve in all of us: The myth is quite simply the story of what it means to be human.

Though not everyone will agree on a common description of what it means to be human, our discussions of human dualism, pride, and freedom make it obvious that the full human is more than a "rational animal" or a "featherless biped." Genesis 2-3 clearly affirms the basic goodness of humans, for we share the spirit (breath) of God as the essence of life. Still, we humans often misuse the gifts and abuse the relationships that are constitutive of our human goodness. Also, our humanity includes the awareness of our ability to grow and respond freely to challenges. Our human fullness includes and transcends the personal and social, the physical and spiritual, the present and future dimensions of human existence.

Dualism, pride, and freedom are certainly basic elements of our common humanity, and from them we can tease out other elements. Humor, for example, seems to be characteristically human. We humans are full of contradictions and unpredictable behavior. We laugh at our mistakes and poke fun at our own pretentiousness. Generated not by inner tension but by inner harmony, the ability to accept our inconsistencies is distinctively human. Humor does not reflect conflict so much as resolution. It proceeds from strength, not weakness. Our ability to take pleasure in our creatureliness is one of the deepest experiences of our full human self. Human life is a journey between two gardens, totally different. The journey has its sacrifices and loneliness, its pain and darkness, but also its ecstasies, and its joy-filled moments of almost unbearable happiness. The human life is to be savored with the pleasure and rejoicing that come with the recognition that we are moving toward the reunion with the Absolute Reality.

Genesis 2-3 is complementary to the creation myth in Genesis 1, with a different view of our common humanity. In Genesis 1, humans are created in the "image and likeness of God;" they are creative and lordly. In Genesis 2-3, humans are gardeners and servants. If we lose sight of either of these two Adams and two Eves, we miss the fundamental paradox of our human condition. Though our heads are sometimes in the clouds, we walk on the earth and are made of clay. Though we dream great dreams and imagine marvels, our basic requirements are very simple. We delight in both creativity and simplicity, in excitement and tranquility.

Since humans are made in the "image and likeness of God," we are co-creators with God. By our responsible acts, in our individual ways, we can make and do things which are "good for food, pleasing to the eye, and desirable for gaining wisdom." Co-creators, we have immense dignity and awesome responsibility. We humans are most creative when we build up and strengthen the relationships that overcome our dualistic separations from the cosmos, from others in society, and from Absolute Reality. When humans are conscious of and consent to their creativity, the world is not immense or unmanageable, society is not an overarching institution unresponsive to our needs, and Absolute Reality is not receding from us, but rather calling us to return to its presence.

The human self is related to the cosmos, society, and Absolute Reality. There are relationships within and between our various dimensions; and beyond and above them all, a powerful mystery. Ancient Hindu mythology has a wonderful image of all of reality as the net of the god Indra — a complex network with a bell attached to each crossing of the strands. Wherever the net is touched, all the bells ring. Human creativity is the conscious ringing of the bells.

First of all, with regard to our relationship to the world, humans are entrusted with cultivation of the garden and dominion over animals, that is, with the sustenance and preservation of the universe. Since we are also "dust," we share existence with all creation. Lordship and kinship are our human ecological dimension. As *humus,* we are able to be "humble," that is, in touch with the earth and with our earthiness. If we are out of touch with our earthiness, we bottle up the divine energies of creativity and imagination. Native American Indians express well the proper human relationship to the earth. Chief Seattle, for example, puts it this way: "The earth does not belong to people; people belong to the earth. . . . This earth is precious to the creator, and to harm the earth is to heap contempt upon its creator.... Our dead never forget this beautiful earth, for it is the mother of the red people. We are part of the earth and it is part of us."

With our human freedom, we have a choice: We can accept responsibility for the world, or we can pollute and and waste the world's resources. Work and labor are not punishments, for Adam was created with work in mind (to till the garden), but there is too often enmity between humans and the world. We have sometimes overdone it with our technology. Our stockpiles of nuclear missiles, for example, are our Tower of Babel. Sometimes we should feel guilty for failing to assume our responsibility and authority, for failing to fulfill the potential of all created things and living beings. Proper human creativity in such situations would not be non-activity, nor a return to a simpler and more rustic harmony with nature. Creativity here entails putting the brakes on and changing the direction, reorienting science and technology to a harmonious relationship with the cosmos.

Second, with regard to our relationship with other persons, humans are entrusted with each other: "That is why a man leaves his father and mother and clings to his wife, and the two of them become one body." Humans have an obligation to others with whom they are co-creators and co-sharers in the nurturing of life. Human fullness and self-realization come only through a society's greater good, through love for others, which entails liberating their potentiality for love, growth, and awareness. Love is the will to extend the self for the purpose of nurturing spiritual growth. Love is the recognition of shared weakness, drawing from the group its creative gifts and powers of healing. Yet humans are free to recognize equality in others or to claim superiority over them. Recognizing equality, we give of the self and grow in freedom; claiming superiority, we remain captives in the garden and fashion a succession of Pandora's boxes with monstrous new problems.

Wholeness includes healing broken relationships. This healing occurs through liberating persons from the cycle of violence, from dependence on others, from social oppression. It means striving for social justice and all the pain that that entails. Most of all, healing means mutuality and companionship between males and females, finding beauty and strength in each other, celebrating the dignity of each other. "Bone of my bone, and flesh of my flesh," Adam exclaims. Man and woman are equal complements, partners in life and in sexuality.

Finally, with regard to our relationship with Absolute Reality, humans are entrusted with the charge to be divine representatives in the world. We humans share the very breath of God and find our fulfillment in the divine nature. We recall that after Pandora lifts the lid from the box, lies, treachery, deceit, diseases, and all manner of evils that could plague humankind fly out. We should also remember that curiosity later overcomes her again when she hears some fluttering against the sides of the box. Convinced that surely nothing worse could happen, she again opens the lid. A small butterfly-like being flutters out and rests on her shoulder: It is Hope, the final gift of the gods. Hope is indeed a human trait and helps to shape the full human self. We humans are constituted not by who we are, but by what we are intended to become. Our selves are determined by discovering our transcendent destiny, interpreting our present and past in the light of that destiny, and then striving to anticipate it. This destiny is the eventual reunion with the Absolute Reality, and we anticipate it when we are the divine representatives in the world.

Humans are free to acknowledge their dependence on God or to claim self-sufficiency. If they renounce their autonomy, the sense that they are master of their own fate, they can achieve reunion with the One, where there will be the overcoming of all dualisms and polarities. But the return to Paradise will not be to the same garden. There is a big difference between the idyllic Edenic past and the peace of the garden of the future. In Eden, peace and happiness are based on childish ignorance; in the future, they are based on freedom. Full human life as a conscious achievement is much more than life in an unconscious garden: Arachne continues her spinning, but it is no longer the same once she has been tangled in the web of human freedom.

## The Happy Fault

Striving to overcome dualism and self-sufficiency and exercising freedom, humor, and creativity are all constituent elements of human fullness. The Christian religious tradition adds still another dimension. In itself, Adam's and Eve's intimacy with God does not imply the divinization of human nature. In the Christian view, this divinization is possible and has been manifested in the God-man Jesus. Divinization is a transcendent goal of human development; it is beyond human achievement and can be realized only through grace, a gift from God. Human wholeness, as it gradually becomes synonymous with holiness, is not possible without dependent freedom, which opens the self to God's activity. Christianity shares this insight with other religious traditions: The Hindu avatars descend from heaven and open the path; the Pure Land Buddhist, Amitabha, releases those who have faith.

In the Christian tradition, the God-man Jesus is called the "new Adam," the new measure of our essential humanity. The promise of what Adam and Eve could become has been realized in Jesus but in a greater way than we could imagine. Not only is there a return to intimacy with God, but a human has actually been divinized. In this sense, the "fall" of Adam and Eve is a "happy fault," for it makes possible a greater human destiny than before. Humans now have the potential of becoming God's children as well as his servants.

This is the good news after the bad news. Jesus is the second Adam: In his incarnation, life of service, death and resurrection, and consequent gift of the spirit, humans have wonderfully and powerfully anticipated the resolution of the contradiction between what we are and what we are called to become. Human possibility to become divine has been established. Humans, through Christ have a "graced" participation in the divine life. When we exercise that potential, in free dependence on God, we accept human life as blessed and as charged with the responsibility to cooperate with God in creating a new Eden. Christians celebrate this event in their rituals of Holy Week, especially on Holy Saturday. They celebrate the new life in Christ, who is the "light of the world" that overcomes the darkness. "Let the earth rejoice," they sing, for "This is the Night." It is the night of celebrating the reconciliation with the One, when heavens are wedded to earth, and polarities are overcome. This is the Night of the Happy Fault, when Christians recognize, consent to, and anticipate their fullness as humans. The fruit of the Tree of Knowledge has never been sweeter.

## Review Questions

1. Why do we distinguish between archetypes and prototypes in regard to myths of creation of the first humans?

2. Describe the major misinterpretations of the Genesis myth of Adam and Eve.

3. What dualisms (broken relationships) occur as a result of eating of the tree of the knowledge of good and evil?

4. Why do you think Arachne challenged Athene?

5. How can it possibly be claimed that the serpent in Genesis 2-3 is a human benefactor?

6. What qualities are essential to being human? Can you think of others in addition to the ones from Genesis 2-3?

7. What does this statement mean: "Human creativity is the conscious ringing of the bells."

8. What is the Christian "happy fault"?

## Discussion Starters

1. "An order without someone to disobey it is somehow incomplete; nakedness without an eye to observe it has no meaning whatever; a heroine is unreal until there is a villain to bring her to life."

2. "People who shut their eyes to reality simply invite their own destruction; and anyone who insists on remaining in

a state of innocence long after that innocence is dead turns himself into a monster.'' (James Baldwin)

3. ''The forbidden fruit — the fruit of guilt through experience, knowledge through experience — had to be swallowed in the Garden of Innocence before human history could begin. Evil had to be accepted and assimilated, not avoided.'' (Heinrich Zimmer)

4. ''Man will never renounce suffering because, after all, suffering is the sole origin of consciousness.'' (Dostoevsky)

5. ''The chief source of man's dignity is his essential freedom and capacity for self-determination.'' (Reinhold Niebuhr)

6. ''Belief in free will comes only from man's need to be given credit for good behavior and achievements.'' (B. F. Skinner)

7. Design a utopian society: How is it governed? What are the religious and sexual and political customs? Who works? Who raises and educates the children? Is there freedom?

8. ''Robbers abound....No one ploughs the land. People are saying: We do not know what will happen from day to day.... The country is spinning round and round like a potter's wheel.... No public office stands open where it should, and the masses are like timid sheep without a shepherd.... Artists have ceased to ply their art.... The few slay the many.... Impudence is rife... Oh that man could cease to be, that women should no longer conceive and give birth. Then, at length, the world would find peace.'' (From an Egyptian scribe 4,000 years ago)

CHAPTER FIVE ————————————————————————

# TRICKSTERS

Religious traditions tell creation myths to bring a sense of order to life and to provide a pattern of orientation in space and time. These myths also describe the separation between Absolute Reality and humans, perhaps due to a process of evolution into higher consciousness or a devolution from some pristine state. We are now going to consider a third element often found in creation myths: the helper in the process of creation commonly called the culture hero or trickster.

This mythic figure in most ancient form serves as a link between the heavens and earth, a channel to the gods. He bestows on humans gifts of their material and spiritual heritage and makes them aware of their godlike knowledge and their responsibilities to civilization. As cultures become more sophisticated, the trickster's role undergoes a transformation. No longer is he pictured as one who helped shape creation and furnish order; on the contrary, he comes to stand for the principle of disorder, irrationality, and arbitrariness. This second form is familiar to us: the trickster as serpent, as spoiler, who plays a variety of mean tricks on the world, and thus introduces disorder.

What the trickster is to myths, the clown is to religious rituals. We will see that clowns, especially at carnival time, help provide with a period of release from rules and obligations of civilized society. By their fun, recklessness, and loosening up of proprieties, they provide feelings of relief and a general relaxation from everyday obligations. By highlighting the contrast between the realm of orderly belief and that of chaotic forces, they show the sense of relativity that clings to all of life and they help revitalize society by calling it to higher truths.

Tricksters and clowns bring out our utopian urge, our desire to live where we are all equals and where there are no social restraints. At the same time, they show the very need for rules, boundaries, and laws in human societies. Tricksters and clowns make it easier for us to live with uncertainty, to be resilient when we encounter difficulties in our plans, to consent to the arbitrary in life, and to admit our own self-insufficiency. They help us make contact with the numinous, integrate the demonic, and assent to the mystery of the universe which forever eludes and surprises us.

## Maui-of-a-Thousand-Tricks

Maui-of-a-thousand-tricks performed many exploits that are still told by Oceanic peoples. Perhaps the most famous story, and the one told with the most variations, describes his theft of fire. In the Hawaiian version, Maui and his brothers see a fire burning on shore while they are out fishing. They try to slip ashore unnoticed to capture this fire, but the birds who made the fire are alarmed, put it out, and fly away to hide. After several unsuccessful attempts to surprise them, Maui hides on shore and sends his brothers back out in the canoe, hoping to fool the birds. They refuse to rebuild the fire, for they perceive that one of Maui's brothers is missing from the boat. At last Maui hits upon a stratagem. He and his brothers set up a dummy in the canoe. Then he remains ashore while the brothers put out to sea again. The birds are deceived this time and build their fire. Maui seizes the moment to grab one of them. He threatens to kill the bird unless it divulges the secret of how to make a fire. At the peril of its life, the bird tells him the correct sorts of wood to use, and thus the mystery of fire is learned.

Another myth of the secret of fire was even more wide-spread. Maui, the much-loved independent child, always full of mischief and able to trick and deceive his elders, usually without hurting them, visits the underworld where he meets with his grandmother, the owner and guardian of fire. When he begs her for a gift, she gives him one of her fingers in which the igneous element is concealed. Thanking her, he wanders out of sight and quenches the fire in a stream and returns for more. She gives him another finger, which he also extinguishes, and in this fashion he obtains all her fingers and toes, except the last. Just what happens next varies according to the storyteller. In one version, his grandmother, angry now, sets the world afire. Maui has to enlist the forces of rain, snow, and hail to save it. Only with a great struggle does he succeed in putting out the conflagration, saving the world from total destruction. In another version, the fire-goddess throws the last of fire into the trees. Since that time these trees have preserved the seed of fire, which can be called forth by friction. In a third version, Maui succeeds in bringing the fire back to earth by himself after he has stolen it. But since the fire is a good servant and a bad master, it burns down many houses before it is tamed as people learn to be more careful.

There are dozens of stories about Maui's exploits in helping to shape and transform the world. In the old days, the sun moved irregularly and traversed the world at speeds much faster than now. The people didn't have enough time to mend their nets or finish their other work because night fell too soon. The sun had to be brought closer to the earth so that it might more quickly heat the stones that the people used in cooking their food. So Maui determined to harness the sun. He resolved to cut off the legs of the sun so that it could not travel so fast. Maui's mother presented him with a magic club that would aid him in this. As the sun came up out of the underworld, Maui noosed its legs one after the other and tied the ropes to great trees. The sun could not get away, and Maui gave it a tremendous beating with his magic weapon. To save its life, the sun begged for mercy. It had been beaten so badly that it was unable to travel as fast as before. Still, Maui released the sun from its bonds only after it promised to go more slowly from that time on.

Maui pulled the land out of the sea with his magic fishhook. His brothers ignored his caution not to turn back to look at what they were pulling, and when they did, their line broke, and the mass of land fractured into the group of islands we find in the Pacific today. In another exploit, he raised the heavens to their present height in the sky. Before this time, the heavens had been held up by plants and trees, which owe their flat leaves to the pressure exerted on them. His greatest exploit, however, was one in which he was not successful: his attempt to secure immortality for humans. He wanted to bring to life those who had died. He determined that the way to do this would be for him to be reborn, and with this in view he tried to reenter his mother's womb. His mother is described as mother earth or as a volcano. Her eyes are bright red, her teeth as sharp and hard as pieces of glass, her hair like the tangles of long seaweed, and her mouth like that of a barracuda. He started the process of reentry, but the chatter of some nearby birds disturbed the mother. His head was crushed by her startled movement. Maui was killed just as the victory over the realm of death was all but gained. Thus there was to be no rebirth for humans.

The cycle of myths about the mischievous deeds of Maui tell us about a graceless creature, much beloved because he reflected the common human frustration with the rules of everyday conduct. A capricious and lovable fool, he broke every taboo ever known, but was always forgiven in the end for his thefts and lecheries. He was wrong to do what he did, but his unconventional actions — especially the gift of fire — had the most rewarding consequences for the human race.

Maui's exploits are reminiscent of Prometheus, the Greek Titan who stole fire from the gods to bring to humankind. Prometheus was a paradoxical character, as wise and kind as a god, but still less than a god. Manifesting a native sympathy for law and order, Prometheus had originally espoused the cause of Zeus. But when Zeus found people hopelessly faulty, he planned to create a new race in their place, but Prometheus could no longer maintain his allegiance. He broke with Zeus and defiantly became the sponsor of the human cause. Since Zeus had deliberately withheld the gift of fire from humans, Prometheus, moved with pity, stole the fire from the hearth of Zeus (or from the fiery chariot of the sun, or from the workshop of Hephaistos, depending on the version) and gave it to humankind. Through this theft, humans were enabled to begin life anew and, little by little, to evolve the arts and crafts.

But Prometheus paid the penalty for stealing fire. Zeus had him chained to a barren rock at the edge of space and time and appointed an eagle to gnaw at his liver, consuming each day what had been restored during the previous night. His fate was somehow appropriate. He loved humans very much and became involved in their lives. Thus he was destined to remain just out of their reach. Still, his spirit was not dimmed, for he was armed and comforted with the "foreknowledge" (as his name itself implies) that someday he would be released and that Zeus would be dethroned. In due time, he knew, Hercules would kill the eagle and break his shackles.

Myths about the theft of fire could be multiplied, but Maui's and Prometheus's exploits are sufficient to show the central place of the culture hero and the trickster in furthering creation. Fire is a most fortuitous gift for humankind. For example, the Greeks regarded all fire as originally divine, as the strongest and most subtle force of nature, and a most potent factor in the advance of humanity. Of course, we understand fire today as combustion, and we put it in the dictionary rather than in mythology. Still, we read these stories and ask ourselves, "What's it all about?" And the way we use archetypal characters such as Maui and Prometheus tells us something about ourselves in our relationship to the Absolute Reality and to the cosmos.

Maui and Prometheus are both culture heroes and tricksters. They are both a link between heaven and earth, a channel to the gods. Their stories are about the interaction of the gods and humans. Fire was an appropriate gift to bring, since it has always been associated with the divine. Some felt that in discovering fire, humankind could rekindle the power of the sun-god himself. Fire then, like the gods, was both feared and desired. As the gods' secret, it could be both comforting and terrifying. Maui and Prometheus gave humankind a gift to reduce the power that fate and chance have over humans, who now have the power to determine their own destiny. Maui and Prometheus thus lead them out of an ignorant, innocent state, and give them godlike knowledge and an awareness of the responsibilities of civilization.

# From Culture Hero to Trickster

To refer to Maui and Prometheus as both culture heroes and tricksters is not accurate. The culture hero and the trickster really represent two quite distinct eras in the development of myths. Within the void or chaos, which is nearly always the starting point of creation myths, were contained the principles that would eventually be distinguishable as opposites, differentiating between persons and things. Looking at this vast horizon of "no meaning," the early religious traditions attempted to provide some clue to the order that must be there. They devised myths to explain how the world and its inhabitants came to be. They treated basic elements, such as fire and water, not just as accidental aspects of life, but rather as important natural forces established at the beginning. Their myths provided clues about the source of evil, the separation from the Absolute Reality, and usually promised some kind of Golden Age where conflict and strife would end. The begining of life, its present condition, and its future fulfillment were all brought together in their stories.

The myths looked for the relationship between people and the world, for harmony within the totality of each person's environment. They told of the roles and regulations that made their lives together coherent instead of chaotic and deadly. Their social arrangements were made intelligible by attributing them to the gods. The myths of the early traditions helped to give order and structure to their world and brought meaning and purpose to life. In their attempt to define and structure their world, they provided themselves with an appreciation and understanding of areas outside human control that affected their well being and destiny. They tried to discover a universal order that transcended all the separate parts of reality, to find some all-encompassing unity. They attempted to order their world by finding the source of unity that lies beyond the complexities, changes, and limits of this world.

In describing the process of creation, the cosmogonic myths serve primarily to bring order out of the chaos the people found all around them. In their myths of the formation of the cosmos and of the first humans, they somehow involved the all-encompassing unity that brings order to their universe. This unity, this Absolute Reality, was often directly involved in the origin of particular components of the world: the sun and the moon, animals, and humans. In many creation myths, however, this Absolute Reality plays only an obscure part. In some myths its role is relatively passive, and in others it doesn't appear at all. Once the primary creation has occurred, much of the work of shaping, assisting, and furnishing creation is attributed to another figure. This figure is the culture hero, a powerful figure that almost totally replaces the Supreme Being as the creator.

In his original significance, the culture hero transforms the world after its creation or assists the Absolute Reality in the act of creation. He may dive to the bottom of the ocean to bring up the first bits of earth, or he may put salmon in the rivers, or stars in the sky in a non-geometric pattern, or make rivers flow in one direction or the other. He changes the shape of the landscape — putting waterfalls here and hills there — and divides living being into animals and humans. In a word, he is the originator of many of the present conditions of nature.

This figure is called the culture hero, not because of what he does in shaping the cosmos, but because of the boons he brings to humans. He is the bringer of culture and the source of uniquely human institutions, such as agriculture, or language, or the technique of brewing beer. He bestows on humans their material and spiritual heritage, their arts and crafts, their laws and ceremonies. He is the mythical link between the original sacred realm in which time and space were first formed, and the mundane secular world of ordinary human life. From this "other" world he steals daylight, or the sun, or water as gifts for humankind. Typically he is the bringer of fire, that energy that turns the raw into the cooked, and rocks into metal. He is a monster slayer, helping rid the people of giant cannibals and other monstrosities. He is the agent of change, the transformer. He sets free humans who have been enclosed in a cave or imprisoned by monsters. He is the archetype of the hero, the giver of all great boons, the teacher of humanity.

As the creation myths became more and more complicated and as rituals were developed to bring some institutionalization and stability to the culture, it became obvious that no stories of a culture hero could adequately capture and explain the world sufficiently in terms of human knowledge. In trying to bring order to their world, the religious traditions unknowingly pointed to the very need for disorder. What this meant for the culture hero was that, in time, he came to be seen in conflict with the creator.

Perhaps the culture hero was seen to have a twin, Prometheus is one example, one bringing good and the other evil, one productive and the other destructive. Prometheus' dull-witted brother Epimetheus — "afterthought" — dispensed various qualities to animals such as swiftness, courage, and the like. He left nothing for humankind. So Prometheus gave them an upright posture like the gods, enabling them to survive.

But most often the culture hero is pictured as being in enmity with the creator. He degenerates into a symbol of what is evil and distorted in existence — a far cry from his earlier role as bestower of a cultural and spiritual heritage. He becomes responsible for inflicting misfortunes on humans, sometimes, it appears, intentionally. In his futile competition with the supreme being, he came to represent the somewhat capricious, dangerous, malevolent aspect of the supernatural.

The serpent in Genesis 2-3 has much in common with this degenerate culture hero. Tempting Eve to eat the forbidden fruit with the promise of godlikeness, he is responsible for destroying the perfectly harmonious relationship between the creator god and the first humans. Through him, death comes into the world, women suffer in childbirth, and men earn their bread by the sweat of their brow. Pandora, too, shares some of these characteristics. Her box marks the end of the Golden Age. Like the serpent, she is responsible for the destruction of sacred time and the human idyllic state. Through her, mundane time is initiated, and along with it, disease, labor, and death.

Evil and disorder could not be swept away as myths looked to find total order in the universe. The devilish individual, the spoiler who played a variety of mean tricks on the world, became more and more prevalent. Far from the original culture hero who displayed some of the more ideal characteristics of the supreme being, this irreverent and unpredictable being displayed ludicrous weakness, great deficiencies, and clumsiness in his competition with the divine being. And yet, he is still portrayed as a wonderfully comic figure, who knows nothing and yet everything, both manlike and animallike. He epitomizes the spirit of disorder and is the enemy of boundaries and definitions. He is ambiguous, arbitrary and capricious. The deeds attributed to him, the activities he is supposed to have set in motion, are not the result of some master plan or carefully calculated purpose or unfolding cosmic destiny. They are disagreeable and unintelligible events, due to his weakness and fumbling, or they are the result of chance events, accidents, and mistakes. His stories personify our human inability to give reasons for things that settle once and for all why there is something rather than nothing, or why this particular thing rather than another, or why there is an incredible variety of things.

In the myths of religious traditions, the culture-hero-become-trickster is unmistakable, but his actions vary according to the cultural context. As a trickster, the comic side comes through, rather than the devilish. He is the image of the actual conditions of human life.

In primitive religions such as the North American Indian traditions, the trickster is variously Raven, Coyote, Great Hare, Old Man, or The Foolish One. He is a spider, a mink, a blue-jay, a bat. Sometimes humanized and ennobled, the figure is usually the earthy, greedy, sensual child-animal who believes everything, tries everything, and finds nothing unnatural. A vagabond, erratic in purpose, he is exposed to all kinds of tortures. He survives by his own cunning and prowess. With his power as shape shifter, he has the capacity to turn himself into a variety of forms (perhaps becoming a bird, or invisible) to escape punishment for his tricks, sly jokes, or malicious pranks. He always manages to survive, to pick up the pieces and move on to another picaresque adventure. Thrown into existence, he seems doomed to learn through trial and error. He takes life as it comes, in all innocence, and never seems to learn from his experiences.

His left hand doesn't know what his right hand is doing. He is sly and stupid at once, with a spice of idiocy about him. He is woman-chasing, gluttonous, scurrilous, playful, knowing nothing of good or evil. Wandering from one adventure to another, he is an itinerant hero with no clear place or clearly defined social identity. He fends for himself in a world of competing forces, with no foreknowledge of how best to proceed. He seems to hover between worlds, dwelling in a world of his own, a world without boundaries. Though he is easily outwitted, he is never entirely defeated or dispirited. He possesses a certain resiliency, taking the bounces as they come. Getting in and out of tight spots, continually bungling or being hoodwinked, he gropes and grasps his way along, wresting survival from nature.

In the historic religions, there does not seem to be much room for the primitive form of the culture hero or trickster. Still, he is always present under some guise. In Hinduism, for example, the aspect that quickly sticks out is that of the change and unpredictability of the great Shiva. Shiva creates and destroys, gives gifts and destroys evil forces. Shiva evokes images of a wild dancer with serpent hair, companioned by a retinue of ghosts. His consort is the grim Kali with her bulging eyes and tongue hanging out to lap the blood of her victims.

In Judaism, the trickster element is not so much the serpent, which is often called the Devil and confused with Satan; rather, it is the element of deception, found in many of the family stories in Genesis. The frequency with which the trickster role is enacted suggests that deception was socially legitimated behavior available to both men and women within the social structure. Thus Jacob tricks his father Isaac, and Rachel tricks her wily father Laban; Abraham tricks the pharaoh, and Lot's daughters trick their father. In Christianity, the trickster's arbitrariness is the theme of the song Mary sings in Luke's infancy narrative. The proud will be scattered, and the humble shall be exalted. Also, Jesus performs in the manner of the culture hero who creates good things for humankind from his own deprivations. He suffers and, in dying, gives a share of his life.

## Clowns and Carnivals

The culture hero and trickster developed in proportion to how much order and purpose the various religious traditions attempted to bring into their teachings, rituals, and myths. They welled up in the unconscious as a sign of the inherent human repugnance against putting too much order in life and a sign of the natural rebellion against a life that is totally predictable or one-dimensional. They are the mythical vehicle for persons to come to terms with the arbitrariness of life without any elaborate attempt at rationalization. Culture heroes and tricksters are a way of underlining that the whole of a culture is an artifact whose structure is logically arbitrary: It could have been otherwise. Not only is the non-rational a part of life, but the very fact that we have chosen one lifestyle and world view rather than another is itself non-rational and arbitrary.

Culture heroes and tricksters are paradoxical. They bring
the gifts of civilization, and yet they break every taboo and shatter
every moral boundary that civilization sets up. While bearing
the gift of fire, and with it, reason and enlightenment, they represent the principles of inevitable chaos, disorder, and the irrational. More than symbolizing human complaints and despair
over the basic needs and difficulties of life or human attempts
to rationalize mysteries, the culture hero and trickster are
reminders of the original unity of humans with Absolute Reality.
They conjure up images of the separation from the original
oneness and recall human hopes for some kind of perfect world
other than the one we know and experience every day. They
serve as a release from the pressure of having to find a reason
for everything in much the same manner as many today try to
outwit evil forces, encourage good fortune, and obtain guidance
by a miscellany of techniques, such as reading tea leaves or
diligently consulting the daily horoscope or engaging in State
lotteries.

Rituals in many religious traditions also celebrated the
nostalgia for paradise and provided a sacred period of release
from the roles and obligations that came with civilized society.
These rituals, with clowns and other masked figures playing the
key role, were associated with springtime and harvest rituals,
where the joy of life was paramount and the renewal of life
through food and fertility were celebrated. Trying to recapture
and reinstate a Golden Age, a time or condition in which limita-
tion and renunciation did not exist, the people permitted
debaucheries of every kind and transgressions of what, at other
times, were the most sacred sanctions. This festival was a time
of parenthesis, a holiday period in which nightmare images
sprang to life and released a breath of madness. The mechanisms
for this uninhibited world of carnival were similar everywhere —
in the Greek Dionysian orgies, the festival of the Saturnalia in
Rome, the Feast of Fools in France, and many other comparable
rites of reversal.

In the Revels of Dionysius, the ancient Greeks stalked the
alleys and squares of Athens in honor of the god of wine,
madness, and rebirth. This ritual centered around the mystic
experience of death and rebirth associated with the springtime
regeneration of the earth. Masked and shrouded in animal
skins, a whirling procession of men in women's garb blended

enthusiasm, merrymaking, violence, eroticism, and the ridiculous into a profound drama of death and rebirth. Groups of women streamed out of Athens in disguises and roamed the mountains for several days, tearing to pieces with indescribable savagery any living animals they caught. These festivities centered on the god Dionysius who, born with goat's horns, brought up as a girl, and raised on honey, was driven mad by the goddess Hera and wandered over the world with a wild mob of satyrs, bringing people the gift of wine and leaving a trail of murder and insanity in his wake.

These gruesome activities were softened when they were translated to Rome. They became the rituals of the Saturnalia, a festival celebrated at the winter solstice. Rather than destructiveness and unbridled license, the emphasis shifted to fun and reckless spirits and a general loosening up of proprieties. There was a humorous reversal of roles, for example, where slaves were served by their masters (a practice still evoked on Boxing Day in England and in Sadie Hawkins dances). The annual feast commemorated the reign of Cronos (or Saturn), a time of release from everyday obligations (as some still do on Saturn's Day, Saturday). It was a momentary return to a Golden Age when all persons were equal and the good things of life were held in common. It was a time of happy anarchy, a time when no war could be begun nor criminals be punished (for what was war and who were criminals in the Golden Age?).

Early Christianity also had ritual ceremonies that abrogated rule and provided for a reversal of socially accepted roles and values. The old pagan festivals were again transformed. Saturnalia became Carnival (*carne vale* means "Farewell to the flesh") and was moved to the days preceding the lenten period of austerity. This ritual period grew wilder, madder, and more menacing with the centuries, culminating in the medieval Feast of Fools and Feast of Asses.

The Feast of Fools was an obscene and blasphemous burlesque of the ceremonies of the church. A ritual of undisciplined wildness, unrestrained wantonness, and irresponsibility, it was a mockery of the ecclesiastical structure. The priests who took part elected a Pope of Fools and appeared at the liturgy either wearing masks or dressed as women. While the priest celebrated Mass, the people danced, played dice, and sang indecent songs. At the singing of the Office for the Feast, the priests and clerics again donned monstrous masks and danced in the choir. They incensed the congregation with stinking smoke from the soles of old shoes and roused the laughter of bystanders with indecent gestures. In the later Feast of Asses, an ass, or a man wearing the mask-head of an ass, was introduced into the sanctuary during Mass. The Song of the Asses was sung, accompanied with the congregation chanting "hee haw, hee haw." At the end of the Mass, the celebrant, instead of singing "Go, the Mass is ended," brayed three times, and the congregation, instead of responding "Thanks be to God," also brayed three times.

The more ridiculous the ritual, the greater the enthusiasm with which it was celebrated. Such rituals were eventually banned, but only over the course of centuries. Even then, many of the practices were retained in profane theatricals. Indeed, many of these elements, stripped of their ritual context, still survive today. April Fool's Day with its pranks, and New Year's Eve with its paper hats and charades are only pale reminders of the medieval Carnival. But the giants on stilts with hideous grinning masks, crudely fashioned dragons and misshapen beasts, horses trampling on crowds, men painted up as women and women swaggering in men's clothing, and the general drunken revelling that occur during Carnival time in New Orleans and Rio and during *Fasching* season in Germany are direct descendants of these medieval rituals.

Ritual clowns still survive today, in particular, among many of the North American Indian tribes. Playing out their hilarious activities during the public performances of annual festivities, these clowns perform an important ceremonial role. Their buffoonery and frivolous pranks help ease the pressure brought on by the tense and solemn atmosphere during the sacred ceremonies. Early observers were slow to recognize the importance of the clowns' religious role, probably because their sensibilities were threatened by the shocking behavior and because they felt such conduct had no place in civilized society. They did not realize that it was precisely because of their deviances from the norms of social behavior that the clowns stimulated feelings of relief and malicious joy among the people.

The ritual clowns go by different names in the various North American religious traditions, names such as Funny Men, False Faces, Fool Dancers, or Contraries. Their humor often centers on gluttony. They are willing to do anything for something to eat, and they eat constantly throughout the days of ceremony, consuming amazing quantities. Their fare is often dirt, live mice, sticks, stones, or whatever is considered offensive and defiling. Their sexuality is exaggerated. They enact skits portraying aspects of human sexuality, or they appear nude and engage in explicit sexual activities, even in the most sacred places during public ceremonies. Their antics are often done expressly to annoy spectators. They might smear mud or excrement over their bodies or drink urine and pour it on one another. They might drop live coals or ashes on people, scoop handfuls of cinders and spray everyone in sight, or plunge their hands into boiling water to demonstrate their power. Sometimes the clowns will act in a contrary fashion. They might reverse the world of language by talking backwards and saying no when they mean yes, or they might ride backwards on a horse, put their boots on the wrong feet, or wear heavy clothing in summer.

## Social Reversal and Release

Maui and Prometheus were helpers in the process of creation, bringing to humans the gift of fire, a symbol of enlightenment and civilization. With the beginnings of civilization, life became more complicated and sophisticated. The Golden Age, a time of simplicity and innocence, faded away. People lost their close union with the creator, the Absolute Reality, and with it their sense of harmony and balance with the world and with each other. Chaos dominated, and they had to introduce more and more order, rules, and regulations into their society for things to run smoothly. In the attempt to dispel disorder, they almost shut out an essential part of their lives. Taboos became rigid; guilt and embarrassment accompanied their human clumsiness; and the arbitrary and unpredictable had no legitimacy.

The tricksters, clowns, and carnivals came along with the phenomenon of cultured societies. The more primitive groups had no need for an outlet against too much regimentation and reason, for the return to chaos was something that loomed over them at every hour. In cultured societies, however, these figures developed as social outlets for humans to protest against the obligations connected with their social order. The movement from culture hero to clown was the movement from ethical lawmaker to ethical lawbreaker.

With their excessive behavior, the tricksters and clowns are earthy disruptive merrymakers who help elicit an ambivalent laughter from the members of cultures and religious traditions. They stimulate feelings of relief and malicious joy in a ritual context because of their many deviances from the norms of social behavior. They know the taboos and can break them with impunity. Though their function includes entertainment and comic relief, it is much more profound than merely providing a spirit of play in a world of seriousness. Their role is essential and full of religious significance. In poking fun at the establishment, whether at police officers, priests, or politicians (as the comedians — our modern tricksters — do very well), they might appear to weaken the very fabric of society, but actually they are revitalizing it by calling attention to higher truths.

During the 1968 student riots in Paris, someone had scribbled across one of the large advertising signs that line the subway walls: "Attention all anarchists. There will be an organizational meeting next Monday night at 7:30 in the foyer of the Sorbonne." Paradoxical as it was, the students felt that they needed to organize, even in the very act of trying to bring down the organization. In their protest against regulations that are concomitant with living in a civilized society, they institutionalized their protest against that institutionalization. This was a mythic act worthy of tricksters and clowns.

As soon as the conditions of stability for living in a civilized society become oppressive, then the need for a compensating period, a time of anarchy and license, however brief, becomes manifest. Most societies recognize this need and channel it, containing it within the specified dates of their local calendar. We see this, for example, in the revelry of Halloween, and Mardi Gras, and New Year's Eve, and even in the pageantry of the Superbowl. Tricksters and clowns manifest the human desire and human struggle to be free of rules, to be unbound and without limitations. They personify a utopian urge to return to a time prior to obligations, a desire to be unconfined, even while admitting that we have to live by society's rules if we are to escape chaos. Ironically, they offer relief from too much order, and relief from too much freedom. They question our established ways and our ability to question.

Tricksters and clowns, as well as our modern comedians and political cartoonists, are profaners, offering an ironic and essential contrast between the realm of orderly belief (with its tendency toward the one-dimensional, the reliable, the dependable), and the realm of chaotic forces (with its celebration of ambiguity and randomness). They act as an officially sanctioned exception clause, keeping society from taking itself with ultimate seriousness. They profane the ideologies and myths of society and balance excessive order by conveying a sense of the relativity that clings to all of life.

In their revelry and mock ridicule, the tricksters and clowns turn the distinctions of rank and status upside down. They deflate the pompous, skewer the self-righteous, and chide the hypocritical. They subject authority figures and ceremonial regulations to wild burlesque, enabling people to give way to great outbursts of pent-up repression. They temporarily turn society inside out with the shrewdly permitted license of the holiday of the vacation period. Striking a blow against law and order, they reach out for a state of pure freedom, a return to the time prior to repressive laws and other civilizing influences. They reverse social roles and social norms in the extravagant joy of overthrowing those restraints and inhibitions that are the price for civilization. The world becomes, for the moment, a place where discrepancies disappear and all become equal. The joy of the beginning, which has been irrevocably lost from the earth, is made present for the moment. In the dissolution of the stiffened traditional order, there is a reactivation of the boundless power and creativity of the beginning.

The real irony, though, is that by doing the forbidden, by representing the forces of chaos and disorder, the tricksters and clowns are thereby creating a meaningful world. By openly flaunting social customs and compromising cultural values, they are actually revealing the very need of the boundaries that give order. By flaunting cultural restraints, they make people aware of their need for restraints. They encourage assent to the regulations of society by negative example. Their actions discourage actions by exposing them. They reinforce the status quo in the act of providing temporary relief from it. They introduce and define elements of a culture's world view in the act of defiling them. Their "civil disobedience" presupposes authentic civil obedience and recognizes the authority and office both of the state and the religious tradition as legitimate but to be taken with provisional, rather than ultimate, seriousness.

## Laughing at Ourselves

Maui and Prometheus and their successors, the tricksters and clowns, keep us from taking ourselves too seriously. In offering themselves as objects of laughter, they take upon themselves the imperfections of us all. They are the foil for our own insecurity. We jeer, knowing that their failures are really our own. They poke fun at our grandiose schemes by showing that some, after the fashion of the Merry Prankster, Till Eulenspiegel, and the bumbling TV detective, Columbo, will achieve through their bungling and stupidity what others fail to achieve through their best efforts. How clumsy we really are. Who of us hasn't held the door open for someone only to have it slip out of our hands just as they are walking through it? Who hasn't offered a box of candy to another, only to have it drop out of our hands at the worst possible moment? We cannot tame or order or control everything. The best laid plans go awry. The tricksters and clowns point to our own need for resiliency when we encounter difficulties in our plans and fail to carry them off smoothly.

The tricksters and clowns are teaching us about ourselves. Many of their purposely exaggerated actions mock those needs and drives which are distinctively human. Often gluttonous or greedy to the point of destroying what they are unwilling to share, often making the same mistake repeatedly in the failure to see the obvious, they are reminding us of a childlike element in ourselves. They are saying that we are all too often too serious. We have forgotten how to be children. Sometimes we should have no aspirations beyond the present moment. Occasionally we have to defy the universe to live in joy, and for that moment at least to ignore any ultimate purpose in life. When children are outsmarted or act stupidly, they are not entirely defeated nor dispirited; they bounce back without grudge or malice, a little bruised or hungry perhaps, but also a little wiser. They don't feel hemmed in by regulations. If the score is lopsided in their pick-up ball game, they'll quit, choose up teams again, and start over. Children are not weighed down by misfortunes or limitations or by the apparent inequities and injustices of life. For them, life is a challenge and they make a game of it. Winning or losing — these both lead to laughter as well as to tears and dismay.

The trickster and clown enable us to embrace ourselves and each other as humans. They reaffirm our human condition and reduce life to the basics. Our requirements are simple: a good meal and restful sleep, freedom from anxiety and bodily problems, the enjoyment of sex and the laughter of children, the satisfaction of work and the pleasure of play, the conviviality of friends and internal peace.

Still, we cannot be "up" all the time. Some moments are moments of unrestrained joy; at other times we are sluggish, gloomy, grave, leaden. We are at times jovial or saturnine, moonstruck or mercurial. Recognizing our basic needs and realizing that we cannot always achieve them, we consent to a larger vision of humanity, a more inclusive acceptance of the many-sided self and other selves. In this, the world does not seem as inflexible and confining as it did before.

In the celebration of our common humanity, we find that being human is not a heavy weight that drags us down or lays a curse on us, but something potentially delightful. We are saying yes to the tricksters and clowns in ourselves, clothed in the awkward innocence of essential humanity. Not a lofty comedown from some idealized image we have of ourselves, it is a reaffirmation of our totally human condition, not as impure, or profane, or shameful, but as fundamentally good.

The trickster and clown not only give us a larger vision of our common humanity, they also bring to consciousness many of the human instincts of our undeveloped state. They provide at once a mockery of the over-heroic life and a corresponding mockery of a life that is merely natural. The tricksters, and especially the clowns in their rituals, open us up to another reality, the dimension of the numinous and the mystical. By evoking fright and terror, or by prompting laughter, they open people to experience not mediated by rational or scientific explanation. They bring the primordial, subliminal elements of our selves to the conscious level in a mythic or ritual setting.

The trickster and clown often represent behavior that is not approved by our conscious minds. The more civilized we are, the more we pretend to ignore their importance, or even their existence, usually with disastrous consequences. We have to somehow make room in our selves for the reality they evoke — the reality of demonic power, of Satan, of suffering. Rather than trying to explain away all the manifestations of the demonic (due, we might say, to black cats, rabbit's feet, jinxes, gaffes, bad luck), the trickster and clown mythically and ritually express our need to admit and to harmonize it into our lives. They give the demonic its due, and help us integrate it rather than repress it. They represent the goblins and ghosts of Halloween night that balances with All Saints' Day; the suffering of Good Friday that balances with Easter; the fun and games of Mardi Gras that balances with the austerities of Ash Wednesday. By recognizing the demonic both in our unconscious and in the world, we admit our own self-insufficiency. We acknowledge that ultimately we have no control over the world and open our selves to help from a savior in our quest for the religious self.

## Topsy-Turvy World

Admitting the demonic in ourselves, we recognize that no matter what efforts we take at shaping things into a rational, orderly, meaningful whole, life is not intelligible or predictable or just. Although we may attempt to define the significance and value of this or that aspect of life or assign causes or develop a logic of relationships, we recognize that a fundamental arbitrariness is quite transparent. No matter what stories we tell to bring purpose and order and no matter how "advanced" our technological society, we still cannot control the quirks and accidents of life. The need for balance always asserts itself. There will always be the rich and the poor, the advantaged and the disadvantaged. Some of us will live short lives, others long lives. Randomness sorts us into the intelligent and the retarded, the attractive and the unattractive.

The tricksters and the clowns help us to come to terms directly with the unpredictable. They make us accept arbitrariness as essential to life itself. The theologies and philosophies of the world's religious traditions, which define cosmic order, divine plans, historical patterns, and ultimate destinies, are all attempts to help us cope with this uncertainty. By contrast, the tricksters and clowns do not offer some well-hidden cosmic plan nor do they attempt to justify the ways of the gods to our ways. Theirs is not the language of sin and judgment, of providence and predestination, of karma and reincarnation, of the fates and the stars. They invite us, instead, to play in the rough and tumble of life, without glossing over what is not always pleasant.

The tricksters and clowns live in us all, for they represent the principle of uncertainty, and their manifestations are universal. We conjure them up when we cross our fingers, knock on wood, blow on dice, or buy dashboard saints. We acknowledge them when we admit down deep that no matter how much structure and order we give to our lives, no matter how much meaning and direction we see or think we see, no matter how successfully we believe we are making progress, our lives and our stories still manage to move in mysterious and unforeseen ways. We consent to them when we admit that no matter how much progress in science and technology we have made, we cannot bring things under control. Paradoxically, the more we bring greater predictability and security to our lives, the more we expose our selves to the unpredictable: What would nuclear winter, power blackouts, and oil tanker spills have meant to those in earlier cultures?

Order and chaos are both essential for our full selves. We can never say that a time will come when there is absolute predictability, when precise calculations will eliminate all the element of mystery. If we were to demand such absolute points of reference, then we would opt for absolute monotony. We would refuse the adventure, risk, challenge, and drama that the trickster and clown personify and completely close our selves off from, and not be free to truly laugh before, the mystery of the universe, which forever eludes and surprises us.

Consenting to the arbitrary in our lives, we are playing the game for the sake of the game. Rather than striving for a perfectionism that can infect or cramp our lifestyle, rather than being involved in cutthroat competition, we can now celebrate our common humanity. Instead of having to be experts, pursuing even our hobbies with a vengeance and treating our play and our games as a burdensome job, we say yes to the curious business of being fully human. When we realize that there are no ultimate answers, and that the thing to do is to live, we are freed from the burden and the awesome responsibility of having the last word. We are freed from the impulse to play God relative to the universe. Being human is not a curse, but potentially delightful, a "happy fault." Those who recognize and consent to the tricksters and clowns inside themselves are saying yes to all sides of their humanity and are not pretending to a divinity that they have not yet attained. They embrace themselves as they are.

# Review Questions

1. Why do you think trickster myths are so prevalent in world mythologies?

2. Trace the development from culture hero to trickster.

3. What are the major characteristics of the trickster? Which of these elements do you find in yourself?

4. What are the major functions of tricksters in myths?

5. What is the relationship between tricksters and clowns?

6. Explain: By representing the forces of chaos and disorder, tricksters and clowns are creating a meaningful world?

7. Explain: Tricksters make it easier for us to live in a topsy-turvy world?

8. What is the nature and purpose of the ritual of carnival?

# Discussion Starters

1. "The source of unhappiness lies in man's effort to control his destiny, thereby impeding the natural flow of spontaneous events."

2. "I find comfort in things like earthquakes and eclipses of the moon because I have no hand in them. They relieve me of responsibility. I find comfort in fatalism and inevitability." (James Taylor)

3. "It is always good to be distinguished by something. I ask nothing better than to be pointed out as the only one in our serious age who is not serious." (Kierkegaard)

4. "The moment you begin to tell your stories you may find that memory is a trickster who picks and chooses scenes. What happened to you in the past has yet to be determined."

5. "In Trickster is embodied the human struggle against the confinement felt by being bound to place, even within the obvious necessity of such definition in order to prevent chaos. In many of his adventures, Trickster permits people to experience the vicarious thrills and freedom of a utopian existence. But his folly reveals the very meaning of the boundaries that give order to human life." (Sam Gill)

6. "In the fragment of a lost play by Aeschylus, the bisexual god Dionysus is greeted by cries of 'Where have you come from, man-woman, what is your country? And what is that garment?' — questions which incidentally might well be addressed to a contemporary teenager. This deliberate confusion of sexes is also a part of the basic aim of Carnival which seeks, however crudely, a dissolution of the stiffened traditional order, a reversal of all accepted values, and a reactivation of the boundless power and creativity of the Beginning." (Alan MacGlashen)

7. "For those who require clean lines, precise calculations, absolute points of reference, and clear and distinct ideas, clownish revelations may not be so amusing. But for those who are not pretenders to thrones that are not theirs or to a divinity they have not attained, or even to some superior form of humanity, the clown enables us to embrace ourselves and one another as the luminous lumps that we are." (Conrad Hyers)

8. "In Halloween a strange alliance is formed between the innocent and the wicked, between children and witches.... Their masks insure the children anonymity and endow them with the powers of monsters and supernatural beings.... They purge the community by the terror of trick or treat, as if a touch of sin and evil were necessary for building community: There is always a happy fault at the heart of any religious system." (Victor Turner)

9. What movie and TV characters today remind you of Trickster? If you could meet one of the tricksters in religious myths, which one would you choose? Why?

————————————————————————

# CHAPTER SIX

# THE HERO'S CHILDHOOD

The profound human questions we find in creation myths — Who are we? What is the purpose of human life? Why are humans separated from Absolute Reality? How should we understand the arbitrariness of life? Why are there evil and death in the world? — also appear in hero myths. The hero is the one who has succeeded through a quest, a search, a series of tasks in adult life in bringing meaning to the life of those within the culture.

Stories of the hero encapsulate a culture's attitudes toward reality and provide a paradigm for people to follow in their own lives. Myths of the hero's quest remain pervasively influential, coloring a people's world vision and helping them to interpret their experiences. His adult quest, perhaps searching for a Holy Grail, the Golden Fleece, absolute knowledge, or perfection (whether in love, or politics, or war), provides a pattern to organize the way we perceive facts and understand ourselves in relation to the world.

Theseus slaying the monster Minotaur in the Labyrinth, Psyche searching for reunion with her husband Eros, Odysseus encountering various difficulties in his attempt to return to his wife Penelope after the battle of Troy — these heroes help people explore and ascertain those areas of their inner selves they feel only scantily related to. The hero myths make the way known from one mystery to another in their lives, guiding them safely on the way from one stage of life to the next, easing their stresses and fears. Myths of the hero give glamor and panache to ordinary human lives, which are so mild by comparison, and they enable people to participate in a life cycle greater than their own. They dramatize the value of life-enhancing qualities such as courage, justice, sacrificial compassion, good judgment (rather than brute strength), modesty (rather than rashful boasting), and enthusiasm (rather than reluctance).

The hero has broken past those barriers that have limited the people, encountered and struggled with the unknown, and returned to the community with a gift to be shared by all. By exercising similar courage and imitating his actions, others may also participate in this boon. If his trials and tasks concern the definitive overcoming of evil or death, then the hero is also a savior, and he makes it possible for the community to break through, as the hero did, to the transcendent, redemptive experience that brings wholeness to their religious selves. Myths that deal directly with this savior aspect of the hero will be treated in later chapters. For now, we restrict ourselves to those stories of heroes that offer exemplary patterns for achieving wholeness in psychological and religious development. Hero myths include the stories of saviors, those heroes of religious traditions who are instilled with divine power insofar as they embody those same qualities of life found in all heroes. They include Jesus struggling with demons and preaching the kingdom of God, Moses overcoming the pharaoh's threats and leading his people from oppression and slavery to the Promised Land, and Gotama, the Buddha, showing the Middle Way between a sensuous life and an ascetic life to true Enlightenment. Here they share the hero's boon with the people, but it is much greater than some life-enhancing quality, for it is the gift of the revelation of the Absolute Reality that dwells in all people.

This chapter looks at just one part of the hero's life, his childhood, from conception through adolescence. These myths, universally found in cultures and religious traditions, are a preview of the hero's entire life. The entire pageant of marvels, culminating with the great central adventure in adulthood, are foreshadowed in the very early myths of the hero who is endowed with extraordinary powers from birth, or even from conception. With the hero's birth, a special manifestation of the immanent divine principle has become incarnate in the world. This is underscored in stories of virginal conceptions and virginal births. Early on, the hero has to confront evil — poisonous snakes, a frantic tyrant, a jealous god — often a hint of his future quality as a savior. The hero has to prove his self through confronting these evil forces, or perhaps through receiving some kind of divine blessing. In youth, the hero will perform prodigious feats and manifest a dramatic thirst for adventure, but occasionally he does not succeed (perhaps wrecking a chariot, flying too close to the sun) because he has not fully matured yet, and lacks a balance in his personality. The childhood cycle concludes when the hero is recognized, after a period of obscurity, his true character is revealed, and his heroic powers emerge into full bloom.

## Gotama, the Buddha

Gotama, the Buddha, is the central hero in both Theravada and Mahayana Buddhism. His pivotal religious experience, his enlightenment, was a liberating insight into both the causes of suffering in the world and the means of escaping from this suffering. Meditating on aging, disease, and death, those experiences of ordinary life from which Gotama's royal father had sheltered him early in life by surrounding him with pleasures and distractions, he decided that the way of a life of sensuality could not help him solve the riddle of the meaning of life. Renouncing his wife and child and worldly goods, he became a wandering beggar and set off to apprentice himself in meditation and asceticism. But his teachers could not bring him the dispassion, the tranquility, the liberation he sought.

His enlightenment came later: The dramatic perception that although all of reality is painful and fleeing, there is a way of escape from it. Humans can escape the terror of aging, sickness, and death by withdrawing their concerns and anxieties about them, that is, by no longer desiring youth, health, or even life itself. Attempting to get rid of these desires is the pursuit of Nirvana, a complete break from the realm of space and time, a break from the cycle of birth and death and rebirth. The quest of achieving Nirvana involves penetrating the illusion of the goodness of human existence. It involves removing the ignorance that makes sensual pleasures, financial success, prestige, and other human goals seem good. It pursues a Middle Way between sensuality and extreme asceticism, a way the Buddhists call the lifestyle of the Noble Eightfold Path.

The accounts of the Buddha's quest for enlightenment are heavily embellished by the religious faith of those in the Buddhist tradition. Stories of his birth and early childhood, as well as of his final days and final release, all take on greater significance insofar as they are seen in the context of his quest for enlightenment. The stories of his early childhood, which are the focal point for this chapter, are found in several of the Buddhist scriptures, and in particular in the *Buddhacarita*.

The birth of Gotama, the Buddha, occurred in this way. Having successfully performed the deeds of several previous incarnations, the time had come for him to return to earth for the last time. He considered the time, the tribe, the mother, and consented to be born in order to become fully enlightened.

Conception is described as taking place at the time of the midsummer festival. The beautiful Queen Maha Maya lay on her couch and dreamed that she was carried away to the Himalayas where she was bathed and laid to rest on a heavenly couch in a golden mansion on Silver Hill. The future Buddha, who had become a white elephant bearing in his trunk a white lotus flower, seemed to touch her right side and enter her womb. When she awoke, she related the dream to her husband who asked his wise counsellors for an interpretation. They announced that the queen was pregnant, and that if her child would adopt the life of a householder, he would become a universal monarch; however, if he adopted the religious life, he would become a Buddha, removing ignorance, folly, and sin from the world.

At the moment of his incarnation, the heavens and earth showed miraculous signs: the dumb spoke; the lame walked; musical instruments played of themselves; the earth was covered with lotus flowers; trees put forth flowers. In all, there were dozens of miracles. Queen Maha Maya carried the child and, just prior to delivery, went to visit her family in a neighboring village. Along the way, she knew that the time for giving birth had come. She took hold of the branches of a tree and delivered, standing up. The child was received by angels in a golden net, who showed it to the mother saying, "Rejoice, O Lady, a great son is born to you." The child stood upright, looked in all directions, took seven strides and declared: "I am the supreme in the world. I am born to gain enlightenment for the benefit of the world."

At the time of the birth, a certain hermit, rapt in contemplation, learned the cause of the rejoicing. He came out of his trance, went to the palace, and asked to see the newborn child. When the young prince was brought in, the hermit bowed to the child. He then announced that he had had a vision and in it he had perceived that the child would become a Buddha in his present existence.

On the fifth day, the naming ceremonies were performed and the child was called Siddhartha. On this occasion, eight fortunetellers were brought in and seven foresaw that the child would become either a universal monarch or a Buddha, but the eighth was sure that he would become a Buddha. Gotama's father asked what his son might see that could possibly make him want to give up the household life. The answer of the wise men was "the Four Signs," that is, a man worn out by age, a sick man, a dead body, and a hermit. The king then resolved that no such sights would ever be seen by his son, for he did not wish him to become a Buddha but desired that he should rule the whole world. Seven days after the child's birth, Queen Maha Maya died and was reborn in the heaven of the Thirty-Three gods.

While still an infant, the baby Gotama was left unattended beneath the shade of a tree on the occasion of the Ploughing Festival. His father inaugurated the plowing, and his nurses prepared the food. After a while, it came to the attention of the nurses that though time had passed, the shadow of the tree had not moved all afternoon. The shadow had remained immobile, protecting the child who sat with his legs crossed, fixed in a yogic trance.

As the prince grew, his father built three palaces for him, where he dwelt according to the seasons. Here he was surrounded by every luxury, and thousands of dancing girls were appointed for his service and entertainment. He was a quick learner and excelled in the martial exercises. His father protected him from all experiences of age, sickness, death, and monkhood, lest he should be moved to thoughts of life renunciation. Thus, while still relatively young, Gotama exhausted for himself the fields of fleshly joy.

This is not the end of the story, however, for Gotama had been born under a divine sign, and his heroic quest was not to be achieved through sensuality, violence or war, but through contemplation. What prompted his adult quest? What brought him out of his childhood adolescence and to the brink of his adult task?

On one of his occasional chariot rides outside the palace walls, he saw a decrepit old man, broken-toothed, gray-haired, crooked and bent of body, leaning on a staff, trembling. He asked his charioteer who the man was and, hearing the answer, said, "Shame on birth, since to everyone that is born old age must come." When he abruptly returned to the castle, his father extended the guard over him. Gotama went for another ride to the park, and this time he saw a diseased man, thin and weak, scorched by fever. This time he said: "If health be frail as the substance of a dream, who then can take delight in joy and pleasure?" On a third occasion, he saw a corpse followed by mourners weeping and tearing their hair. He made inquiry, returned, agitated in heart, saying, "Woe to the life so ended. Would that sickness, age, and death might be forever bound." From then on he sought a way of deliverance. Driving forth a fourth time, he met a mendicant friar, a *bhikku,* dressed in religious garb, with downcast eyes, carrying a beggar's bowl. Asking who the man so calm in temper might be, he learned that he was a monk who had abandoned all longings and led a life of austerity, living without passion or envy, and begging his daily bread. The thought of retiring from the world was a pleasing one for Gotama. He gradually realized that through him, the bond of mortality would be loosed and the veils of ignorance would be rent asunder, since he would be completely fulfilled in the way of wisdom. Everyone who had faith in him would be "saved" from the three evils (sickness, old age, and death) without exception.

## Heroic Origins

Though particular details in the myths of the Buddha's birth and childhood are unique, similar patterns can be found in the myths of the hero springing from widely scattered religious traditions and cultures. The emphasis in the early childhood myths will be upon the special qualities that the hero exercises in that society. Thus Gotama is the Buddha, the "enlightened one," who dispels ignorance. Similarly, Jesus ("Yahweh saves") is also Emmanuel, "God with us." The hero is born under mysterious or unusual circumstances (perhaps there is a virginal conception or the birth is announced in spectacular dreams and prophecies). He may be the son of a god or of royalty, marked for greatness by a special sign (the naming of the child; the mother's early death and removal to heaven; the miracle of the shadow that doesn't move). While still quite young, he is often placed in harm's way, having to face monsters or other evil threats that will help him later to lay claim to his heroic role by his adult tests and trials.

Myths throughout the world agree that the hero has to have an extraordinary capacity right from his birth in order to face and survive his experiences. By making the boy the father of the man, the religious traditions create stories that anticipate the greatness of their hero. Since the hero touches a darkness unexplored, the myths symbolically express the sense that the hero is essentially mysterious from the very beginning. The myths provide a didactic explanation for the believing community, rather than being childish fantasies or lies. They point to the hero's greatness, to the victory he will eventually achieve, the victory they all can share in.

The miraculous events at the conception and birth of Gotama find their parallels in many cultures. The virgin mother of the Roman god, Attis, conceived him by eating an almond or, in another version, by putting a pomegranate between her breasts. A feather between the breasts helps conceive the Toltec-Aztec god, Huitzilopochtli, which is not surprising when we recall that the Aztecs often symbolized the divine, immortal part of a human as a precious feather. The Greek hero, Perseus, was conceived after the god Zeus came to Danae as a shower of gold.

Many instruments were causes of unusual impregnation: the wind, sunlight, a blade of grass, a pebble, a magic apple (sent by Freya, the Norse goddess of fertility), a pine nut (Tewa Indian), an emerald. Horus, the Egyptian hero, was conceived when his resourceful mother, Isis, found and assembled the pieces of Osiris who was murdered, chopped up, and scattered by his evil brother, Set. Gathering all the pieces except the penis, which had been eaten by a crab, she enlisted a skilled craftsman to make a wooden phallus and by using the arts of love she enabled the body of Osiris to beget upon her the holy child, Horus. Athena, the Greek goddess of wisdom, was not born of a female at all, springing full grown from the forehead of Zeus.

Gotama was sheltered from the evils of old age, sickness, and death, encountering them only in his adolescence. Much more common is the hero who must face danger at a very young age. Like many infants who were destined to become heroes, Horus was born and reared in a secret, humble place — the delta marshes of the Nile. Set, his wicked uncle, took the form of a poisonous snake, slithered into the marshes, and bit the infant. As Isis frantically watched her child writhing in pain, the gods came to her aid. A messenger came from the sun god and declared that the child was so special that if it were to die, then the sun itself would stop. Similarly, Heracles, while still an infant, strangled two serpents — their eyes shooting flames, poison dripping from their fangs — that had been placed in his nursery.

Most often the early danger is abandonment, usually because the hero's birth contravenes a prohibition by a wicked ruler. Gilgamesh, for example, was thrown by his guardians from the acropolis for fear of the king. A keen-eyed eagle saw the boy's fall, and before the child struck the earth, it caught him on its back and set him down in a garden with great care. He was then raised by the lowly overseer of the garden. The twins Romulus and Remus were subjected to a purificatory rite of passage when they were released into the natural flow of the river. They floated for a while, and when the water receded, their tub knocked against a stone and capsized. The screaming infants, stuck in the river mud, were rescued by a she-wolf who nursed them. While she licked them clean, a woodpecker guarded them and carried food to them. They were eventually found and raised by a lowly shepherd couple.

Although not really abandoned, Moses, too, was placed on the Nile. He was concealed in the bullrushes because Hebrew women were forbidden by the pharaoh to have children. The pharaoh's daughter noticed the child and was filled with pity for it. Without knowing who she was, the princess told Moses' sister to find someone to suckle the child. Moses, whose name means "drawn out" (of the water), was thus raised by his own mother. Sargon, set adrift by his low-born mother on the Euphrates, was found and raised by a farmer, with the great goddess Ishtar protecting him. Sigurd, the great Scandinavian hero, was put in a glass vessel and cast into a stream by his father, Sigmund, who had killed his mother, believing her unfaithful.

Krishna, an avatar (incarnation) of the Hindu god Vishnu, was born in a jail where a wicked enemy had confined his chieftain father and mother. A loyal landowner on the other side of the river was able to secretly exchange the baby for another infant. Krisha was thus brought up in exile as the son of the cowherd. A goblin, Putana, disguised as a beautiful woman, but with poison in her breasts, came to visit. She entered the house where Krishna was being raised, made herself very friendly, and presently took the baby in her lap to give it suck. Krishna drew so hard that he sucked away her life, and she fell dead, reassuming her hideous form. A hint of the savior qualities of the hero, Krishna, is manifested even at this very early age, for when Putana's foul corpse was cremated, it emitted a sweet fragrance. The divine infant had given the demoness salvation when he had drunk her milk.

The baby Buddha, sitting fixed in a yogic trance, had power over the shadow of a tree. Similarly, myths of the child-hero abound in anecdotes of precocious wisdom and strength, as well as prodigious feats in later childhood. We saw earlier how the Polynesian hero, Maui, snared and slowed the sun to give his mother time to cook her meals. The Tlingit Indian Root-Stump (so called because his mother had become pregnant when she swallowed some root juice) grew very fast and was tough. When playing on the beach one day, a monster who had been killing his people grabbed the boy. Root-Stump rapidly grew roots in every direction, pulled down this monster and broke it into several pieces.

The Irish hero, Cuchulain, held the field against fifty boys when they attacked him with clubs and spears. This boy-wonder, with his early thirst for adventure, got his name ("Culaine's dog") when he had to serve in place of a watchdog that he killed by thrusting a ball into its mouth, seizing its hind legs, and battering it against a rock. The Hebrew King, David, whose older brother calls him an "impudent young rascal," claimed that he had killed lions and bears in guarding his father's sheep. He disdained the sword, spear, or dagger, refused to put on a bronze helmet or coat of mail, and instead attacked the Philistine enemy, Goliath, with a sling and five pebbles. Hitting the giant in the forehead, he grabbed Goliath's sword and cut off his head.

Myths of later childhood often directly point to the central deed of the hero. Theseus had no difficulty recovering the sword and sandals from the rock, showing he was the equal of his father who had put them there. Having grown up strong, athletic, intelligent, and courageous (attacking what he thought was a real lion when he was only seven), he was able to prove his royal roots, to find his self, when he heard the story of his birth. He was well prepared for his later exploits, which would be beneficial for the society of Athens. In ridding the land route to Athens of Procrustes and other robbers, he would make the way safe for other travelers. In killing the Minotaur, that monster at the center of the incredibly complex Labyrinth, he would free Athens of its obligatory human sacrifices. In giving Athens a democratic government, he would make the people there citizens rather than slaves.

Krishna's precocious knowledge also foreshadowed his future greatness. While still a young lad, he told the herders that they were wrong to offer sacrifices to Indra, the god of rain. Indra was not supreme, for the rain and prosperity they sought depended on the sun, which drew the waters and made them fall again. Telling them to turn their attention to a mountain, saying it was more worthy of their honor, he took the form of a mountain god and received their offerings. Indra, enraged, discharged a deluge, seemingly the end of the world. But Krishna filled the mountain with the heat of his inexhaustible energy, lifted it with his finger, and told the people to take shelter underneath it. The rain struck the mountain, hissed, and evaporated, none of it touching the community of herdsmen. Krishna, of course, was already preaching the message that he had come to earth to deliver. His advice was that the Way of Devotion (Bhakti) must begin with reverence for everyday objects — mountains, for example — rather than with remote gods or vague concepts. Since the divinity is immanent in all persons, it is manifested through any object profoundly regarded. Furthermore, it is the divinity within each person that enables them to discover the divinity without.

Early in life the heroes' qualities are already manifested. For Krishna, Horus, Theseus, the Buddha, and many other mythic heroes, childhood is a time of extreme danger and obstacles, a time of touching the unexplored darkness. The child-hero has to enter a zone of unsuspected presences, which may be benign as well as malignant. Extraordinary capacity is required to face and survive such experiences. Very early on he shows those qualities that will be manifested in his adult quest or tasks. His future greatness colors these early myths, and they convey a definite sense of his coming greatness, whether bringing enlightenment to others, leading them out of slavery to freedom, or proclaiming to them the message of the divine life that they have within.

## Infancy Narratives of Jesus

The myths of the early life of Jesus found in the infancy narratives in the gospels of Matthew and Luke share many of the themes of the heroes of other religious traditions. These two narratives are intended to be theological prefaces to their gospels. They are faith proclamations, theological expansions on the already developed belief in the divine sonship of Jesus and in his role as Messiah. By immediately noting that neither Mark nor John provide any account of Jesus' birth and early childhood, nor any evidence of a particularly unusual birth or childhood to accompany Jesus' title as Son of God, it becomes obvious that both Matthew and Luke were freely inventing details to underscore their beliefs. Though they may have known eyewitnesses who could provide historically reliable facts about the early life of Jesus, they felt justified in creating incidents that would point out the kind of hero Jesus was to be: the Messiah awaited by the Jews, but rejected by most of them; a king and savior of all, one identified with the poor and outcasts, who paradoxically reversed the values and goals of the people. Their infancy narratives are quick to proclaim his supernatural origin and character and his early awareness of his function in salvation because they are framed within the context of his subsequent passion and death and, most importantly, his resurrection.

While agreeing on Jesus' heroic role as savior, Matthew and Luke paint two very different pictures of his birth and early childhood. Anyone who attempts to approach these infancy narratives literally has a difficult time harmonizing the biographical details. Here are just some of the differences we find in the first two chapters of each of these gospel writers. For Matthew, Jesus was born and lived in Bethlehem for at least two years (when the magi arrived from the East); for Luke, the story begins in

Nazareth, and Jesus' parents go to Bethlehem for only forty days, until Mary's purification. Matthew pictures the annunciation of Mary's pregnancy as made to Joseph, citing his embarrassment. Luke's announcement story centers on Mary, citing her greatness. Matthew, writing for Christians who had previously been Jews, shows that Jesus is the fulfillment of many of the prophecies of the Jewish Scriptures and models his story on parallels from the childhood of the Jewish hero, Moses, especially his early escape from evil by the flight into Egypt. Luke, writing for all Christians and proclaiming that Jesus was born as a savior for all people, traces Jesus' lineage back not to Moses, but to Adam, the "father of all mankind." Matthew's eyewitnesses are the non-Jewish magi (members of the aristocracy). Luke's witnesses are poor, lowly people and shepherds (members of a despised class). Matthew stresses the evil that Jesus faced; whereas, Luke's text is filled with the good news, a joyful spirit.

That the infancy narratives of Matthew and Luke are expansions on their faith in the heroic role and resurrection of Jesus becomes more apparent if we look at each of them in more detail. Matthew's goal was to reassure Jewish Christians and gentiles who had recently joined them that the Jews had not lost their heritage. Jesus was the fulfillment of everything they looked for in their Scriptures. Matthew will thus evoke the Jewish hero, Moses. Just as Moses escaped the slaughter of the baby boys by the pharaoh, so Jesus escaped the slaughter of the innocents by the wicked ruler, Herod. (For this reason, Matthew will later have Jesus bring the new Law to the people in the Sermon on the Mount, just as Moses brought his people the Law from Mount Sinai). As the expected Messiah, Jesus' lineage is traced by Matthew back to King David (the king from whose line the Messiah was expected) and to Abraham (the traditional father of the Jewish nation). Since Matthew traces the lineage of Jesus' genealogy through Joseph, his story of the virgin birth has as its major theme not the virginity of the mother, but rather its fulfillment of a prophecy from Isaiah.

As often occurs in heroic birth myths, a miraculous event accompanies the birth. In Matthew's version, this episode concerns the visit of the magi, those star-gazing astrologers from Mesopotamia. This group (neither kings, nor three, according to the text) had followed a star in the sky, convinced that it would lead them to a newborn regal hero. Desirous to offer him their treasures and pay him their homage, they displayed a steadfast faith in the Messiah, a faith that Matthew starkly contrasts with the infidelity of the Jews who refused to accept Jesus and his hero's messianic role.

The mood and message of Luke's infancy narrative are very different. Luke never mentions Joseph's embarrassment over Mary's pregnancy, nor the slaughter of the innocents and the flight into Egypt, nor the visit of the magi. His story, told from the point of view of the mother, is more intuitive, subtle, and subjective. He brings out the significance of the hero, Jesus, by contrasting his birth and early childhood with those of John the Baptist. His narrative is quite stylized, using patterns we have seen in other heroic myths: A heavenly being appears, the birth of the son is announced, the name is determined, and his future is revealed. It also uses a pattern found often in the Jewish Scriptures: God's call, the expression of doubt, doubt removed through explanation, and a sign given to ratify the call.

Luke celebrates the good news of Christmas, the wonderful tidings of salvation, that a savior has been born for all people. His narrative centers on spirit-filled people, eagerly expecting the Messiah and welcoming him with love and joy. He praises the greatness of the virgin mother in the "Magnificat," the prayer she sings when she receives the announcement of the divine origin of Jesus. Luke makes no effort to dress up the obscurity and lowly estate of Jesus' birth. Indeed Luke stresses the poverty of Jesus, to which all Christians are called. His parents are poor, taking temporary lodging in a stable; his early days are unattended, except by the poor and despised shepherds. His parents' offering in the temple is two turtle doves instead of the usual lamb.

The hero's childhood stories often include episodes that point to his future role; the Jesus stories in Matthew and Luke are no exception. Stories of his name are one example. The first of Matthew's references to Jesus' name occurs when the angel, appearing to Joseph, says that "Mary shall bear a son, and you shall give him the name Jesus (Savior), for he will save his people from their sins." Later, in the context of Jewish prophecies, Matthew says that Jesus shall be called Emmanuel, which means "God is with us," and he shall be called a "Nazarene," that is, one who is specially consecrated to God.

In Luke, the angel appearing to Mary says that the child to be born of her shall bear the title "Son of the most high," the "Son of God." Angels also refer to him as king over Israel forever, as the deliverer, the Messiah, the Lord. Another significant incident in Jesus' childhood occurs in Luke, when Jesus goes up to Jerusalem at age twelve for the Passover festival. When he stays behind, his parents find him only after three days, sitting in the temple surrounded by teachers, listening to them and asking questions. All who heard him were amazed at his intelligence and the answers he gave. When asked by Mary what he was doing, Jesus replied, "What made you search; did you not know that I was bound to be in Father's house?" Jesus is shown proving his self, preparing for his adult task to perform the mission from his Father. Luke repeats twice that Jesus was growing up, advancing in favor with God and men.

## Virgin Births

Why are stories of the hero's virgin birth so prevalent? Why is the hero so often an only child, with his virgin-mother either dying shortly after giving birth (as Gotama's mother was removed to heaven seven days after his birth) or remaining in an immaculate state after the birth (as is implied in the infancy narratives of Jesus)? Why do so many stories of divine origins involve some kind of "sacred marriage" through which the divine male, in human or other form, impregnates a woman, either through some normal sexual intercourse or some substitute form of penetration? Why the feathers? The pomegranate seeds? Why is Mithras born of a rock; Adonis, of a tree? Why, in Judaism, does Yahweh play a special marvel-attended role in the birth of Isaac, Abraham, Moses, Samuel, Samson, and so many others?

So many of these myths developed many centuries after the events they depict. They come late in the tradition, long after the achievements of the hero. In all these stories, the virgin birth is just one of the elements of belief that constellate around the hero, showing his far-reaching importance. It is one of the stories that embellish the traditions surrounding the unfathomable mystery of the hero's salvific task. The meaning of the virgin birth myth consists in how it reflects the religious tradition's belief in its hero's role as savior, as one who combines both divinity and mortality. The story functions to express how they understand their god's (or gods') intentions regarding them and humankind. No human father is said to have begotten the hero; instead, there has to be a special divine act in order to bring out the special manifestation of the immanent divine principle that has become incarnate in the world. Thus the hero both shares and identifies with the human condition, but also transcends it, having a special connection with the Absolute Reality.

In the Christian myths of the virgin birth, Jesus is constituted the Son of God. What was proclaimed about Jesus' relation to the royal David and to the Spirit was pressed back even to his conception. Thus the story about the purity and innocence of his mother is really a statement about the child. The miraculous event remains focused on Jesus to show that he was not some kind of divine phantom (never born in the flesh) nor was he born just like everybody else. The virginal conception was a visible sign of God's gracious intervention in connection with the becoming of his son. It is an effective, interpretive sign of the eternal divine sonship.

In suggesting that the story of Jesus' virgin birth is properly a story of the son and not the mother, there are two possible areas of misunderstanding. First, this is not meant to detract from the marvelousness of Mary, the mother of Jesus. Her role as mother, which became much larger over the centuries, is more than a projection of mere human motherhood. Statements about her virginity are really statements about her spiritual purity and total openness to divine activity. She incorporates many of the traits of those mother goddesses who are the source of all motherhood. The ultimate spark of life, they are involved directly in human affairs, yet also transcend them, producing life in a medley of ways. Second, those scientific attempts to explain the virginal conception by parthenogenesis in animals or by cloning are irrelevant. They are well-intentioned misunderstandings of what the religious tradition intended, namely, that the birth of the hero is an extraordinary activity of the creative power of the Absolute Reality, as unique as the original initial creation. Attempting to explain the virgin conception or virgin birth as a phenomenon of nature reduces their meaning, tantamount to denying them altogether.

The hero's life cycle provides an exemplary pattern for the persons within the culture or religious tradition. What is the significance, then, of divine sonship? It is to recall that divinity is manifested in each person. Though they have been separated from the Absolute Reality, there is a spark, a seed, an element of the divine within the core of each self. To celebrate this virgin birth of the hero is to recall this element and to remind the devotees not of what they are, but of what they can become. It serves to remind them not of the narrow perspectives of their own lives, but to involve them under the aegis of a greater purpose and thus enhance their existence.

Specifically, for Christians, this means that Christmas, as the celebration of the incarnation of the God-man, is the proclamation of their belief that God is present not just to Jesus, but in every Christian, now. Just as the infinite Absolute Reality was found in the finite human Jesus, so human life is deified. Christians have entered a new stage of history, for to be fully human is to be divine. Celebrating Christmas, then, is not so much a feast to celebrate the birth of a poor child in a manger as much as it is an anticipation of the future resurrection triumph over despair and death. Celebrating Christmas is celebrating the fact that it is possible for humans to experience the Absolute Reality, God, as present in the world, in historical and finite events. The real meaning of human life, Christians are saying, is that God enters into it.

## Hopes for a New Beginning

Gotama is described as issuing from his mother's womb like a man coming down a staircase, stretching out both hands and feet, unsmeared by any impurity from his mother's womb. Nevertheless, to honor the future Buddha and his mother, there came two streams of water from the sky to refresh the two of them. This hero, though human, is somehow untarnished by human failings. The streams of water are not only to honor the hero and his virgin mother; they express the human longing for a new beginning, the primordial hope for a second chance. The purification process is similar to the one of the flood in the myths of creation. All humans wish to be children again, with no false, masklike front. They all wish to be innocent, reflecting on the outside what they feel on the inside, with no dichotomy between appearances and reality. The naked child does not have to rely on an outer front, for there is direct and immediate contact with the inner world. There is a longing for childlikeness (spontaneous, creative, imaginative) as the very reverse of childishness (infantile, regressive, dependent). The innocent child is the efficacious child, for his power comes not from worldly experience, but directly from the Absolute Reality. In the innocent child there is a divine wisdom at work that protects and rewards the youth for its purity, that provides a special skill that will make survival plausible. There is a force, a magic potency of innocence, which is a source of power and a source of the continued protection of the divine father.

The longing for a new beginning, for an age of innocence, is also stressed in the infancy narratives of Jesus, especially in the song that Mary sings, the "Magnificat." Her spirit rejoicing, she recalls the many blessings that Yahweh has brought her people, the many wonderful dealings with humanity. She sings of how the Holy One, the Absolute Reality, has intervened in human affairs, putting to rout the arrogant of heart and mind, bringing down monarchs from their thrones, lifting high the humble. He satisfied the hungry with good things and sent the rich away empty. There is a kind of left-wing, subversive tone in this hymn that cannot be overlooked. All merely human order is challenged, and the powerful, selfish, and violent are turned upside down. Nothing merely human is ever complete and final. The song alludes to the adult task of the hero Jesus to bring about the ultimate manifestation of the kingdom, where human greatness counts as nothing, where all share a certain nothingness before God, for even the lowliest is of immeasurable value. The song proclaims the religious tradition's hope for a new beginning, a reversal of the leaders of human greatness. It joyfully sings of God's embrace of all, but especially the sick, the weak, the powerless. The song extols God's encompassing of all of life, his eternal yes to all people and all places.

The task of the hero, Jesus, is to make this kingdom real. Incarnating the very qualities of tenderness and compassion — far from the virtues of the conquering hero — he will gather the poor and outcasts around him. He will announce a kingdom where the integrity and worth of every person, thing, and moment, however lowly, may be defended and become the object of special wonder and delight. It will be a kingdom in which the foolish are chosen to shame the wise, the weak chosen to shame the strong. It will be a kingdom of the "chosen" where the chosen are selected not on the basis of having the most to offer, but rather because they have nothing to offer but their innocence, their nakedness, their very selves.

## Monsters and Evil Forces

The child-hero must face monsters or other evil forces very early in life. Endowed with extraordinary powers from the moment of birth, his first struggles are anticipations of the great central adventure, that great struggle that will eventually provide a boon for the culture or religious tradition. The Buddha story is not really an exception, even though his royal father does everything possible to have Gotama avoid seeing evil. Gotama does face evil in the form of old age, sickness, and death; and his struggle to understand them will eventually bring him to enlightenment. Jesus, too, faces evil forces: Herod, the tyrant-governor who sees Jesus as a threat and thus seeks to have him slaughtered along with innocent children. Jesus' circumcision not only calls attention to his solidarity with the human race, but anticipates his passion as he sheds his blood for the first time.

Why do religious traditions almost universally invent monsters? Tyrants? Jealous fathers? Demons? Why does the hero have to face evil at such an early age? What do they signify? What purpose do they serve? Most generally, the monsters are simply the embodiment of evil. Wreaking universal havoc, hoarding the benefits of society, sometimes demanding human sacrifices, they lurk in outlying regions. Through malice or desperation, they set themselves against the human community. They have to be cleared away. Furthermore, the tyrants of the human kind, usurping to themselves the goods of others, are the cause of widespread misery. These, too, have to be suppressed. The elementary meeting of the hero with monsters and evil tyrants is a preview of struggles to come. Facing a monster in early youth is a sign of the hero's future greatness, a sign that the gods are with him in his future tasks. The monsters will not provide the struggle that marks the pinnacle of the hero's career, but they are very dangerous foes in a sort of preliminary skirmish. These foes are so dangerous that they are the foes of the gods, too, capable of battling with and defeating the most powerful of deities.

Sometimes the monsters are a way for a religious tradition to recognize and picture those mysterious forces they don't have much control over, the "unknown" in their selves. Psychologically, they are a people's way of acknowledging that there is no such thing as total protection from evil (whether monsters, tyrants, suffering, old age, death); evil must be accepted as a part of the natural arrangement of things. Whether the monsters symbolize external or internal dangers, the hero knows that the monsters are there to be killed. And, most important, once he has slain them, he knows that the power that was theirs belongs to him. By killing these evil, chaotic, deformed monsters, the hero is slaying the animal within his own nature. He takes on their power, helping to kill the monstrous and wild desires and instincts in others.

Sometimes the struggle against evil and monsters is unsuccessful, either because the monster is so great or because the hero is too weak. What the myths seem to be saying here is that the child's growth into maturity and adulthood is a struggle; it takes time and cannot be pushed too fast. The growing child has to take on power gradually, not recklessly, otherwise he will be overwhelmed. Growing children are vulnerable and helpless while they develop and acquaint themselves with the enormously complex world. The process of growth is slow and painful. For example, many a father naturally feels twinges of jealousy, sometimes bitter, as the son, once dependent and worshipful, promises to equal or outshine the father's achievements, just as the father's own strengths begin to wane. And yet, part of reaching maturity is repudiating the parents' protection, and in some sense supplanting them. The old king must die before the shining prince can take over. There is an inevitable tension — evil between the father and son, and the son will always be the natural victor in the course of life.

All children have to face the dilemmas of childhood, perhaps changing schools, moving from one town to another, leaving the familiar world for an unfamiliar one. Because they cannot realize that the new will become as familiar as the old, because they cannot see beyond their immediate world, the new world is both fascinating and dreadful. Each new world demands that they learn new relationships, but this is difficult since they have no long-range pursuits to carry them beyond the immediate situation, no focal point to carry them above the monster-dangers.

And yet, paradoxically, because these monsters and dangers are both fascinating and dreadful, children will seek them out. As generations of loving parents know, childhood is always very risky; and the more special the children seem, the more they need stimulation and actually seek out dangers when life becomes dull. They seek the joy of having tempted and conquered chaos. Loosing and then subduing the monster is a freeing, exalting experience. Their relationship to the unknown as they grow into adolescence is one of wonder and fear, of daring and venture. If no ferocious dragon lurks nearby, they will call out to them: pressing the accelerator, making cutting remarks, taking up hang-gliding. In plunging themselves into such danger, they are not seeking destruction, but rather recognizing the inevitability of chaos, evil, and suffering as a part of the human condition.

## Initiation as Anticipation

Monsters are a curse to themselves and to the world, and the havoc they wreak is universal. They make people cry out from the housetops and from their hearts for that redeeming hero, the carrier of the shining blade, whose blow, whose touch, whose existence will liberate the land. In confronting and controlling what terrorizes the people, the hero is initiated into his role as savior. Struggling against the monster, or performing some other task of adolescence (we recall Theseus obtaining the sword and sandals from the rock), the hero is following through on the natural process of self-realization. It helps him find his real self and what his task in later life will be. It helps him "prove his self."

Gotama was hailed at his birth as the one who would save many from folly. It was foretold that if he retired from the world, he would roll back the clouds of sin and ignorance away from the world. Even at his birth, he was associated with the lotus flower, which, as a symbol of wholeness, anticipated his savior's role.

Anticipations of messiahship similarly accompanied the story of the birth of Jesus. His names all point to this future role. It should come as no surprise that Jesus, in early adolescence, should be in the Temple "going about his Father's business." As he was growing in wisdom and favor, he was already God's son, preparing for his role of making the kingdom a present reality, of doing what God himself is doing — loving, caring, forgiving, serving. Jesus sought his father in the Temple episode when he was old enough to express in word and work his self-consciousness and self-identity. Longing to overcome the separation from his father, he anticipated his suffering on the cross, which was the supreme event in the Christian religious tradition in overcoming the separation between the Absolute Reality and humans.

Part of the hero's childhood tasks is "finding his roots" and establishing his origins. He has to accept his background as part of accepting his self in order to develop and actualize that spiritual energy so necessary for a successful life. In applying the hero's struggles to our own lives, we see that these myths are valid in helping us understand our own growth, describing every child's eventual victory over parents, every generation's progressive conquest over the previous one. The myths also reflect the universal human wish to somehow share a divine lineage and somehow find a way to deserve and live up to it. Also, just as the hero's struggle anticipates the later struggles, so early childhood struggles can be the inspiration to find a meaningful life through a search, through a quest. If, in sharing in the myths of the hero, we add glamor to our own necessarily restricted lives, then in our own initiatory struggles, we can compel ourselves forward, adventuring into the realm of monsters where all things are uncertain, provisional, and subject to question. It keeps us on the edge, opening ourselves continually to further questing, so that our lives will always retain a sense of destiny and mission, filled with enthusiasm and refreshment as we take on the tasks of the full adult life.

## Ritualization

In the myths of virgin birth and childhood initiations, the hero shows the continual triumph of new life over death. He emerges victoriously reborn. This new life also recurs at each new phase of his development throughout life. By continually conquering the unknown, as monster or as evil, he continually transforms the self through whatever rite of passage is appropriate for transversing the corresponding stage of his essential development. Overthrowing and reconciling the monsters and evils within himself, the hero helps release the spiritual energy that enables him to lead a successful life later.

Ritual celebrations of heroic births and childhood rites of passage are the means for people to participate in the life cycle of their heroes. By recalling their heroic deeds, persons become conscious of themselves as formally connected (through the repetition of similar acts and the assumption of similar roles) and materially connected (through history, through the generations) with their primal heroes. In performing rituals and retelling the myths, they remind themselves of their own religious selves, their own share of eternal life that is made real at this moment. Rituals ground the Absolute Reality in the relative. Just as the hero broke through to the transcendent and achieved the real self throughout his life, so do others in their rituals break through to their own immanent divinity.

This breakthrough to one's real self occurs not only in those community rituals that commemorate the religious hero, but also those that directly involve each individual. Like the hero of their religious tradition, each person goes through a series of rebirths from childhood to adulthood. This rebirth is formally ritualized at important times, whether in rituals such as circumcision and Bar Mitzvah in Judaism, or baptism and confirmation in Christianity. In these rituals the child often takes on a new name — a new self — a new strength that will help in the struggle from the world of childhood to that of adult responsibility. In much the same manner as the annual celebrations of our own birthday, which are an expression of our own hope for a new beginning, these rituals recall who we are and renew our determination to ''prove the self'' throughout our lives.

# Review Questions

1.  What is the purpose of the miraculous events so early in the hero's life?

2.  How do you explain the many divergences in the two gospel narratives of the birth of Jesus? What is the essence of each narrative?

3.  What is the purpose of virgin birth myths?

4.  Why does the hero face evil so early in life?

5.  What are some of the rebirths that each of us goes through as we move from childhood to adulthood?

## Discussion Starters

1.  "To become mature is to recover that sense of seriousness which one had as a child at play." (Friedrich Nietzsche)

2.  "The toys children played with did not teach them nearly enough about the aggressiveness, skepticism and hostility necessary for survival on earth." (Kurt Vonnegut)

3.  "The play of children is not play in the trivial sense of that word. Indeed there is no trivial sense except as a reflection of our adult unawareness of what play is. Play is playing-at. It is the rehearsal of various roles and the practicing of these roles in a variety of situations. The very words 'rehearsal' and 'practicing' are misleading; they derive from the adult, retrospective view of the matter. From the standpoint of the child, play is the serious business of life." (Herbert Fingarette)

4.  "To play is to yield oneself to a kind of magic, to enact to oneself the absolutely other, to preempt the future, to give the lie to the inconvenient world of fact. In play earthly realities become, of a sudden, things of the transient moment, presently left behind, then disposed of and buried in the past; the mind is prepared to accept the unimagined and incredible, to enter a world where different laws apply, to be relieved of all the weights that bear it down, to be free, kingly, unfettered and divine. Man at play is reaching out for that superlative ease, in which even the body, freed from its earthly burden, moves to the effortless measures of a heavenly dance." (Hugo Rahner)

5.  "Play reveals the true wisdom of the imagination and points to a reality other than that to which adult members of our culture are brainwashed. Current utopian dreams and creative efforts at social change fail because they assume that the present organization can be changed and that the

overthrow of all oppressive powers will guarantee a better order in their place.''

6.  ''Observing such festival as were superstitiously kept in other countries to the great dishonor of God and offense to others — any such day as Christmas or the like — either by forebearing labor, feasting or any other way is to be made a finable offense.'' (A law in the Massachusetts Bay Colony)

7.  ''The entire theme of the Incarnation is the transformation of mankind into God — the birth or awakening of the divine and eternal nature in man as his true Self.'' (Alan Watts)

8.  ''Jesus represents a confrontation of God with oppressive forces. Jesus precipitates the suffering of innocent children, the division of families, the overthrow of religious and political kingdoms. It is indeed a paradox that the birth narratives, which announce a joyful event, should also report such widespread suffering.''

# THE VISION QUEST

Although breaking away from home is a very exhilarating experience for many of us, it is a time of heightened vulnerability. Young adults doing this are exposed to a wide variety of experiences and encouraged to entertain as many possibilities for themselves as they can. During this period, we are urged to slowly expand our self-perceptions and to gradually choose our life work from among the many possibilities we come into contact with. This period of life is a time for getting in over our heads, and then struggling until we are able to get our feet on the ground, to feel the strength and security of our new stage of existence. After the appropriate passage of time, we are ready for the next step, and there is a ritual of "graduation" where both our rights and responsibilities toward society are recognized.

Part of our decision for our adult task and lifestyle is in determining what not to do. When overwhelmed by life's possibilities, we have to decide which will be ignored and which will be pursued. The period of young adulthood is the time for pulling away precisely to see what the various possibilities have to offer, so that we can finally limit the self to doing what is most characteristic and appropriate for it. This is learned by experiencing some of the paradoxes and absolutes of life, by feasting and fasting (studying during the week and playing on weekends), by living on the heights and traveling through the depths, by ascending to peak experiences and descending into dark caves. This is the time of discovering and determining the self, a lonely, introspective time for attempting to achieve an inner and outer coherence. Looking at the past and picking details that will support a future that will be meaningful, and looking at the vast panorama of possibilities of the present, we try to find a task, a work (some would call it a vocation or a mission) that will be enjoyed, and earn us the self-respect, support, and loyalty of others. The process goes on for years, till we emerge and tell the world, with a vengeance, who we are, and announce what has been brewing in us for some time.

There is a period of transition for all of us prior to our adult careers, a time where we are caught between our past achievements and our future possibilities. It is the period when, like a high-jumper, we want to retreat before taking the leap into adult life. This period of transition is the time to see the past in order to own it, the time to awaken within the religious self all the riches that the past has incorporated. Although its purpose is to reappraise the life-structure from a heightened awareness, pulling away can also bring much loneliness and isolation. Pulling away helps to get rid of a lot of pressure, but for many it is felt as a time for rebellion against the parental environment, a period of relative isolation in which all estrangements seem greater. Still this time-out has to be taken so that the larger framework of life can get settled, so that we can once again devote ourselves to details we can manage. After a while, if the retreat has been successful, we can rededicate ourselves to our adult tasks with a period of energetic and goal-oriented activity.

Prior to their heroic task, heroes in the major religious traditions usually withdraw from the world to meditate in preparation for their later deeds. In the archetypal circumstances of this stage of meditative withdrawal, the hero retreats to a dark forest, or a cave, or a wilderness, where he breaks past the horizons of the created world; and after facing dangers and undergoing trials from demons, he passes back in a spiritual rebirth to his mundane existence.

For each of us on our own quest for the religious self, we retreat into our ourselves, struggle to clarify the difficulties and possibilities before us, and attempt to eradicate them by giving battle to the demons of our own culture. If we are able to absorb and integrate the new forces we encounter in our retreat, then we experience an almost superhuman degree of self-consciousness and masterful control.

Initiation into heroic adulthood occurs along a broad time spectrum. Buddha and Jesus are generally considered to have been in their thirties, whereas in the ritual vision quests of the North American Indians, those who embark on the quest in order to take on the power of the "shaman" (the medicine man, the witch doctor) are often hardly into their teens. Buddha withdrew to the forest because he did not feel that either a life of sensuous luxury or a life of excessive asceticism was a valid way to seek enlightenment. Jesus withdrew to the desert after he had come through an initiatory baptism from John, and learned that he was the beloved Son of God. The young Indian males underwent several days of fasting on their vision quest, not because they had experienced the joys and disappointments of adult life, but because they were on the edge of adulthood and their elders felt that they were particularly apt to encounter the numinous in their spiritual rite of passage.

The hero, if successful, emerges as a shaman, that is, as one who has had a direct experience of the unknown in himself and can now convey that power and share that experience with the community. As with all the major rites of passage, there is a losing of the self in order to find the self, a putting aside of potential for worldly power in exchange for the joys of the spirit. The retreat involves physical and mental suffering. The god within is not so easily born. The transition from the old to the new usually involves a period of testing, a time of wandering about, in indecision, in apparent conflict with demons. There is a struggle to give coherence to what is happening, for many times the heroes do not know they are headed for a special task for the community, or even want it or seek it.

Though the archetypal struggle of the heroes lasts for days or weeks, the moratorium in our own lives is usually much longer, even going on for years as we become conscious of and gradually consent to our developing religious self. During this withdrawal, we are tempted by demons, those forces that deter us from our tasks and from a genuine experience of our inner selves. Occasionally, the temptation on this inner journey for some persons is to look only inward for self-satisfaction and personal achievement, rather than gradually turning outward to discover what we can do for our society and for the world. This should not deter us from the withdrawal, however. In fact, ideally, there will be an occasion for a moratorium periodically, a "religious vacation," a retreat, all through our adult lives, a time to break away and reenter this numinous experience. Many seek this moratorium by going on a religious pilgrimage, perhaps to Rome, Jerusalem, or Mecca; more frequently, however, religious persons do it by observing a ritual period of time — Lent comes to mind — a time for slowing down and recharging their religious selves.

## The Temptations of Jesus

Jesus' 40-day period of fasting in the wilderness just prior to his public ministry, his adult task, is his heroic withdrawal. Jesus has gone to the Jordan River to be baptized by John during a general baptism of the people. John the Baptist has announced that it is an opportune time, the time when all will see God's deliverance. The people are on the tiptoe of expectation. When Jesus approaches, John tries to dissuade him but baptizes him saying that he is doing it in order to conform in this way with all that God requires. John tells the people that he baptizes them with water, but that there is one who will come after him, whose task will be to take away the sins of the world. As John performs the ritual baptism on Jesus, the heavens open and the spirit of God descends in a form like a dove. A voice from heaven proclaims: "This is my beloved Son; on him my favor rests." Jesus has come to John and learns that much is expected from him: He is the Son of God. This calls for a time for reflection and prayer as Jesus always does at critical moments in his ministry.

Jesus returns from the Jordan River and pulling away from his friends is led by the Spirit up and down the wilderness for forty days. Indeed, the Spirit is his inspiration and is responsible for the temptations. All during his journeying he has nothing to eat, and at the end of it he is famished. This is the cue for the devil to enter. The devil first tells him: "If you are the Son of God, then turn these stones into bread." Jesus, in the turmoil of trying to decide what this being "the Son of God" might mean, quotes from the Scriptures he knows well: "Man cannot

live on bread alone. He lives on every word that God utters."
Next (following the story as told by Luke) the devil shows Jesus
in a flash all the kingdoms of the world in their glory. "All this
dominion will I give you and the glory that goes with it. They
are mine to give to anyone I choose. Just pay me homage and
it shall be yours." A second time Jesus fends off the demon by
quoting the Jewish Scriptures: "Do homage to God and worship him alone." Finally (again following Luke), the devil takes
Jesus to the holy city, Jerusalem, and sets him on the railing
of the temple. "If you are the Son of God, throw yourself down.
Angels will support you, for fear that you should strike your foot
against a stone." A third time Jesus recites Scripture: "You are
not to put the Lord God to the test." With this exchange, the
devil departs, biding his time.

This incident of the retreat to the wilderness and the three
temptations, developed in skeletal outline in Mark's gospel, is
expanded by Matthew and Luke in a way consistent with the
purpose of their stories and their theological visions of Jesus.
Matthew and Luke freely invent details, even reversing the order
of the temptations in order to put the most important one last.
Matthew recounts last the temptation to dominate the world from
the top of a mountain, thus recalling Jesus' role as the new
Moses, the lawgiver on the mountain, reliving the primordial
event of the Exodus. Luke, on the other hand, reserves for last
the temptation to jump off the temple railing, recalling the central importance of Jerusalem as the locale of the passion and death
of Jesus, the first stage in the history of salvation. Both Matthew and Luke suggest that the Spirit drives Jesus into the wilderness. Just as the Israelites, after crossing over the water of the
Sea of Reeds, are led into the desert and are tempted there, so
Jesus begins his own Exodus, putting his life under God's
scrutiny. Their 40 years of wandering through the desert and
the 40 days that Moses spends with Yahweh on Mount Sinai
are all evoked in Matthew's and Luke's narratives in the 40 days
that Jesus passes in the desert.

Not having eaten for a long period, Jesus gives himself to
the vulnerability that comes to all who suffer extreme hunger
and physical weakness. He feels deeply in himself the extremity
of these needs. His own physical need is the context for the first
temptation to turn stones into bread. Think of it. If he is indeed the Messiah, the Son of God, it would be nothing for him

to supply his own physical needs and those of others. To be able to supply them during his ministry with material abundance, initially in food, would be to outdo Mammon. Later he will feed a multitude of people with bread, but this would come from very little bread, not from stones. He does not succumb now, though, for to turn stones into bread would be giving in to the seduction of being a Messiah who would live in ease and comfort rather than be a suffering servant. Jesus refuses to use divine power to eliminate the evil of poverty or to transcend the human situation by providing instant foods or instant gratification. The problem of life, he learns in his withdrawal, is not overcome by eliminating evil, but by living in the midst of it with a lively faith in God — not by bread alone, but by every word God utters.

All the kingdoms of the world — in a flash, on a mountain — all this dominion is the devil's to give. Think of it. Just by being subordinate and ready to obey the devil now and help him in his political power play, Jesus would find the route to power. At the slightest concession to the road of political-religious power, the people would applaud him, drag him into it, make him king. He could be a political Messiah, a status seeker who could rule the world in a flash. But Jesus does not give in to the temptation to be a political Messiah, to rule the world by using the same power other kings have. He rejects the dream to rule the entire world and the lure of the prospect that limited resort to dark actions might make possible a wide wielding of power for good. He rejects the lure of the means-to-the-end. To do so would be manipulation of others, a flagrant violation of respect for freedom and for an open future. It would be to break the connection with the Father, something that Jesus refuses to do now, and later, when in his heroic task he will be dragged down by the weight of the world on the cross and again tempted to forsake his father.

Throwing himself down from the Jerusalem temple as a test to gain certainty of assurance in advance about the outcome of his heroic task seems like a suicidal impulse. Think of it. People would rally around Jesus if they were assured in advance of the success of his ministry. After his death-defying leap, the people would believe that he could do anything. If he could demonstrate mastery over death, then there is no law of nature that he could not defy. Jesus could use this gaudy show of the miraculous to galvanize a nation and instill in them a dogged confidence to press through periods of extreme national risk. But Jesus does not give in to this headiness, this exhilaration of danger. Instead, he confronts death from a different direction. He sees his ministry as one of healing disease, raising the dead, challenging death's institutions and its agents. The success of his task is in being nailed to a cross, by letting himself be cast into death's realm, trusting in God his Father to raise him up.

In each temptation the devil comes to Jesus with a possibility that is ingeniously close to the heroic task that Jesus is in the process of discovering as God's way for him. Though the opportunities for violating his ministry are abundant, Jesus discovers that he can achieve his heroic mission by refraining from actions that would,. by worldly standards, normally lead to it. In his wilderness withdrawal, Jesus turns from the current cultural expectations about messianic fulfillment — miraculous acts, interventions, assumptions of temporal power — and points to the realm of God as more inclusive. The devil tells him to give the people food, but Jesus offers them the eucharist; the devil offers political rule, but Jesus is a different kind of king; the devil tells him to defy death, and Jesus dies on a cross. So great a reversal from tradition is involved here that Jesus puts his life on the block to perform his heroic task.

The wilderness temptations are a rite of passage for Jesus. Coming after his response to John's call for repentance, Jesus' experience is one of gradual self-discovery, of the nature of his career as Son of God and his task as savior of the human race. He emerges from his desert encounter to proclaim the good news that the time has come and that the kingdom of God is at hand. The main lines of his subsequent career all radiate from this decisive starting point. Through all his wanderings, his teaching in the synagogue, his eating with sinners and picking grain on the Sabbath, Jesus shows a deepened sense of inner authority and peace. He knows that the struggle will continue, for "the devil departed, biding his time," and indeed, his struggle will be primarily with the devil. Jesus invites sinners and outcasts to join in the festivities of God's kingdom and brilliantly designs parables to evoke a new vision of human possibilities, a kingdom and a vision that are present in a world where evil still remains.

## The Hero's Temptations

The classical heroes also pass through a period of time during which they sharpen their awareness of their impending task and responsibilities. Destiny summons them from the pale of society to a zone unknown (a distant land, a forest, a cave, a lofty mountaintop) for a period of time between innocence and experience. Muhammed in his Night Journey, which Muslims still commemorate, withdraws to meditate in a cave and enters into a trance, traveling not only to Jerusalem but throughout the cosmos. Experiencing direct knowledge of the Other World, seeing the worst that people could suffer and anticipating the bliss in store for the righteous, he resolves to bring to all people the message of total submission to the one compassionate God, Allah.

Young North American Indian warriors, especially the Sioux and other Plains Indians, often withdraw to the wilderness on a lonely quest where they fast and torture themselves, hoping for a vision that would give them the power to become mighty warriors. Their quest often involves initiation rituals where they learn the roles expected of them as adults. Through frightening, painful ceremonies, which often included sacrifice, their fathers communicate a masculine power to them. The young boys apply themselves to learning secret myths and passing through rites of passage to satisfy the unspoken need to discover their adult roles in the tribal society.

Because this period of withdrawal is a time of heightened vulnerability, there is often a temptation to refuse the call to action. Moses, for example, casually strolls in the wilderness, tending the flocks of his father-in-law, when a passing phenomenon, a burning bush, catches his wandering eye. His curiosity lures him away from the frequented path to see this wondrous sight. He then experiences the birthright of his ancestors Abraham, Isaac, and Jacob, a direct experience of the numinous. Through this encounter his heroic duty becomes clear: He has to alleviate the misery of Yahweh's people in Egypt by rescuing them from the power of the pharaoh.

There is immediate reluctance on his part: "Who am I that I should return to Egypt?" That is, why should he give up his life of security; why should he return to the scene of his crime where he murdered one of the Egyptian guards? This is Moses' struggle with the demons within himself. He knows what is expected, but still offers excuses three times. He first refuses to surrender to an unknown God, saying that he doesn't even know who he is speaking with. Yahweh brushes this off, telling him that it is he, the Absolute Reality, who is speaking with Moses. Moses then tries to shift his doubt onto the people by protesting that they will never listen to him. Yahweh, however, shows him the effective power of his presence by momentarily turning a staff into a snake and briefly making Moses' skin diseased, as white as snow. Finally, Moses asks Yahweh to send somebody else, using the excuse that he is not a good speaker. Though Moses cries out from the depths of fear, saying that he can only stutter, Yahweh responds that he will have Moses' brother, Aaron, do the speaking. Having exhausted his excuses, Moses sets off for Egypt on his heroic task of liberating his fellow Israelites. To his credit, once he starts out, he does not turn back.

In the case of Gotama's period of withdrawal, the temptation is not due to reluctance, but to the demon, Mara. The future Buddha's early life has been spent surrounded with pleasures and the good things of life. Although he lives in luxury with a happy wife and child, nothing seems to please him. On various trips away from his royal castle, he has seen old age, suffering, and death, and a yellow-robed ascetic. In his great renunciation, he later thinks that perhaps the ascetic life might be the way beyond old age, suffering, and death, so he slips into the routine of the wandering hermit in the forest. For six years he follows various teachers, undertaking such extreme asceticism that he almost dies. Still, he doesn't find the way out of suffering, so he determines to focus on intense meditation. He makes his way to the Tree of Wisdom, resolved to achieve enlightenment.

Mara the fiend summons his demons, mounts his war elephant, and comes after him with temptations. Mara first takes the form of a messenger who announces that an enemy has taken Gotama's palace and wife and begs him to return to restore law and order. Rather than deter him, this message makes Gotama even firmer in his resolve to attain a higher and better state. Next, Mara uses the elements of nature to dissuade him: a terrible whirlwind, a rainstorm, showers of rocks, deadly and poisoned weapons, burning ashes and coals, a storm of flaming mud. All of these, however, do not disturb the future Buddha.

Finally, Mara brings in his strongest forces, his three daughters who use all the arts of seduction known to beautiful women. The daughters offer him their companionship, appeal to him with the songs of the season of spring, and exhibit beauty and grace, but Gotama is not moved. He conquers the temptations, declaring that pleasure is fleeting, whereas death, sickness, and age are permanent realities. Overthrowing the tempter, he achieves enlightenment during the night. He remains feeding on the joys of contemplation for seven weeks. Then he begins his heroic task, preaching to his disciples the Deer Park Sermon, in which he expounds the Four Noble Truths of Buddhism.

Examples of temptations during the withdrawal period, or at the time of the call to the heroic task, could be multiplied. Odysseus, for example, is an ancient draft dodger, attempting to avoid the Trojan War by trickery. He feigns insanity by plowing the seashore. Achilles, too, is a war resister, dressing himself in a woman's clothes so that the ambassadors of Agamemnon will not recognize him during the draft call. These heroes do not succumb to the temptation to refuse their call to action, however, and do commit themselves to their adult deed.

If we were to refuse by giving in to the evil monsters within ourselves at the time of our own withdrawal, we would block the release of that spiritual energy that will enable us to lead a successful life. We would lose the power of significant affirmative action and, instead, become victims to be saved. We would succumb to those material and sensual forces that would deter us from experiences of deaths and rebirths in our lives, those honest experiences of the inner self so necessary to the process of self-realization and wholeness. We would develop a kind of inertia that would make it difficult to challenge, much less change, our current attitudes. We would carry on, lazy and self-satisfied, content with the small self, as though our present system of ideals, virtues, goals, and advantages were to be fixed and made secure forever.

## The Shaman's Withdrawal and Vision

In his temptations, Jesus goes to the depths and the heights, receives spiritual wisdom, and then returns to the world to teach what he has learned. Throughout his ministry he often goes off alone, to be rejuvenated through meditation, and then returns to his small community of followers to teach them through stories and actions. He brings to his disciples a new power, the power of healing and a new vision, the vision of the immanence of the kingdom of God. Very similar to this pattern of separation and return, the process of initiatory death and rebirth, is the vision quest of many North American Indians, especially the Plains Indians. In this lonely puberty watch, young men go off alone to an isolated spot in the wilderness where they fast and pray to prove their worthiness. They inflict uncompromising ordeals and tests on themselves for several days. They continue this strenuous, liminal solitude between boyhood and manhood until they have a vision, perhaps of a certain plant or animal, which then becomes their guardian spirit. Then they return to the tribe to receive a new name taken from the plant or animal that would be their guardian spirit from then on. Now they are fully reborn as new persons and are received into the adult community with appropriate rituals. They are now ready to live as responsible adults for the sake of the community. Black Elk, the holy man of the Dakota Sioux, had his great vision when yet a boy. He saw himself as the ''Sixth Grandfather.'' Grandfathers symbolized the god Wakan Tanka, who was venerated as being loving and compassionate, full of years and wisdom. Black Elk thus saw himself as the spiritual representative of the earth and of all people. His vision blessed him with the power to become a great holy man, a shaman, in whom the roles of teacher, healer, and wise man were wondrously mixed.

Some youths receive their vision during a near-fatal sickness rather than through withdrawal, fasting, the sweat bath, or other initiatory ordeals. When physical energy is lost in their sickness, there is a possibility for an increase in spiritual energy. If the youngster can transfer attention from outside profane matters to inward sacred images, which then takes on the character of therapeutic agents, he can combat his sickness. If he can develop the capacity to transcend the natural, to conquer the appetites of his own childhood, and to exist on a higher level where will power and spiritual strength are required, then he might succeed in curing himself. Curing himself, he would have power over the sickness and might become a shaman, or medicine man. Passing from death back to life again, he personifies a healing force.

The shaman represents one of humanity's most ancient visionary methods of entering non-ordinary reality and exploring the hidden universe usually glimpsed only through myths and dreams. His withdrawal and return is a journey to acquire a new power and a new vision, to heal and maintain health. His religious sensibility and insight into the dark interior of human nature, though sometimes used for black magic, witchcraft, or other harmful purposes, are a gift to the community. Like Jesus, the Buddha, and Moses, the shaman has faced up to the temptations of demons and taken on their powers within, thereby turning the potential for hurting and for destruction into a healing gift for the community.

The shaman's power of healing, though occasionally obtained through inheritance or election, usually comes when he has succeeded in curing himself. He knows the mechanics of illness and can use this knowledge to cure physical illnesses and to guide others in their spiritual rites of passage. By his songs, stories, drumming techniques, and skills in divination, he calls the community's attention to the supernatural forces at work. In his struggles with sickness, with the monstrous and devilish forces in his visions, he opens himself in the depths of his solitude to the mystery of being and confronts the emptiness in his self. He integrates his conscious and unconscious worlds. Now he takes responsibility not only in solitude for his own spiritual life but also responsibility in public for his society. Though personal and solitary, his vision is for the sake of others. His charism of healing is exercised in community, and his healing ritual is the exercise of a religious power for others.

Jesus, Gotama, Moses, and the shamans all experience a similar withdrawal and return with a new power and a new vision. They are all heroes who have struggled with demons and taken on a numinous power they can now transmit to others. They now have to make the meaning of their sacred vision a part of people's lives by awakening the dormant spirit in the persons they touch and by bringing them into contact with the creative and re-creative forces of reality. They have all experienced an ecstatic withdrawal, a "magic flight" to the unknown, and they have the equally magic ability to return to their selves, renewed, with a numinous power to mediate to the community.

Their demonic struggles during the withdrawal on the threshold of their heroic tasks portray the perils and redemption of each of us. These heroes personify the essential developments and conditions of each person's existence. Their withdrawal echoes our search for self-realization, our attempts to find a meaningful life and become our full selves. Again and again we suffer spiritual convulsions, and each time, with luck, we are revived. Through a cycle of suffering and health, temptation and intrigue, weakness and innocence, despair and guidance, we are tempted to be content with a shrunken self, a withered version of our possibilities; and if we are successful, we grow and gradually perceive and then appropriate the power of the unseen, but real spiritual world.

Our own primary vision quest is the withdrawal, a moratorium, when we take time out to prepare ourselves for our life's work and to accept the responsibilities integral to the freedom that comes with adulthood. If we succeed against the demons, we not only determine our careers or jobs, but we realize that our future depends on the development of a sense of personal participation in history, and we relate the whole range of roles we engage in to the religious self each of us is called to be. This inner quest is not restricted to the threshold of adulthood, however, for we have a period of testing at all the moments of crucial decisions in our lives. Our desert experiences each time are a letting go — throwing our selves from the temple railing — of our selfish inertia. They are an abandonment to the inexhaustible unknown, the deliberate slowing down to become attentive to the presence of the numinous within our selves. They require effort to get through the dry spells, agony, and discipline for the long haul.

If our periodic withdrawals are successful we gain an awareness of our lifestyle and abilities. We are revitalized and develop a sense of humor at the expense of boredom and exhaustion. If we can find a center of repose, an oasis within, we can link together the isolated experiences of our lives into a pattern distinctively our own. We then overcome the temptation to merely copy someone else's lifestyle, hoping to escape the necessary inner struggle and conflict necessary for self-realization and wholeness. At the same time, for our lifestyle to be personal and not destructive, we have to remain open to the new and unexpected. Openness to the spontaneous and changeable cushions us against future shock. Like Jesus, Gotama, and Moses, we have to expect surprises. The returns may bear little resemblance to things expected. If the inner quest is truly heroic, it will be successful only through a struggle. Miraculous cures, success in business, or college scholarships may not materialize from some outside power, but we may experience inner peace, infinite and sublime patience, and a new zest for living. Withdrawing for meditation and prayer, we may not always get what we pray for, but we will get what we really need. Returning from those periods of withdrawal-meditation-prayer, if our own quest is successful, we don't run away from the world but give ourselves over to it, like Jesus, Gotama, and Moses, and their disciples. We have the courage to act and to continue to act in spite of evils around us, bringing love and compassion to others.

## Rites of Passage

The baptism of Jesus and his withdrawal into the desert are his initiation into adulthood. After his submersion into the watery chaos in the ritual of purification, he emerges to a new life in the spirit. He experiences the voice of God giving him his unique self-consciousness and calling him to his heroic task, his special vocation. The withdrawal and struggle with the devil in the desert strengthen his convictions for his future ministry. His initiatory experience is an example of a ''rite of passage.''

We humans have a penchant for elaborately ritualizing the transitional experiences of life. Because transitions may not be successfully negotiated, they are fraught with danger. Rites of passage are designed to provide the corporate, not to mention divine, aid needed for individuals for moving through childhood into adolescence, from youth to full maturity, finally from life to death, and perhaps, to new life altogether.

Rites of passage are rites of transformation that often accompany changes of place, state, social position, and age. The most important ones occur at birth, puberty, marriage, and death — those critical moments all societies ritualize and publicly mark with suitable observances to impress the significance of the transitions on the individual and on the community. Through these rituals, the community symbolizes the danger and loss involved in the passage, helps protect the individual amidst the terrors of the change, and facilitates successful negotiation of the transition. These rituals are a positive experience, setting aside the transitional period, between the more ordered and stable periods of life, as a sacred time to get in touch with the deeper, non-profane values in one's own life and community.

Rites of passage have been described as dramatic rituals of death (self-destruction) followed by new birth (self-expansion) or as rituals of growth from a stage of existence controlled by impulse and primal drives to a state of existence ordered by covenants and social norms.

The most generally accepted explanation of what happens in a rite of passage, however, is developed in the threefold framework of separation, marginality, and incorporation (or crisis, struggle, and return) that has been formulated by Arnold Van Gennep and expanded by Victor Turner. The first and third stages, the separation and the incorporation, provide a frame for the second, liminal stage. In the separation, the individuals are detached from the group, from their earlier fixed and stable condition. Out of the ordinary flow of life, they experience loss and disorientation. In the incorporation their passage is completed. The ritual subjects are in a stable state once more, with clearly defined rights and obligations, expected to behave in accordance with certain customary norms and community standards. In this resolution of their passage, they have let go of their former state and are accepted as belonging in the new one. It is the second stage, the intervening marginal period, that corresponds to the myths of the hero's withdrawal and struggles.

Similar to the period of the hero's withdrawal, persons are in a spiritual desert or wilderness during the liminal stage of the rites of passage. For a varying period of time — days, months, years — they are in a state of ambiguity, passing through a realm with few or none of the attributes of the past or of the coming state. In their withdrawal from outer activities, they are "betwixt and between." No longer identified with their past involvements or projects, they have passed from the familiar, with its known points of reference and safety, but not yet passed into a new position assigned by custom, convention, or ceremonial. They are threshold beings in the realm of pure possibility, at sea with their selves and their world. Like those going through adolescence, divorce, or a career change, they exhibit behavior proper to both states (both child and adult, married and single) without having worked either one through, thus confusing themselves and others. It is a time of decisive change, with possibilities for better or worse, a time of great opportunity and great danger.

Paradoxical as it may seem, the liminal time of confusion and undoing, of dissolution and decomposition, is also a time of growth and transformation, of reformulation of old elements into new patterns. It is a time for decision making, when the initiates can be assisted to make some of the most fundamental decisions of their lives. Only by deciding which of the many possibilities they will ignore and which they will pursue can they realize their inherent potential. In their willingness to enter the unknown, they become defenseless, weak, and stripped of whatever status and authority they may have acquired. Their time of exposure to the numinous makes them vulnerable to the diabolical powers that threaten to destroy and break apart their entire world. If they are successful in struggling against these destructive aspects, they begin to appreciate the need for structure. They participate in the discovery of new symbols that will hold all things together and in the building up of a very special community (so special that Turner referred to it as a *communitas*) where they are bound together with strong emotional ties, not merely for the duration of their initiation, but for their entire lives.

## Pilgrimages

A pilgrimage is a powerful example of the rites of passage and illustrates well the paradoxes of the liminal stage. Pilgrims are betwixt and between, journeying to a place where the human and the divine meet. Just as the heroes on the vision quest set forth on an interior spiritual pilgrimage, so the pilgrims physically traverse a mystical way. A pilgrimage is a transforming journey similar to the process of human growth toward wholeness because the pilgrims voluntarily undertake a dangerous passage, a liminal experience in leaving their normal world to enter another realm. They form a *communitas,* traveling past boundaries, often even national ones.

In the major religious traditions, pilgrimages perform a function analogous to that of the initiation rites, vision quests in primitive cultures. The pilgrims enter a new, deeper level of existence than they have known in their accustomed milieu. Similar to the ordeals of tribal initiation, they undergo privations and struggles — the temptations of the pilgrim's way. They leave their familiar lifestyle for a time and join an egalitarian community on a liminal, cleansing, transformative journey toward a sacred place.

Pilgrimage shrines are centers of spiritual renewal, even for those unable to make the actual physical journey. Indeed, the primary purpose of a pilgrimage is the interior journey, and all persons with the proper disposition can refocus their spiritual vision without an actual visit. Stressing this spiritual purpose of the pilgrimage as a rite of passage, we can defuse some of the criticism that has been occasionally heaped on them. It is sometimes asserted, for example, that they are plastic and predictable voyages, tours without tears, where travel companies pamper tourists with personal fancies, allowing no unforeseen adventures between departure and arrival and eliminating delays and discomfort.

Actually, similar criticism has been made over many centuries. In early Christianity, for example, Gregory of Nyssa claimed that Jerusalem was a city of cheating and poisoning and denied that there were any spiritual benefits to be found there. Calvin claimed that they were vestiges of primitive religion and that they hindered the process of salvation, making people waste time and energy that might be more profitably used.

Of course, some of this criticism was, and still is, justified. Medieval pilgrims received special privileges (such as relief from the burden of paying taxes and benefits from a system of indulgences whereby they obtained forgiveness of sins) and the element of commerce (buying cockle shells at Compostela, or a distinctive cap and staff at Canterbury) has always been present, diminishing any interior conversion that might be experienced.

Pilgrimages are found in all the major religious traditions. In Judaism, pilgrimages have been made for thousands of years to Mount Zion in Jerusalem, the site of the immanent presence of their god Yahweh among those faithful to the covenant; their pilgrimage of ascent up Mount Zion is a ritual commemoration of the Exodus. The Exodus was their community rite of passage from slavery in Egypt to a new life of freedom in the Promised Land. They became a religious people during this passage. The first stage of their rite of passage was the separation from the land of their birth and from the state of slavery to their Egyptian masters. Crossing the threshold waters of the Sea of Reeds was death-threatening but also life-promising, for it was their way to freedom.

The second stage, the liminal, was their period of wandering in the desert, still nowhere near the Promised Land. During this period of trial and testing, there was much murmuring and doubting. They wandered, vacillating, for 40 years, suffering hunger and thirst, losing their sense of direction as well as their sense of their selves. When their spirit reached its low point, Yahweh called their leader Moses to the heights of Mount Sinai to provide them with a new style of life, in code and convention, that would mark them as a special *communitas,* as his Chosen People.

The third stage of their communal rite of passage, the incorporation, was fully established with the death of Moses and their entry into Canaan. From then on they have relived the Exodus each year in the Passover ritual, not as individuals, but as a people. Not much later, they began making pilgrimages to Jerusalem.

The Japanese also show reverence for the mountain as one of their pilgrimage shrines. A mountain summit is liminal, the dwelling place of the gods, the meeting ground between this world and the next, between the sacred and the profane. They customarily pause halfway up the mountain in joyful anticipation of the culmination of their pilgrimage. They recognize that the effects of the pilgrimage have to occur along the way. Interior renewal and ritual contact with the numinous must come before they arrive at the top of the mountain. Their pause on the way fills them with a joy that sustains them as they continue their struggle upward.

As for the Hindus, their sacred pilgrimage sites are much more extended than the mountain or the temple. Thus the River Ganges is a place of encounter with their gods. Even to follow the course of the river along either bank, stopping at various sacred spots to read or hear sacred myths and to engage in prayer, is a pilgrimage. The river, though dirty and filled with refuse, is permeated with the divine essence and capable of cleansing them spiritually.

The importance of the pilgrim's inner change during the liminal period is perhaps best illustrated, however, in the Hajj, the pilgrimage to the Muslim holy city of Mecca. The Hajj, one of the Five Pillars that support the religion of Islam, is supposed to be undertaken by all physically and financially able Muslims at least once in their lifetime. The desire is so great and the space so limited, however, that many of the more than a million who make the pilgrimage each year are assigned by lot. Muslims come to Mecca from every Islamic nation, race, and sect, from "each distant point" as the *Qur'an* has it. They come to the Kaaba, the center of their spiritual journey, where the divine intersects with the human, in the hope of mercy and forgiveness from Allah.

Their intense preparations — their separation — give evidence of the changes occurring in them. They don a white seamless garment, which removes all traces of status, occupation, and place of origin. All wear the same dress and worship as absolute equals. Though they have diversity as individuals, they have unity as pilgrims. The special pilgrim's robe helps them become totally conscious of the divine encounter and their unworthiness for all that Allah has done for them. Thus they shout the ritual acclamation, "Here I am, Allah, at thy service" to express their response to Allah's summons and to reinforce their desire to be of service to others along the way.

Of the actual pilgrimage itself, which takes more than a week, three ritual actions deserve special mention. One is the "circumambulation" where the pilgrims walk around the Kaaba, the sacred stone, seven times. It is as if they are drawn by a magnetic attraction to the Divine Force at the center of their universe. A second ritual is the stoning of the pillars at Mina, which represent Satan and the forces of evil. In throwing the 70 small stones, the pilgrims hope to purify themselves and to destroy some of the shadows, temptations, and evil impulses within. The major ritual, though, the central act that cannot be omitted, is the journey to Mount Ararat(note the importance of the mountain again) some miles away from Mecca, for the "standing." This is the high point of the pilgrimage, where the vast multitude stands before God on the barren desert landscape from noon until just before sunset, united together in total submission to Allah, in a prefiguration of the Last Judgment. All their ordeals and struggles of the pilgrimage — and their lives — are offered to Allah at this liminal moment.

As for the incorporation, the return to their communities, the pilgrims keep their garments as a remembrance of the strength and vigor of the spectacle, of how they were caught up in a real feeling of unity during the week-long ceremonies of encircling the sacred shrine and standing at Mount Ararat. Many of them express signs of pan-Arab unity, but more important, there is often an expression of the rearrangement of thought patterns and the tossing aside of convictions previously held.

Testimonials to a radical change of heart away from prejudice and hatred — as in the autobiography of Malcolm X, for example — affirm that all humans are truly equal, that there is the oneness of God and the oneness of humankind.

The liminal stage of rites of passage is a time of paradox. This is especially true for the pilgrimages in all religious traditions. One paradox is that of *joy and suffering.* A pilgrimage that stresses only suffering, irritation, discouragement, and penance, but neglects to bring out the joy of fellowship and sharing, is lopsided. Joy comes to pilgrims not only from "conquering the enemy" but from entering a different threshold, a shrine that represents a place both in and out of time, a threshold between two worlds, where the pilgrims have a direct experience of the sacred. This joy is contagious and is shared with those who have not undertaken the spiritual journey.

A second paradox is that of *unity and diversity.* Though they come from different nations, cultures, and value systems, the pilgrims profess the same faith, are heirs to the same hope, and practice the same love. In spite of different social lives, social classes, and role expectations there is a type of bonding as they move toward a common sacred source of healing and renewal. Regardless of social customs, laws, norms, there is an equality in sharing a common predicament, and the pilgrims become all things to all people, in real identification with the poor and the oppressed.

A third paradox concerns the *present and future.* Pilgrims transcend time; their world is open to expanding horizons. They find meaning not only in remembrance of the past, nor in particular attention to the present, but also in their openness to the future. They are conscious of moving from a determined past and consent to a future that is free, exciting, and unpredictable. Living with the ambiguities of the present, which is never final or ultimate, they are open to the promise of a venturesome path that varies and changes with every unexpected obstacle and turn in the road. Still they are certain of the outcome: "Those who lose their selves shall find them." With their direct experience of the numinous, they are both in and out of time.

The *way and the goal* is a fourth paradox. Pilgrims are persons on the way, passing through lands sometimes not their own, seeking the goal of wholeness and self-realization in relation to the divine and to other persons. They seek the goal to which their spirits point the way. There is an indescribable thrill in nearing a shrine: The whole environment motivates the pilgrims as they come closer. It is as if the divine were presiding over their movement, continually calling them and urging them forward. They experience the presence of the numinous not only at the shrine but even as they move along the way to the goal. The "way," however, as it is understood in the various religious traditions, is a symbol of the presence-yet-absence of the divine. If persons don't experience the numinous on the way and find the unknown in their everyday lives, they will never arrive at the goal. The way is the goal.

The final paradox deals with the relation of *shrine and home.* Though pilgrims set their sights on the shrine, they cannot remain there without abandoning their other responsibilities. The ultimate purpose of their pilgrimage, it turns out, is not at the shrine, but back home after all. Yet, they have to leave home to learn what was there all the time. To refuse the homecoming would be to cut the self off from the experience of the shrine, similar to the hero on the vision quest who refuses the call to his heroic task. The encounter with the numinous at the shrine is real, but it cannot last. It is removed from the everyday experiences of home, and it is at home that the effectiveness of the encounter has to be realized. The experience at the shrine is the model, the paradigm, of what the home experience must be. Pilgrims take a risk in leaving home, and now they have to take another risk in returning home. Their journey is thus a circular one: a going out and a return, but a return with a new vision and a new resolve. The pilgrims leave home to find God; arriving at the shrine, they find that God has continued to move ahead of them and is now calling to them from their own homes, from the centers of their day-to-day activity.

## The Ritual of Lent

Most of us undergo rites of passage, both religious and secular, at crucial times in our lives. The liminal experience of a communal pilgrimage or of a personal vision quest, however, is not so common. For Christians, a close approximation to these heroic rituals of withdrawal is the ritual season of Lent, when they commemorate and celebrate the 40-day period of meditation of Jesus prior to the beginning of his public ministry. "Lent" means "lengthen" referring both to the lengthening of days in early spring and to a time to slow down, to meditate. It also means "lean" and was set in the lean time of the year, the months of spring when the food supply was scantiest. It was the time following the excessive debauchery of the time of carnival (which means "goodbye to the flesh" or "goodbye to meat"). Christians took this natural "time-out" period of this voluntary mortification (that is, "dying to the self"), which they share in common with all the major religious traditions of the world, and made it a time of preparation for ritual initiation into the community and for the joyous celebration of new life at Easter.

The emphasis in the lenten ritual is not primarily on sacrifice, on "giving things up," but rather on retreat and meditation, similar to the heroic vision quest. It is the time for development of the spiritual life, a special time for encountering and taking on the power of the divine. Reacting to their busy schedules and sensing their bodies' and spirits' need for quiet and reflection, people find in Lent the time for deep reflection on their lives, their faith, and their position in the world. It is a time out, a withdrawal to liminal time, always to return. It is a fixed period to withdraw from ordinary occupations to go on a pilgrimage to the strange and promised land of the soul.

Lent is commonly a time for Christians to "mortify the flesh," perhaps by fasting (that is, cutting down on food) or sometimes abstaining from eating meat. This serves personal and communal purposes. On the personal level, it is a type of preparation for death, a dying to the small self for the sake of the larger self. When real hunger and a feeling of tiredness and exhaustion are involved, it helps a person become conscious of dependence on God, of a sense of human limitations and self-insufficiency. More generally, fasting puts the self in an open, receptive condition, ready to accept divine activity. On the communal level, fasting sensitizes the self to the terror and desperation of those who have nothing to eat. It is the expression of solidarity with the world's hungry people (to the extent that people don't give in to the temptation of using fasting as a dietary fad or as a salve for guilty consciences). More generally, fasting is a way of protesting against any unjust social order, against a world in which there are haves and have-nots.

Whether persons become involved in the lenten ritual or not, we all need time out for our own vision quests. For us, it will be those special times and places (our desert, our shrine) when we can find our selves. It will be those occasions when we can just let our watches wind down, eat when we're hungry, sleep when tired, wake when rested, do a great deal of things we call nothing. Our vision quest occurs when we can knock down the metronome of our social existence and vacate the premises of our ordinary lives. Getting back to simplicity, we can find the center, the still point of our selves, which is waiting to be rediscovered, the still point that we can touch when we are at rest.

When we pass over the threshold to the unknown, to the Kaaba at the center of our existence, there is often a flooding of new possibilities. We need this vision from time to time, for without such a vision, our lives would be mundane and parochial. We need different perspectives to break out of the drab one-dimensional self-limitations that we construct for our selves. Liminal situations give us the capacity to see the self in new and broader and more appropriate perspectives. In our liminal experiences we get an approximation, however limited, of our place in the cosmos and our relation with the numinous and with others. With the vision gained during our liminal periods, we can develop the necessary correctives to stay on the right course to perform our own heroic tasks, to enlarge our spiralling self.

## Review Questions

1. What is the significance of each of Jesus' three temptations?

2. Explain: "The wilderness temptations are a rite of passage for Jesus."

3. What are the purposes of the vision quest among North American Indians?

4. Why are persons particularly vulnerable at the time of the liminal stage of a rite of passage?

5. What are the major elements in the Muslim "hajj"?

6. Explain the various paradoxes in any pilgrimage.

7.  What are the personal and communal purposes of the Christian season of Lent?

## Discussion Starters

1.  "A bright college student is one who realizes that he has not yet fully developed his potentialities, who experiences a tremendous amount of energy, and who has only a vague idea in which direction he wants to go. Thus he hopes to find three things: a) competence, which enables him to cope with the demands of society; b) control, which provides him with channels for his unruly impulses; and c) vocation, which gives him the convictions that he is called to do what he feels vaguely attracted to." (Henri Nouwen)

2.  "Physically, today's adolescents mature faster than their parents did. They also exhibit a superficial knowledge of sex and other 'adult' experiences. But in matters of emotional development — the ability to set one's own goals, to tolerate frustration, to postpone gratification, to take responsibility for others — today's students are significantly less mature than their parents and their grandparents were at the same age."

3.  "The world is not what it appears to be. Behind this surface life, where we experience the play of life and death, there is a deeper life which knows no death; behind our apparent consciousness which gives us the knowledge of objects and things there is pure consciousness. Truth is experienced only by those who turn their gaze inward."

4.  "Young people are too all-or-nothing, too certain: I've always felt that I must never be too completely sure of what is right. Let belief be tempered by discretion." (J. K. Galbraith)

5.  "Philosophy can really give us nothing permanent to believe either; it is too rich in answers, each canceling out the rest. The quest for meaning is foredoomed. Human life means nothing. But that is not to say that it is not worth living." (Peter DeVries)

6.  "In many so-called primitive cultures it is a requirement of tribal initiation to spend a lengthy period alone in the forests or mountains, a period of coming to terms with the solitude and nonhumanity of nature so as to discover who, or what, one really is — a discovery hardly possible while the community is telling you what you are, or ought to be. He may discover, for instance, that loneliness is the masked fear of an unknown which is himself, and that the alien-looking aspect of nature is a projection upon the forests of his fear of stepping outside habitual and conditioned patterns of feeling." (Alan Watts)

7.  "Once upon a time, I, Chuang-Tzu, dreamt I was a butterfly, fluttering here and there, to all intents and purposes a butterfly. Suddenly, I awakened. Now I do not know whether I was then a man dreaming I was a butterfly, or whether I am now a butterfly dreaming I am a man."

8.  "The adventure of change may be a tragic adventure for many — a sad uprooting of cherished customs and instituions. Yet change is the one constant of history. Not a decade has gone by in our nation's history in which we did not undergo new experiences and seek new challenges." (Robert F. Kennedy)

9.  Draw up a personal coat of arms. What images and symbols will you use to describe yourself in relation to your work, study, love, home, religion? How will you group these elements together? In pairs? Apart? What other elements will you include? What mythic figures will you depict?

# CHAPTER EIGHT

# THE HEROIC TASK

Human lives are in every instance far more complex, elaborate, subtle, and indeterminate than any model can provide. Models can give us perspectives on our lives but not absolutely unchallengeable descriptions or prescriptions. Myths of heroes are such models, relevant for those experiences we have along with everyone else. Heroic myths provide a pattern for organizing data, a common thread for analyzing our reactions to our experiences as we pass from one stage of life to another. We are the heroes. We are Rama, or Odysseus, or Parsifal, for example. By understanding their heroic tasks or quests, we know more about what our universe looks like and our place in it.

The theme of the hero's quest is among the earliest and best developed myth-narratives formulated by religious traditions and cultures. The quest pattern is known to us all, for it is the pattern of our own experience. The hero is not only the one who acts for all of us, who stands in our place to face dangers and risks, but his quest is really a model of our own quests. In the *Odyssey* and *Aeneid*, in the struggles of Perseus and Theseus and Heracles, in Parsifal's search for the Holy Grail, we see enlarged in story form the pattern of our own experience. Again and again, like the hero on his quest — entering the unknown, struggling with what lies there, finding something of value, and returning with it to the community — we find ourselves facing the unexpected, with its risks and opportunities. Heroic myth stories help us to create and interpret our own lives; they make us conscious of our various possibilities, both comic and tragic, and help us consent to experience them. The more we know about the hero's quest and the more we identify with it, the more it helps us compensate for the insignificance and banality of the humdrum existence from which, in reality, very few of us can escape. Looking at the hero's trials and participating in a life cycle greater than our own gives glamor to our own restricted quests and to the seemingly mild tests of everyday life.

Though the entire life of the hero is often considered a quest, our interest here is with the central task-struggle-journey that marks his adult life. The hero has gone through the period of withdrawal, the period of meditation and vision quest, and now he has to perform his adult task, the deed that will bring a real boon to the community. He has to prove his self with an action of universal importance in the prime of his life. He has established his origins by finding the divine destiny within the self, and now he has to act on that destiny. The quest is always toward a goal and should be distinguished from mere adventure, which may be undertaken for any number of reasons and may lead anywhere. The grave and serious nature of the undertaking contrasts with what may well be frolic in an adventure. The quest is always marked by a sense of struggle, of imminent or actual danger in which all of the hero's will and power will be called forth in order to push on. The hero's quest goes beyond self-fulfillment, culminating in a boon (gift) that has social and cultural value for the community as a whole.

## The Ramayana

One of the most beloved myths in India and Southeast Asia is the love story of Rama and Sita found in the *Ramayana*. The *Ramayana* holds great religious significance as part of the Hindu sacred literature (which includes the *Vedas, Upanishads, Puranas,* and the *Mahabharata*). Dating from about 200 B.C., it exists in different versions with many additions by later generations.

Rama, along with Krishna, is a human avatar, incarnation, of the god Vishnu, the "preserver of the world." He embodies the Hindu virtues, including a sense of duty and even-mindedness. Though Rama is a savior, it is his human quest that concerns us here. During his heroic odyssey, he meets many types of people who open his eyes to the nature of things. His strange adventures — living in a hermitage, fighting a battle with demons, and losing his wife — give him the wisdom and knowledge that eventually enable him to regain his country, throne, and wife.

Rama was sent to the world to save it from Ravana and his demons, who harassed the holy hermits and kept them from offering sacrifices to the gods. Rama was the handsomest and strongest of the four sons of the king since his mother had taken more magic potion from Vishnu than the women who bore the king's other sons. When Rama grew to manhood, he heard of Sita, who was beautiful, talented, and virtuous. Her royal father had resolved that whoever could bend a bow would have Sita for a wife, knowing that no ordinary mortal could possibly accomplish it. Rama bent the bow with such strength that the weapon snapped in two, and Sita became his wife.

The heroic crisis in Rama's life was precipitated when his father proposed that Rama should be crowned his successor. One of the queens, however, exploited her special position to prevent his succession to the throne. Because she had been promised two boons by the king, she demanded that her son, Bharata, should be made regent and that Rama be exiled for 14 years. Though the king was sad, he had given his word and had to fulfill his promises. As a dutiful son, Rama prepared to go into exile. Claiming that a wife's place was with her husband, Sita and Rama's brother, Lakshmana, both insisted on accompanying him. The three left and stayed at the hermitage of a holy man. Meanwhile, Bharata refused to accept the kingdom won so unfairly and set out to find Rama to ask forgiveness for his mother. Rama, however, had given his word to his father and remained in exile. Bharata placed Rama's sandals on the throne as a symbol of his right to the kingship and himself lived a hermit's life.

A demon-maiden fell in love with Rama. Spurned by him, she sought revenge and asked her brother Ravana (the demon-king of Sri Lanka) for help. Ravana's power was so great that it could be broken only by an alliance of men and monkey people.

He sent a demon disguised as a deer to lead Rama astray while on a hunt. When he failed to return, Lakshmana went in search of him. Meanwhile Ravana came in the form of a hermit, and when Sita showed him hospitality, he assumed his horrible form as a ten-headed demon. He proposed that she become his wife, but she poured scorn on him. He lifted her by force into his chariot to take her to his kingdom. Sita threw off ornaments toward a group of monkeys so that news of her abduction would reach Rama. Put into Ravana's harem under strict guard, Sita was given a year to make up her mind — marry him or die — but she spurned his advances with utter contempt. Rama, learning from a vulture of her imprisonment, allied himself with the monkey people.

Hanuman, the leader of the monkeys, was a valuable ally. On a spy mission, he went to Sita and told her of Rama's plans. Then he mischievously began destroying Ravana's city, tearing up trees and pulling down buildings. He mocked Ravana's army as he continued his destruction. He was finally caught but escaped and set the whole city on fire with burning rags that had been tied to his tail.

Though Rama wanted the waters to part so that he could cross directly to Ravana's island, he had to build a causeway. At last he and Hanuman's army of monkeys besieged the city, and a great battle raged for days. All the demons except Ravana were killed, and he and Rama engaged in single combat. Ravana had ten heads, and when one was cut off, another grew in its place. Rama, however, had a powerful weapon, a magic spear from Brahma, and was able to kill Ravana.

Freed, Sita rushed into Rama's arms, but he was cruel and cold. He said she could no longer be considered his wife since she had been defiled by another. Because Rama was adamant in not listening to her pleading, Sita asked for wood to build a fire so that she could call on the gods to prove her innocence. When she threw herself on the flames, the flames lifted her from the ground and set her down in front of Rama. Because she had proved in ordeal by fire that she was still virtuous and worthy to be his wife, Rama embraced her joyfully.

Rama and Sita returned home, along with Lakshmana, and Rama became king. Rumors began to fly around, however, that Sita had been unfaithful. Since no one had seen the trial by fire except Rama and Lakshmana, there was no one to vindicate her, and she was sent into exile. Sita went to live in the ashram of Valmiki (who would compose the *Ramayana*) and shortly afterward gave birth to Rama's sons. When these sons grew up, they came unknowingly to Rama's court and sang the story of Rama and Sita. Rama claimed them as his sons and sent for Sita. When she was again asked for a proof that she had been true to her marriage vows, she refused to accept the man who had twice accused her of unfaithfulness. She cried out: "Mother Earth, if I have been pure, take me unto yourself." The earth opened and Sita disappeared into it.

Rama went mad with rage and despair, and his friends feared that he would take his own life. But Brahma suddenly appeared to him and gave him this message: "Have you become so wrapped up in the world of illusion that you have forgotten who you are? You are the great Lord Vishnu, and this body you are in is only a temporary form you assumed in order to destroy Ravana. This woman you called Sita was an incarnation of your eternal wife, and she awaits you in your heavenly home." Rama was again at peace and soon after disappeared from the earth into the heavens where, as Vishnu, he continues to watch over the world and wait for another time when he must come to earth again to save it from destruction.

This hero's story is traditionally interpreted as placing before us the ideal of a harmonious pursuit of the principal goals of life, especially Dharma (duty and righteousness) and Moksha (liberation of soul). Happiness is based not on material possessions and environment but on proper human relations and performance of one's duties as a member of the family and the community. Thus Rama's submission to his father's decision and his struggle against the forces of evil and adversity, and Sita's obedience, patient suffering, and above all, faithfulness make them exemplars of ideal behavior.

Other Hindu religious ideals are also apparent. There is emphasis on proper social order and the orderly functioning of society. There are repeated references to the human will's subservience to the divine order and the power of destiny — karma — over people's lives. Though Rama occasionally swerves from these canons of conduct, he exemplifies the qualities of courage, truthfulness, generosity, forgiveness, deep respect for elders, and honoring one's word at all costs. The message he receives from Brahma at the end regarding the illusory nature of the world is the boon he leaves for the community: even-mindedness in success and failure, in joy and sorrow, in opulence and poverty is conducive to liberation and happiness.

## The Heroic Monomyth

Perhaps to appreciate better what we can learn about ourselves from the hero Rama, it would be useful to look at elements from the *Ramayana* from the perspective of Joseph Campbell's monomyth of the hero. In *The Hero With a Thousand Faces,* Campbell has provided a schematic summary of the interpretative elements that function typically in heroic myths.

During Rama's 14-year exile, he had to go to the demon kingdom to rescue his wife Sita. In the *call to adventure* of Campbell's hero, this is where the hero sets forth from home, with its protective but unchallenging milieu, and is lured or voluntarily proceeds to the threshold of adventure. In a condition of need, a crisis, with a symbolic deficiency — perhaps a golden ring is missing, or the people are living in a wasteland, or a monster is threatening the lives of those in the community — the hero is called to action. His call may be voluntary (Theseus desiring to go into the labyrinth to kill the Minotaur), involuntary (Odysseus being carried over the seas by the winds of the angered god Poseidon), or due to mere curiosity (Moses exploring the burning bush). In any case, the hero's activities must be directed toward some goal outside himself to lead to his authentic wholeness.

Rama learns of Sita's whereabouts through the vulture messenger and arrives at the demon kingdom through the aid of the monkey, Hanuman. These are examples of the *protective figure* that helps the hero as he journeys to the threshold of adventure. This protective figure may appear as a wizard, a hermit, a shepherd, or perhaps as talking birds in the forest. In some religious traditions, this helper may be a guru, a teacher, a ferryman, or a conductor of souls to the underworld (Hermes-Mercury). Perhaps the protector may be a goddess who lures, guides, or bids the hero to follow her wisdom and take her as she is, without undue commotion and with the kindness and assurance she requires. The protective figure aids the journey, whether in time or space, encouraging the hero in his uncertainty (for he cannot be certain in advance of success or failure).

All of this is necessary for the hero to establish his separate identity as a person of exceptional courage or wisdom.

Though Rama would like to take the easy way out and have the waters parted to the island of Sri Lanka, he has to build a causeway to the devil's kingdom. The *passage of the threshold* is never easy. Usually the passage to the other world involves getting past preliminary dangers. The realm of the unknown may be guarded by gargoyles, dragons, lions, or cherubim; perhaps there is a drawbridge, or Scylla (the six-headed monster) and Charybdis (the giant whirlpool). The hero has to defeat, or at least conciliate, these powers before he can encounter the object of his quest-struggle-trials. This passage over the threshold is a kind of self-annihilation, either inward or outward, a contest between contradictory forces within the self, which the hero must face before he can perform his life-renewing act.

After a long difficult struggle, Rama defeats the ten-headed demon Ravana. This he does with divine help, the sacred weapon of Brahma. This is the *hero's task,* the central act of the heroic quest, the struggle within the struggle. Beyond the threshold, the hero journeys through a world of unfamiliar forces that present him with his supreme ordeal. Such a series of tests would screen out someone unworthy, but in them the hero is revealed. The hero may have to slay a dragon, rescue some beleaguered maiden from unspeakable fate, fetch a cup of the water of life from the well at the world's end, or measure the dark in the belly of the whale. The hero Theseus, in order to prove himself worthy to be the heir to the throne, killed the robber Procrustes to make the road safe for travelers, killed the monster Minotaur which lived at the center of the labyrinth, and had to find his way back by means of the single linen thread of Ariadne. The hero Heracles, to be cleansed of the frenzied crime of killing his wife and three sons, had to undergo twelve tasks of labors, including killing the Hydra (a creature with nine heads and poisonous breath), obtaining the girdle of Hippolyta, the Queen of the Amazons, picking the golden apples of the Hesperides, and bringing back Cerberus, the dog that guards the underworld. In these and similar struggles the hero comes to wholeness and a new relationship to the world and is made suitable for his role within the culture.

Having conquered the demon, Rama rescues Sita, who proves to be a boon for the people as the queen of their kingdom.

The hero thus *receives the boon,* which is for the common good of the society the hero belongs to. Once he has proved he is worthy of it, he receives this gift from the gods and goddesses. It might be a miraculous energy, or wisdom, fire, Golden Fleece, or perhaps a peace pipe. Intrinsically, this gift will be an expansion of the hero's and the people's consciousness and their very being, through illumination or transfiguration.

Finally, there is the heroic *return.* Rama returns after fourteen years to reign as beneficent monarch. He winds up where he started, but with a difference. If the divine powers have blessed the hero in the struggle, as with Rama, he returns under their protection and as their emissary; if not, he flees and is pursued with further adventures and escapades, often with the "good" gods fighting the "bad" gods who try to set up magical obstructions to his return.

Sometimes the reintegration with society is difficult. Perhaps the desire to return has been lost, or perhaps he fears he will be misunderstood (Moses was reluctant to return from Mt. Sinai because he felt the people would never believe him). Still, the return has to be made for the heroic task to be complete. The boon must be shared for the quest to be successful; only then is the society re-created, only then does the hero spiral his egocentric nature, his small self, into a larger self that is identified to some extent with his culture.

The basic elements of Campbell's paradigm we have outlined in skeletal form — the call, the protective figure, the passage over the threshold, the task, the boon, and the return — reveal the way each of us must travel toward wholeness. In the hero's struggle we can anticipate the outlines of our own quests. This holds true whether we tell of a specific task (Rama defeating Ravana to rescue Sita) or of the quest of an entire lifetime (Rama incarnated to struggle against demons, in which case the boon is the message that he receives from the god Brahma about the illusory nature of the world, and the return is his ascent to the heavens).

The major benefit of this model has been well stated by Joseph Campbell:

> We have not even to risk the adventure alone, for the heroes
> of all time have gone before us; the labyrinth is thoroughly
> known: we have only to follow the thread of the hero path.
> And where we had thought to find an abomination, we

shall find a god; where we had thought to slay another, we shall slay ourselves; where we had thought to travel outward, we shall come to the center of our own existence; and where we had thought to be alone, we shall be with all the world.

The outward adventure of the hero reflects an odyssey of the spirit through which the hero in each of us explores the wilderness of his own selfhood. No one else can go where we must go; no one else can wrestle with our freedom and our dreams for us. It is both the heroic burden and the crowning gift of each of us to go on our quest for the self; it is our capacity for being heroes.

## The Heroic Pattern

Many of the experiences of our lives are disjunct. Experiences seemingly not connected come together as each of us realizes that the hero in the myths is really our selves and that the hero's actions are reminiscent of the activities in our own lives. Before looking at other benefits of this heroic model, I would like to introduce a second, similar pattern, one allied to the rites of passage we considered in the previous chapter. This second pattern highlights more the ritual element of the heroic quest. Religious traditions often ritualize the hero's quest either to commemorate their reception of the divine boon or to provide a pattern for the initiatory rites of other members of the society. Ritualizing the hero's quest and boon are both a commemoration and a preservation of the tradition.

During their exile, Rama and Sita had many adventures, and the places where they stayed are today reverently visited by throngs of pilgrims. In fact, in India each fall, the myth of the *Ramayana* is acted out in the ritual of Ram Lila. For over a week, segments of the story are acted out in songs and dance in religious fervor and excitement, becoming especially vivid at the moment when Hanuman, the monkey, burns down the demon's kingdom. The people's involvement in the ritual pageantry of the victory of Rama and the forces of good over the demons and the forces of evil is their own rite of passage. In this and similar rituals in other cultures, the dramatic re-enactment helps conduct the people across thresholds of change and growth, both in their conscious and unconscious lives.

Similar to rites of passage, the hero's quest contains a crisis, an initiatory struggle, and a return. First, the hero is forced, due to some need, to leave the security of home. He then undergoes a series of tasks on his journey, generally for the community's benefit. Finally, after a symbolic undergoing of death in his trials, the hero receives a boon from the gods which he brings back to the people in his triumphant return. These are all vividly demonstrated in the heroic struggle of Perseus.

1. *Crisis:* The people are worried that Perseus's mother will have to marry the tyrant Polydectes, and the only way that this can be forestalled is for Perseus to bring him back the head of Medusa (a winged monster whose very look could turn man to stone).

2. *Initiatory Struggle:* First journeying to the land of the dead, he finds several boons that will help him: The gifts from the gods include winged sandals, a shrinkable pouch, a cap that makes him invisible, Hermes's sword, and Athena's breast plate. With this divine aid, he is able to trick Medusa and cut off her head.

3. *Return:* After saving princess Andromeda (who has been chained to a rock as a sacrifice to the sea serpent) and marrying her, he returns home with Medusa's head, and all Polydectes's cronies are turned to stone when he takes the head out of the bag. Perseus and Andromeda then live happily as king and queen.

The reason for introducing this second heroic pattern, similar to the rites of passage, is to remind us again of the key moments of liminality. It is precisely at those marginal points of transition between stages, those moments between the secure past and the untried future, where the mythic images spark and ignite new self-realization. These are the moments where, precisely through clashes with the unknown, the person dies to the old self and is born to a new self. From this perspective, the quest becomes a series of transformations, and each liminal moment becomes the grist for the mill of other similar transformations in the quest for wholeness.

The hero, and each of us, becomes separated from the ordinary flow of life with concomitant losses; in his struggle, he is betwixt and between, neither where he was and not yet what he will be; in his re-incorporation, he lets go of his former state and grows into a new one. In his crisis, the hero becomes aware of forces he cannot handle alone; in his struggle, he takes on the power of these other forces and incorporates them into his self; and finally, he returns to his community, a new self in a new relationship.

The two liminal moments are crucial: the first, when the hero commits himself to change his situation of existential need and, thus, permits new growth in the self; and the second, when the journey begins to reverse itself, that moment at which the task is finished, an insight attained, or a new power appropriated, and the hero begins the return with his gift for the community. These liminal moments are moments of grace, when the up-and-down, the now-and-then, the past-and-future come together, and the hero passes to a new stage of personal and human wholeness.

Both patterns of the heroic quest help individuals understand, appreciate, and consent to the human tasks in their own lives. Hidden in the adventures of the hero are the answers to life's questions, but none of these questions can be tackled until the individual is willing to undertake the quest. And there will always be stern tests before any concluding formula can be uttered. There are no automatic successes. Any victory must be dearly, rather than cheaply, won. Indeed, evil is a necessity in the hero's world, present under the aspect of terror and the imminence of defeat. There is no way to discount the reality of these risks and dangers or to guarantee the outcome before the very end. But the quest has to be undertaken, and there has to be a willingness to give of the self before a person can grow, before arriving at a "oneness" or reunion with all creation, with the spiralling self, and with the numinous forces active in each life. It is the giving of the self to the quest, the consent to the struggle, that opens up possibilities for a fuller life and a new relationship with the world.

Though we share in the hero's physical triumphs, their validity depends on the spiritual effects. Ultimately, the goal of the hero's quest, and ours, is self-realization, a keener self-understanding that resolves our lives in new directions. The hero's quest corresponds to our subjective experience of life. In reliving it, we do not escape to a world of fantasy but to a world through which we begin to see our own world more clearly. By participating in the hero's struggles and triumphs, we probe our spiritual nature and come into contact with the mysterious other world of the human soul. We find strength for our own struggles, our sojourn through sorrow, our attempt to define the nature of good and evil, the quest for meaning and happiness. We find courage to continue our quest to work well and love well and to meet the still greater challenges that run the full gamut of human existence.

Participating in the hero's quest helps us in our movement from consciousness to consent throughout life, for example, in moving from the awareness of our sexuality to our consent to intimacy with another, from the consciousness of death to consent to our own mortality, from our first job to consent to our life's work. Sharing the hero's quest helps our maturation from concern for the self, to concern for the self and another, to concern for the community — the ever-expanding self and circle of concern.

The two heroic quest patterns provide another benefit for us by dramatizing the value of life-enhancing qualities in our journey from childhood to adulthood, from arrogance and foolishness to humility and wisdom. The *Ramayana* extolled duty, submission to divine will, and concern for proper social order. Other cultures or religious traditions might highlight the courage to undertake a risk, or to labor and struggle against monster forces for the benefit of society. Evident, too, is the joyful disposition of the hero, not a joy apart from sorrow, but a joy distilled from the experience of agonizing choices and painful awareness of the errors in human decision making. Occasionally, too, the hero will show sacrificial compassion: Jesus, for example, not only cooperated in the events leading to his death but to a large degree he engineered them, as if he were acting out a painful but urgent ritual. Ingenuity is another heroic virtue, a certain resourcefulness in escaping from danger or overcoming the villain, a mental agility as thrilling as his physical prowess.

Other life-enhancing qualities are manifested not as virtues in the hero, but as flaws to be avoided. For though we create heroes through whom we can vicariously live out our fantasies of glamorous living without hardship, we also inevitably find ways to knock our creations off the pedestal, to show their weakness, folly, and commonness. Good judgment, for example, is more important than physical strength (Heracles and Samson may have been strong, but their strength was as often a source of harm as of benefits). Modesty is more important than the hero's idle boasting, which often precipitates struggles not related to the quest. Also, confidence and enthusiasm are more effective than reticence or reluctance (Moses was an effective prophet in spite of his threefold attempt to get out of the task of freeing the Jews from slavery under the Egyptian pharaoh).

To delve further into some of these life-enhancing qualities that the hero personifies, let us take a closer look at two more hero quests, one from the Greek tradition (Odysseus) and one out of the medieval Christian tradition (Parsifal and the quest for the Holy Grail).

## Odysseus

Homer's *Odyssey,* dating back at least as far as the 8th century B.C., is part of the universal heritage of humanity. More than an epic romance of high adventure, it exemplifies the heroic pattern and points to many of the heroic virtues that make human life admirable. Odysseus goes through the spiritual process of loss and growth (that is, the dying to the old self and the rebirth of the larger self) and as restorer of the kingdom at Ithaca, he incarnates the socially responsible self.

Odysseus embodies several qualities the Greeks admired. Though he was at first reluctant, even feigning madness to avoid sailing hundreds of miles away, he did commit himself to battle, all to vindicate the honor of a minor Greek prince whose wife had run off with an Asian nobleman. A wanderer, Odysseus met emergencies with a cool head and was able to survive hazards by his resourcefulness as much as by his strength. He survived the ten years of battle and the next ten years of wandering through strange seas by his self-reliance and confidence in his own powers against fate, by his cunning and by his courage. Indeed, as the wily instigator of the ruse of the wooden Trojan horse (with the aid of Athena), he was instrumental in ending the war.

He had several soldiers hide in the hollow belly of a great wooden horse. The next day the other Greek soldiers were gone, and this huge mysterious horse was sitting before Troy. The Greeks left behind a solitary soldier, who claimed that he had been destined to be a human sacrifice to the gods, but had managed to escape. He told the Trojans that the Greeks had left the horse in order to placate the angry goddess, but they secretly hoped that the Trojans would desecrate it, earning Athena's hatred. His lies were convincing. In spite of Cassandra's warnings, the Trojans dragged the horse into the city gates to honor Athena. That night, the Greek soldiers crept out, let the rest of the army in, set the city on fire, and massacred the Trojan soldiers and citizens.

Having avenged the honor of Helen's husband in the war at Troy, as told in the *Iliad,* Odysseus desired to return home. This is the crisis that precipitates the many struggles, the heroic tasks, that are recounted in the *Odyssey.* His journey is presented retrospectively as a long and painful return to his homeland, hindered several times by the insubordination or madness of his companions. When they forget their troubles by eating the lotus in the land of the Lotus Eaters, he was obliged to take them back to the boats as prisoners. On the island of Aeolus, they thought that the god's wind bags were full of great treasures. Opening the bags, they let loose the evil winds that flung the fleet far from its goal.

Enticed by drugs and other seductions of the nymph Circe, the companions drank her wine and were transformed into pigs and imprisoned in a pigsty. Odysseus freed them with the help of a magic potion from Hermes but then succumbed to her charms and had to be roused from a long hedonistic sojourn by his homesick and impatient men. Again, on the island of the Sun, the companions destroyed the sun god's cattle, thus incurring his curse and their own death, as they were subsequently destroyed in a great storm.

Three of Odysseus's tasks merit special attention: his adventures with Cyclops, with Tiresias in the land of the dead, and with Calypso. The Cyclops were a race of monsters with one eye in the middle of their forehead. One of them, Polyphemus, entrapped Odysseus and his search party in a cave, threw the men against the wall, dashing their brains out, and ate two of them at each meal. Devising a plan of escape, Odysseus got the Cyclops drunk with wine. Odysseus then said: "You haven't asked my name, but I'll tell you anyway. My name is Nobody." His men took a sharp pole, made it hot in a fire, and drove it into the huge eye which hissed in the heat. When the Cyclops cried out, his friends asked who was hurting him. He replied: "Nobody is hurting me." They hollered that if nobody was hurting him, there wasn't much they could do about it.

The next morning, Odysseus and his men escaped by hanging underneath the Cyclops's sheep as he let them out to pasture.

This episode was just one of many in which Odysseus would mask his identity and give fictitious accounts of himself. On his return to Ithaca, he put on the mask of a ragged old wanderer and told stories of how he was a fugitive killer, a prince down on his luck, a rich youth sold into slavery by his protectors, and a beggar whose former prosperity had taught him the difficulties of fortune.

When Odysseus had persuaded Circe to assist him to find his way home, she included in her sailing instructions a visit to the spirit of the prophet, Tiresias, in the Hyperborean region, the Land of the Dead. Having escaped her charmed circle, he wanted to find out how to appease the sea god Poseidon. But the visit was much more than that, for here he had a vision of his past and of his future. He talked with his mother and his dead soldier friends, Achilles and Agamemnon. Tiresias warned Odysseus that lawless and violent men had taken over his royal hall and were courting his wife Penelope, and that he would face additional difficulties on the sea before his return. The good news was that he would eventually arrive home. Thus reoriented in the Land of the Dead, Odysseus was not afraid to continue the rest of his tasks and struggles to return home.

Many more dangers had to be endured. Odysseus had to stuff his men's ears with wax to pass the Sirens, those beautiful women whose voices lured travelers to their death on the rocks. He had to expose them to the narrow channel of Scylla (a six-headed monster) and Charybdis (a giant whirlpool that could have easily sunk the whole ship), only to be washed up eventually on the island of Calypso where he would remain a prisoner for seven years. Calypso, whose name means "concealer," kept beguiling and coaxing him, hiding Ithaca and Penelope from his mind. A conflict of interest was apparent in Odysseus: He found the goddess both dreadful and fascinating, yet still retained his wish to return home. Though he was held captive by this fascination, he gradually came to realize that he was a mortal and could never live with an immortal goddess. Though he had encountered the divine Calypso, he opted for the mortal Penelope. Conscious of his own humanity, he consented to return to the human Penelope rather than spend an eternity with Calypso. Acknowledging the link between his mortal humanity and his sexuality, he consented to his humanity and was now ready for his return to Penelope.

Having undergone all his tasks, Odysseus is now ready for the return home. Leaving Calypso, he is again shipwrecked, washed ashore, and received warmly by the Phaeacians, who listen as he recounts all his trials. After being nursed back to health, he is transported, asleep, to the shore at Ithaca. In this way Odysseus reaches his much longed-for home without knowing it. On awakening he doesn't recognize where he is, until Athena, the goddess of wisdom and his divine protectress, lifts the fog and shows him his homeland. Athena advises him that more than a hundred men have divided up his land and cattle and even want to force his wife to marry one of them. Though Penelope has put off the suitors by telling them to wait till she has finished weaving a garment (which she then secretly unravels at night), they have caught on to her ruse, and have forced her to choose. At Athena's suggestion, Odysseus makes himself known to a few loyal servants and to his son Telemachus.

Athena's plan calls for Odysseus to disguise himself as a beggar. The suitors commit outrages against this stranger, refusing courtesy and hospitality, and force him to undergo humiliations. Meanwhile, Penelope, forced to marry one of them, decides to have a contest. In an episode reminiscent of Rama and Sita, she will marry the man who succeeds in stringing Odysseus's bow and shooting an arrow through a dozen ax handles. None are able to string the bow, much less shoot it. When the beggar Odysseus asks to try, the suitors object but Penelope says that she will merely give him a new coat and tunic if he succeeds. He performs this task effortlessly, and with the suitors still stunned, he begins killing them. Athena, disguised as a bird watching from the rafters, aids Odysseus by fending off the arrows. In a massacre, Odysseus and his faithful few kill the suitors. At last, Odysseus manifests his true identity publicly.

But this is not enough for Penelope, for she demands her own private test. Unlike Sita who first proved her innocence to Rama and then to the public, Odysseus first proves his identity publicly and then has to do it privately. Penelope had already put him to the test. In addition to the bow and arrow episode, she had casually asked him what her husband was wearing when he departed twenty years earlier, and he had described perfectly the robe she had woven for him.

But she still wasn't convinced. Their son Telemachus is angry that his mother is so hard-hearted, but she tells him, "If he's Odysseus truly home, beyond all doubt we two shall know each other better than you or anyone. There are secret signs we know, we two.'' She then tells her maid to make up the big bed in her room and drag it outside into the hall. Odysseus cries out that it is impossible to move that bed, for he had built it himself using an olive tree with its roots still in the ground. This is the proof she needs. Her knees tremble, for no one but Odysseus could know the secret of the marriage bed, of how Odysseus had built it and rendered it immobile. She throws her arms around him and weeps for joy. At last the return — to their blissful beginning — is complete.

Odysseus finishes his heroic trials and returns home, a larger self. In many quest myths, the hero assumes the throne of the kingdom and claims as his bride a wonderfully beautiful woman he has delivered from imprisonment to some adverse power. We saw this in the *Ramayana*. But Odysseus's quest is different, for the feminine principle plays a much larger role in tempering his virility to make him a well-rounded person. His rite of passage is centered on one woman, his wife Penelope; it is guaranteed by the female goddess Athena who instills in him cleverness, endurance, and adaptability; and it is foiled along the way by the charms of the sorceress Circe and the numinous Calypso. For the success of his quest, he has to become conscious of and consent to the feminine side in himself.

Another element is needed, too, for the success of his heroic quest. Every path toward wholeness requires that persons strip themselves of their ordinary and habitual self in order to truly become a larger self. This transformation doesn't occur without sacrifice, humiliation, and self-denial. Thus Odysseus is Nobody to the Cyclops, loses all sense of direction after visiting Circe, and has to visit the land of the dead (that is, he has to die to his smaller self) to get his bearings once again. At the beginning of his quest, his ships and men are loaded down with treasures; at the end, everything is stripped away, and he is cast ashore naked and exhausted.

At the beginning, he is an egocentric, aggressive warrior; at the end, he has a deepened awareness of the meaning of home and his return there. He has learned, both in his visit to the land of the dead and among the hospitable people of Phaeacia, the model of domestic and community values. And this is the boon he brings back to his own people: In the role he has to play, ultimately, he returns to Ithaca to restore the kingdom and set up the democratic way of life (so prized by the Greeks). This way of life, energized by his responsive and responsible self, is the gift he shares with the community.

## Parsifal and the Holy Grail

Just as Odysseus exemplifies Greek ideals and virtues and symbolizes the person who enlarges the self by losing it, so from a Christian point of view does the medieval hero, Parsifal, in his quest for the Holy Grail. There are as many interpretations of the meaning of this quest as there are versions of the story. It has been suggested that the earliest versions transmitted glimpses of an initiation ritual that blended Christian and pagan ideas, glimpses of a series of initiatory ventures in which the ritual question ("Whom does the Grail serve?") permitted entrance into the sacred mysteries. It serves equally well as another example of the hero's quest, with its attendant crisis, struggle, and return.

The general setting belongs to the cycle of myths of King Arthur and his knights. Full of high purpose, valor, and strength, they all must undergo trials to test their courage, power, and nobility before they can perform their great deeds. The knights all have flaws (such as pride, lust, rashness, vengefulness), but they rise above these faults in the contribution they bring to the kingdom. Concerning the Grail itself, a few knights do attain a partial vision — Galahad (the stainless virgin knight who would have nothing to do with women), as well as Gawain and Lancelot. In the German and French versions, which I will blend together, the hero is Parsifal, the "holy fool," who represents the ordinary person's search for the supreme mystery of life.

The young Parsifal is so dazzled by some knights who ride by that he desires to be a member of Arthur's court. His mother dresses him in fool's garb, hoping that he will be disillusioned with the world and return to her. But she cannot dissuade him and he pulls up roots. Early in his travels, Parsifal is befriended by a woman who sends him off in the opposite direction from Arthur's court, for she fears that in his innocence he will lose his life in knightly combat. He finds his way to the castle of Gurnemans where he goes through training to become a knight. When the rough edges have been taken off and he has finished his training, he is given precise instructions that when he reaches the Grail Castle he must ask the question "Whom does the Grail serve?" Departing, he meets a woman, Blanche Fleur, who asks him to conquer the enemy besieging her castle. He spends the night with her, marries her, and then leaves her.

Continuing his travels, Parsifal comes upon a fisherman, the Wounded Fisher King, who tells him where to find the only lodging in the region. This hostel turns out to be the Grail Castle (also called "Monsalvesche"). The Fisher King presides over this Grail Castle, but he cannot touch the Grail nor be healed by it. He is wounded and his kingdom is a barren, infertile wasteland. This curse on the king and his kingdom can be removed, the court fool had prophesied, only when an "innocent fool" arrives in the court. Thus Parsifal arrives at the Grail Castle for the first time.

His first glimpse of the Grail comes when a procession of youths and maidens carry the object through the hall of the castle. The appearance of the "grail" (literally, a dish) produces a banquet. As it goes through the throng, each knight receives, miraculously, the meat and drink of his choice. Perhaps Parsifal is dazed by all the splendor, by the knights, by all the festivities. At any rate, he fails to ask the question. When he awakens the next morning, he finds that the people of the castle have all disappeared. Then the castle itself disappears, but not before his horse's hooves hit the drawbridge.

When Parsifal first entered Arthur's court, he made a damsel laugh — no small feat, since the woman hadn't laughed in six years. As a reward, Parsifal is told that he can have the horse and armor, if he can get them, of the Red Knight who had stolen a chalice from Arthur. Parsifal seeks out and kills the Red Knight, piercing him through the eye and taking his armor. His brave adventures continue and he subdues many knights. The women he meets berate him for failing to ask the question when he was in the Grail Castle. Arthur sends out knights to search for him so that he can be properly honored, but he is reluctant to go back. After many years of killing, he sees the blood of some geese in the snow. In a trancelike state, he thinks of Blanche Fleur, the wife he left behind, and becomes melancholy. Soon after, a hideous damsel, a sorceress, confronts him and tells him everything he has done wrong — the knights he has slain, the damsels he has left weeping, the lands he has devastated, the children he has orphaned. As the women before her, she tells Parsifal to search for the Grail Castle again, and this time to ask the right question.

His adventures continue, for a short while or a long while depending on which version we read, when one day he meets some pilgrims who ask him why he is bearing knight's arms on Good Friday. He suddenly remembers what he has forgotten all these years and goes to a hermit fòr confession. The hermit absolves him and tells him to go immediately to the Grail Castle. This he does, and this time he quickly asks the question, "Whom does the Grail serve?" The reply is given, "The Grail serves the Grail King." At this moment the Fisher King is healed immediately, and the wasteland and all its people can now live in peace and joy. Parsifal soon has the joy of being reunited with his wife, and they have a son, Lohengrin.

In spite of the considerable variations of detail in the different versions — the role of King Arthur and his court, the identity and relationship of the Fisher King and the Grail King, the timing of his slaying the Red Knight and his marriage to Blanche Fleur (or another), and the wording of the crucial question — the main outline of the heroic quest remains. There is the call to knightly adventure; the advice from the protective Gurnemans, the women, and the hermit; the threshold crossing at the drawbridge; the tasks of fighting knights and searching for the Grail; the return to the castle; and the boon of restoration of the wasteland.

Parsifal's crisis is precipitated when he doesn't recognize the importance of the Grail on his first visit. His task is to ask the question after he proves his fitness through his knightly adventures. And his return, with the boon of health and life to the king and his kingdom, occurs gradually, only after he realizes that knighthood is not enough, and that the answer is really within himself.

What really is the Grail? Though a "graal" was a large "dish" on which meat was served at banquet, the Grail has been considered variously as a cup of wine, a stone, a product of alchemy, a divine person. In any case, the Grail is beyond all earthly joy; it is the source of life, both physical and spiritual. Whatever it is, it is considered to be so profound and mysterious that people believed it worthwhile to spend their whole lives searching for it. Through a play on words, the "sanct graal"

(Holy Grail) becomes the "sang real" (royal blood). In the medieval Christian milieu, the life-giving properties of blood are extended to include the cup in which it is carried. The Grail is to be found in the Grail Castle, "Monsalvesche" (the mountain of salvation), a castle that has to be earned. It is the reward for fulfillment of a quest, not something that a knight can blindly stumble into and fully understand. The Grail doesn't exist in physical reality. It is a powerful inner reality, a mystical perception, a vision of beauty and connectedness. At the heart of mystery, where only a few can recognize its truth, the Grail is the symbol of the supreme spiritual value, attained not by renouncing the world or social custom, but by participation in the pulling of the heart. It is achieved only gradually through self-consistent action.

The Grail myth carries the insight that self-realization does not depend on external qualities such as wealth, position, or physical strength, but rather on private integrity and valor in pursuing great goals. Each of us is on our Grail quest, too, and this quest never truly ends, for it is the quest of seeking to become a fuller self, of penetrating the Grail of one's own being. When Parsifal first comes upon the Grail Castle, he fails to ask the required question because he does not perceive it to be his responsibility. Virtues entailed in the question, "Whom does the Grail serve?" (and its variant "Uncle, what ails thee?"), such as compassion and serving the needs of others, are developed only after a search, only as we learn to turn from the truths we can see to those we cannot see. With our first Grail visit, often in the innocence of youth, we have a vision of our self as unique and very precious. But we can't cope with or fully understand this experience, so we lose it. Much of our adult lives is the time between the two Grail visits, when we search for something that is within us all along.

When we become conscious of and consent to the reality that it is we who serve the Grail, then there is a paradoxical surprise in store: The Grail serves us. Beyond earthly joy, the Grail is the happiness that comes through serving others and healing their wounds. The Grail — happiness — comes when we no longer make it the goal of our lives, but rather seek happiness of others. If we ask the Grail to make us happy, we preclude happiness; if we serve the Grail and the Grail King, we will be flooded with happiness.

In the Christian context of the myth, serving the Grail is doing what God does — healing and serving, forgiving and loving. Failure to recognize this spiritual truth means expulsion from the castle, and the search has to begin again. But the lost Grail can be found again, and the afflicted wasteland can blossom anew. That makes the search worthwhile.

## The Archetypal Quest

Mythic heroes embody the accepted culture traits and the collective achievement of the religious tradition. Thus, for example, the Hindu hero Rama exemplified the ideals of duty and destiny, Odysseus reminded the Greeks of the virtues of a democratic society, and Parsifal recalled the virtues of compassion and service. In the intuitive vision of the world and life that they represent, we see that the individual and society are not in conflict but require each other. That is, the significance of the hero's quest is not in puffing up his imperial self but in spiralling the self into a greater self by bringing a boon to the community. The gift he brings to the community affects his own wholeness. His heroic accomplishments are realized at the cost of his symbolic death: a dissolution of his childish innocence and selfishness and a gradual rebirth into a new world of interdependence.

The adventure elements in the hero's quest — destroying cities, conquering demons, and slaying monsters — serve only a subordinate function. It is the inner component that brings about genuine change and makes the hero's story a valid paradigm for others. That is why the heroes we looked at in this chapter are more than just cultural heroes; they are archetypal. They reflect and symbolize the essential developments and real conditions of every human's existence. They are bigger-than-life figures around whom people of all religious traditions can weave their growth. Through cycles of life and death, good and evil, temptation and intrigue, weakness and innocence, despair and guidance, the myths of these heroes can help every individual achieve harmonious growth as they gradually become aware of the unseen real spiritual world.

The hero myths may not be true stories, but they are not unreal. They are the story of each human soul. They tell us that every path leading toward spiritual wholeness requires that we strip ourselves of our ordinary self in order to become a religious self. Our personal quests for self-realization are heroic to the extent that we attend to the crucial process of crisis, struggle, and return, to the rounds of destruction and re-creation that occur at graced moments throughout our lives. And the quests are successful to the extent that we assume a public destiny and are involved in the fulfillment of all humanity rather than merely our own personal self-fulfillment.

## Review Questions

1. Describe the crisis, struggle, and return of the hero Rama.

2. What are the major stages in the heroic monomyth as described by Campbell?

3. Explain: The heroic quest pattern dramatizes the value of life-enhancing qualities.

4. What is the mythic significance of Odysseus's adventures with Cyclops, his visit to Tiresias, and his stay with Calypso?

5. What is the significance of the Holy Grail?

6. Explain: "Much of our adult lives is the time between the two Grail visits." What is the difference between the two Grail visits?

7. The Parsifal-Holy Grail myth has been called "The Christian myth of the Middle Ages." Show how the answer to the question "Whom does the Grail serve?" summarizes the "truth" of Christianity.

## Discussion Starters

1. "Philosophers have only interpreted the world in various ways; the problem is to change it." (Karl Marx)

2. "Whether I win or lose is not important, only that I follow the quest . . . the effort remains sublime." (Don Quixote)

3. "Man does not always win his quests. Sometimes the hero loses because he is too weak and the task must wait for a stronger man. But sometimes the task itself may be too great. Throughout history man has been very sensitive to his limits and to the differences between himself and his god. Only in the past fifty years has man begun to feel that his only limit is himself." (Barbara Stanford)

4. "The end of life is now not so terribly far away — you can see it the way you see the finish line when you come into the stretch — and your mind says, 'Have I worked enough? Have I eaten enough? Have I loved enough?' All of these, of course, are the foundation of man's greatest curse, and perhaps his greatest glory. 'What has my life meant so far, and what can it mean in the time left to me?' And now we are coming to the wicked, poisoned dart: 'What have I contributed to the Great Ledger? What am I worth?' " (John Steinbeck)

5. St. Paul's hymn in the second chapter of the Epistle to the Philippians is an account of the paschal journey, or hero's quest, of Jesus. Describe the various stages of that quest.

6. "Life is death for those who do not have adventure. Adventure comes to those who are willing to take chances and daring enough to take the risk." (Prince, the musician)

7. "Odysseus heading into the Atlantic was going in the wrong direction, but his errancy was what taught him to value what he eventually found."

8. If you could meet one of the heroes of the classical traditions, which one would you choose? Why? What would you like to ask him? What advice would you give?

9. Have your heroes and villains switched places over the years? Why?

10. What movie and TV characters today remind you of the heroes in this chapter?

# THE GENTLE HERO

Up to this point we have studied the heroic myths as masculine quests. We have overlooked the roles of the women, although the stories, especially in the *Ramayana* and the *Odyssey* (and to a lesser extent the Grail myth), are as much Sita's and Penelope's as Rama's and Odysseus's. When Rama sees Sita for the first time after her abduction, he is overcome by a combination of joy, sorrow, and anger. This is natural, but it is difficult to appreciate his harsh expressions in sending her away because he finds it difficult to believe that she could have preserved her purity while in the demon Ravana's bondage. On this occasion, as on others, Sita displays remarkable calm, dignity, and courage. After telling him in plain language that it is unworthy of him to suspect her, she still prepares herself for the purificatory fire ordeal. Of course, she comes through this ordeal with honor. But her trials are not over. Having convinced him, she is still the subject of uncomplimentary remarks in the community. She is sent away again, though in the advanced stages of pregnancy. On this occasion, too, Sita rises to magnificent heights. Though sorrowful at this turn of events, she appreciates Rama's desire to respect the wishes of his subjects and maintain standards of conduct. So she finds asylum in an ashram and gives birth to her twin sons.

When called back later, she is told she will have to undergo the fire test again to convince the community of her innocence. This is too much. Sita wonders what crimes she has committed in a previous life that she has to undergo such terrible sacrifices to respect ill-informed public opinion. The very thought of another trial is so debilitating that she asks for and obtains deliverance by Mother Earth.

Throughout her ordeals, Sita is the supreme model of the traditional Hindu wife, utterly pure and loyal. She possesses in abundance the qualities to make her immortal among women: supreme faithfulness, infinite capacity for suffering, courage to speak her mind, a high sense of dignity and self-respect. Above all, she submits to duty, not duty concerning war and the affairs of state, as for Rama, but duty to human love and domestic affairs. These virtues ultimately qualify her for relief from mortal suffering. She is the most impressive character in the *Ramayana*.

Penelope, likewise, undergoes a heroic struggle to maintain her loyalty and affection during Odysseus's long absence. Continually besieged for twenty years by suitors who have moved into the palace and devoured Odysseus's wealth, she manages only with difficulty to repel their advances by using the ruse of promising to choose one of them as her king when she has finished weaving a tapestry and then secretly unraveling at night what she has completed by day. Her hospitality knows no bounds. When Odysseus comes back, she listens to his deliberate deceptions, kindly offers to allow him to try to string the bow and to give him a new coat if he succeeds. Then, after Odysseus has slain the suitors, she does not go directly to him. Too many times strangers have come pretending to be her husband. With patience, the gentle approach, she goes over by the fireside and sits down, staring at him. How can she know for sure that this is Odysseus? Though he has proved his identity to the community, she still needs her private test. Only after he reacts correctly in insisting that their marriage bed cannot be moved — a secret that only the two of them could know — only then does she begin to tremble. Her lonely ordeal is now over, and she embraces Odysseus as her husband.

The heroic trials of these women follow the quest pattern of crisis, struggle, and return. Yet there is a difference: Their task is a journey inward, not outward. Obviously, we have to modify our suggestion that growth through the course of the life cycle and progress in the spiritual life are best symbolized in the journey experience. To insist that human lives inevitably echo an external journey and that we achieve transformation by proving ourselves courageously and aggressively winning a boon is too stifling, too one-sided. The journey theme is not essential for the hero's task. Indeed, many of us wander, but we go nowhere. We settle down, but then get up and move on, always looking for something more. We cut our lives up into discrete stages and perhaps never reap the fruits and rewards of quests already completed, since we see them as merely provisional. Isn't there some other way of talking about proving the self in adult life, some alternative to the journey theme?

In the quest myths of Rama, Odysseus, and Parsifal, we saw that even in their external journey, the real struggle was within them as they moved toward adult wholeness. Though it was difficult for them to give up their kingdom, their self-gratification, and their knighting, these heroes did realize that their power was only illusory and not fulfilling. There are other heroes whose journeying is not essential to their task at all. Jesus and the Buddha were both itinerant preachers, but their heroic deed was achieved by preaching and enlightening others. Jesus preached the good news that the reign of God is within us, and Gotama taught that true liberation from suffering comes through overcoming ignorance.

Sita has a crisis with the accusation of infidelity after her abduction, undergoes a struggle in the fire ordeal, and experiences a return either to her husband or to the realm where there is no illusion. Penelope endures the crisis of seeing her husband off to war, the trials and struggles of waiting patiently for his return, and then the joyful reunion twenty years later. Still, the female involvement in these myths is peripheral and static, and there is hardly any suggestion that they grow to a new level of wholeness following the quest. Isn't there some alternative paradigm in which a heroine (a word that is suspect because it often refers to the one who is saved by the hero, rather than to a person of outstanding courage, nobility, and other achievements) can emerge as the model of developing fully human self-awareness? There must be a feminine hero who can evoke awareness in all persons, male and female, of those great motifs in life that transcend personal lives, yet are common to all. The imagination that is truly sensitive to myths should be able to perceive and enter into the task of the heroine, too.

Some exciting things begin to happen when we give up the exclusivity of the journey model and allow another paradigm to assume importance. If we no longer look at life as only a progressively upward movement through journeying and aggressive questing but instead follow a more *gentle* quest for human wholeness, we begin to move away from a basically masculine self-ideal to one more complex, more convoluted, and more human. This new model depicts adult life as a process of enlightenment and growth from unknowing to understanding, and from understanding to consent. Here we don't look at the hero's task as new achievements at all. Rather, it is a development of something already within, the unfolding of dormant powers not yet awakened. It is a matter of realizing (acknowledging and making real) the depths in our souls. An inner room, a circle, a Grail Castle that need not be stormed but can be entered almost at will — these are metaphors that convey a sense of immanence. Questing for them, we do not transcend ourselves to become something new, but we learn to develop the fuller selves we already are.

From this perspective adult maturity and success are achieved not by conquering, overcoming, or snatching a reward, but by protecting and developing the gifts of each in relation to others. There is no competition because there are no individual prizes. Each person is enriched through the mutual development of potential rather than through benefiting at another's expense. The adult quest is not a journey through dangerous realms but rather a slow realization of what is within, reaching out to embrace the universe. It involves coming into contact with our inner center, a way of achieving wholeness by grounding the self on the spiritual powers within.

This model has been suggested by some who are involved in developing human wholeness from a feminine perspective. It adds a very important dimension to our spiritual appropriation of the hero's quest. Indeed, the fullness of the human life might well be understood as a synthesis of these two models, for there are times in our lives when we have to exert control and other times when we have to go spontaneously with the flow. Paying attention to both models, we can unite the dualisms of spirit and body, the rational and the irrational, the spiritual and the social. We balance our efforts to get ahead and to win respect with our attempts to nurture creativity and equality in personal relationships.

## Psyche and Eros

If the hero has a thousand faces, the heroine has scarcely a dozen. Apuleius tells of one of these in the myth of Psyche and Eros in *The Golden Ass,* which has been described as a myth of the union between the human soul and divine love. The myth hints at the divine nature that awaits the soul, "Psyche," that endures long trials and tasks in the service of love, "Eros." It is a tale of the relations of heart and mind, of the human joy born of victorious struggle on the journey from romance to real marriage. Psyche (a word that signifies both a butterfly and the human soul) is the tender person who, freed from her chrysalis, rises to a higher existence where, united with love (Eros) in sacred and mutual marriage, she participates in the joys of the gods.

Psyche is the youngest of three daughters of a powerful king. Her beauty is so radiant that no man will dare ask for her in marriage but will pay homage to her beauty rather than to the goddess Aphrodite (Venus). Her parents exult in the honor paid to her and her sisters, jealous of her beauty, are happy in the thought that they are married but she never will be. Consulting the oracles about Psyche's fate, her parents are told to take her to a mountain top as if part of a funeral procession and to abandon her there until a future husband should come for her. Trembling but resigned, she waits on the mountain, believing that she is doomed to marry Thanatos (Death) or, at best, become the prey of a monster.

Aphrodite, who is jealous of Psyche's beauty, sends Eros (Cupid) her son to inspire Psyche with a passion for the ugliest person. No sooner does Eros see Psyche than he lays aside his bows and arrows and resolves to marry her himself. Enlisting the aid of Zephyr, the gentle west wind, he has Psyche transported to a magnificent palace in an unknown region. She is not discontent with her new life, for she is mistress of invisible attendants, and her commands are instantly obeyed. Her only grief is that she is not permitted to look at Eros. He visits her only at night, saying that he is the husband allotted to her by the gods and at the same time warning her never to inquire who he is, for then she will forever lose his love and become miserable.

In spite of her paradisal happiness, Psyche longs to see her family again to tell them what has happened. The sisters are permitted to visit and envy quickly fills their hearts. Hearing the circumstances of the marriage, they sow the seeds of suspicion that her husband must be a hideous monster because he dreads being seen. They maliciously encourage her to use a dagger to rid herself of this monster while he is asleep. Agitated in her heart, she takes a lamp and a knife and goes to his bed to settle his identity once and for all. Instead of the monster she expects to see, she beholds Eros, God of Love. She attempts to withdraw the lamp, but her hand trembles and drops of hot oil fall on his shoulder. In rage, he goes out, vowing never to return since "Love cannot live where trust is lacking." Psyche tries to end her life by throwing herself into a river, but the waters gently carry her to the opposite shore. Here she meets with the god Pan who succeeds in consoling her with the prediction that she is destined to be happy.

Psyche searches far and wide in search of her husband who, unknown to her, has fled back to his mother. Not finding him, she appeals courageously and humbly to Aphrodite, her jealous mother-in-law. Aphrodite hides her son and receives Psyche only with scorn, telling her that she will have to perform terrible ordeals, four seemingly impossible tasks to win back her husband.

First she has to sort a mixture of tiny seeds into separate piles before nightfall on penalty of death. A colony of ants feel compassion and sort the seeds for her. The next day, Aphrodite, furious that the task has been successfully completed, tells Psyche to go to a field across a river, get some golden fleece from the rams pastured there, and be back again before dark. At the river's edge, reeds whisper to her to wait till the sheep come out of the field, then she can gather the fleece where it has brushed off onto the bushes.

The third day she has to fill a crystal goblet with water from the source of the river Styx. Disconsolate when she finds no place where she can get her foot near enough to the stream, she is helped by the eagle of Zeus which takes the cup, flies to the center of the stream, and fills it for her.

Psyche's fourth task is to make the descent to the underworld and borrow a jar of Persephone's beauty ointment. She sets out on the dreadful enterprise, despairing of success. A boater, her invisible guide and protector, teaches her the precautions to take and warns her of impending dangers. She safely pays off Charon the boatman who ferries the souls of the dead across the Styx to Hades, gives some barley cakes to take away the fury of the three-headed dog Cerberus that guards the gate, and finally reaches the Queen of Death. Persephone gives her the desired jar with the strict instruction not to open it. Scarcely has Psyche left when curiosity and vanity induce her to open it. She is instantly enveloped in a black and noxious vapor, which throws her into a deep swoon from which she might never rise. But Eros, who has recovered from his "wounded love" and escaped his mother, hastens to her assistance. He puts the ointment back, pricks her awake with an arrow, and takes her to the throne of Zeus, proclaiming her as his wife. When he asks for her admission among the immortals, Zeus complies with the request and Aphrodite becomes reconciled with her. Psyche and Eros have a child whose name is Pleasure.

## Psyche's Crisis

Unlike the heroic quest of Rama, Odysseus, and Parsifal, the crisis in Psyche's life is one of relationship. Earlier she has taken the plunge by abandoning herself to her fate on a mountain top, and now, with her husband Eros gone, she is called to take another step toward her full maturity. Her quest of self-discovery is precipitated not by some monster to be subdued or kingdom liberated, but rather when she drops some oil on her husband when trying to know more about him to improve their relationship. Her crisis is an inner path in "trying to prove her self in the adult quest." This is a different quest for wholeness.

Eros leaves Psyche because their relationship is not yet built on mutual fidelity: Psyche is not yet able to let Eros be himself. Early in the relationship, she wants to know all about him, take out all the mystery, and pigeon-hole him once and for all. Most of us have a similar dilemma in coming into adulthood. Our efforts to develop intimate and mutual relationships are stymied by our need to categorize the other person. This dilemma is compounded by another problem — infatuation or projection — where we make an image of the other person according to what we would like to find in him or her, and then put this image on a pedestal and worship it as if it were divine.

Psyche has said yes to the Zephyr wind earlier and has come alive with an energy to tackle life; she has settled in on marriage to someone still unknown, and now the possibility of deep failure presents itself. She has found out, as we all do, that she cannot live in paradise every day. Life is full of such disappointments, and our inner growth will always involve an experience of suffering as the inevitable price of transformation. Her suffering is a pain shared by all mortals who would give birth to a divine world within this physical life and its finite limits. And this particular episode is most poignant, for it is another dilemma at the beginning of many marriages. Until marriage, we seek our freedom to be individuals while, at the same time, we search for someone to surrender this freedom to. It is the very stuff of the quest of the gentle hero.

When Eros leaves Psyche, she is in turmoil and is diverted from committing suicide only on the advice of Pan. The separation from her husband is heartbreaking, but not death-dealing. It is rather an inner crisis, one that demands that she let go of her own narcissistic image in order to grow in personal power, that she let go of her own ideals and seek inner assistance. Psyche has reached the point where she is both humbled and relieved by the realization that what is best for her does not reside solely within her view. Letting go, of course, is not what she would normally feel like doing in this situation, for fear of meeting something worse; but she must let go if she is to be broken up, remade, and restructured as a whole person. Such dying in order to be reborn doesn't mean, however, that she should abandon her commitments recklessly, as she would by jumping into the river.

Till now, her personality flows from her life as a daughter and a wife; till now, these roles have set her spirit on fire, but they are no longer enough. Now empty and motionless, she is called to leave behind previous meaning and definitions in order to go out into the dark with a faith that there is more to her. Early in her quest she has to let go, accept and live through this new experience, painful as it is. She has to turn the situation over to fate and wait on the natural flow of the universe; she has to drop personal control and give herself over to the will of the gods. This is not the time to force logical understanding, but instead to wait patiently and listen to the soft voice within. It is the time to let go of finding a reason for everything and to wait for a wisdom that comes not from logic or action, but from feeling and intuition. Her task is an inward task, and she becomes her true self by patiently letting go and waiting.

It is never more important to be in touch with the self than at this time of life, at this crisis when her present feelings can cause emotional shipwreck. She desperately needs to draw on all the strengths of her past and the potential of her future and focus them on the bumpy present in order to sustain herself through the transition. She has to reassess the strengths of her relationships and accomplishments and confront the limitations of her love and work. Such letting go is dying to the small self, to a life of mere externals, and an opening up to values and choices that flow from her inner resources.

Although the myth is the story of Psyche's growth into a mature marriage, we are not overlooking Eros's need for letting go too. He is not yet ready for full commitment to her either. He is childish and immature and runs home to mother when things don't go his way. He says that their marriage will be a paradise, but all paradises fail; each one has a serpent of some kind in it. He is immature, for he doesn't want her to ask any questions; and when Psyche lights the lamp and sees the god in her husband, he isn't ready to live up to all that that entails. A married couple, the Greeks seemed to know, can remain happy in romantic union only until unmet needs demand conscious knowledge of the lover's real identity.

Psyche and Eros both have to quit clinging to their illusions and projections about each other. They are both guilty of the infatuation that accompanies falling in love. Rather than demanding that each live up to the images of what they would like their spouse to be, they both have to let the other be and enjoy the surprises that the other can bring.

Infatuation develops from being possessed by a distorted vision of what is, a distorted relationship between inner expectations and outer realities. It is like living under the spell of some magical love potion. Falling in love is seeing the world colored and distorted through a gossamer veil of ideals of what we would like our spouse to be. Infatuation projects a highly valued part of the self on someone else where it is then worshipped. The other person becomes an extension of the self, which leads to possessiveness, jealousy, lack of confidence, and anxiety when the other is not present. Infatuation is the initial attraction, the instant desire, the excitement and eagerness felt when we put the other person out of the realm of the ordinary, far apart, where it is impossible to love, value, and respect the person, and to feel the beauty of mutual commitment. Keeping such fantasy qualities isn't workable and cannot last. The transpersonal godlike quality dims, and the down-to-earth person is revealed. The nagging doubts, unanswered questions, and little bits and pieces about the beloved that we would just as soon not examine too closely are brought to light in their own time, and the dream is spoiled.

Psyche's crisis is the very human crisis of trying to find a way to make her marriage work. It is precipitated when she lights the lamp and sees the divinity in her husband. For most of us, however, the crisis is similar yet different. We know the person is human, but we insist on projecting divine images and ideals on the other. The crisis, then, is to translate infatuation into love. Marriage begins with falling in love and must make the transition to mutual loving, if it is to be successful. For a marriage to endure, it must be based on a relationship between a couple who consent to see each other as ordinary, imperfect people who love each other without illusion and without inflated expectations. Love is quiet understanding; it is the mature acceptance of imperfection. It gives strength and bolsters the beloved. Love is friendship that has caught fire. It flames up one day at a time, with a warming presence, even when the two are separated. Love means trust. When one is calm, secure, and unthreatened, the other feels that trust and is made to feel even more trustworthy. Love is an upper, making the other look up and think up, and trust in one's own potential for wholeness, while accepting fears and weaknesses, conflicts and change.

The transition from infatuation to love in marriage is a religious rite of passage. The transition from falling in love to loving means no longer refusing to enter the mystery of a relationship. It is the passage from two independent lives into new and exciting, but confusing, mutuality. In a way, Psyche is right when she goes to the mountain top for her marriage. Eros and Thanatos are closely related, and the journey of love is in many ways a journey to the realm of death. Loving means losing a vulnerably precious sense of the self, being changed through encounters, and a willingness to be influenced by the other. The challenge of intimacy demands gradual self-disclosure and self-modification through interaction with the other, through the strain and exhilaration of mutual influence. But if it is a dying, it is also a bringing to life. True love in marriage bestows life on the other. Words of endearment and encouragement make our everyday lives sparkle and vibrate with excitement.

## Psyche's Tasks

While Penelope was described as sitting patiently at home waiting for the return of Odysseus, and Sita was forced to undergo the fire ordeal on two occasions to prove her innocence, Psyche has to perform a series of tasks before she can conclude her search and find her Love. In the more aggressive quests of the male hero in the last chapter, we saw that they were aided in their tasks by a mentor. Odysseus, for example, visited the underworld where Tiresias instructed him in the principles of democratic society as well as pointing out how he must voyage to return home safely, and Parsifal had some of the rough edges of knighting taken off by his visit to the castle of Gurnemans. Mentors are not there to solve all our problems but to show during a period of crisis and struggle that we are not all-powerful, that we cannot solve all the world's problems, that we will always have to live with mysteries in our lives. A mentor is not someone who will perform our task for us, but someone we can bounce off our joys and hopes and fears.

Psyche's mentor is Pan. Pan dissuades Psyche from drowning herself in the river and gives her advice to pray to the god of Love. Prayer becomes the way of deliverance for Psyche, for it enables her to see herself as she is and the world around her as it could be. This seeking of help is a crucial turning point in her quest, one of the major moments in moving toward wholeness. Through her prayer, Psyche realizes that her mother-in-law, Aphrodite, is not only the source but also the way out of her difficulties. Through her prayer, too, the god of Love, Eros, becomes attuned to her distress and will later aid her by instigating help for her in each of her tasks.

To her credit, Psyche goes to Aphrodite, for this is a challenge not everyone will accept. Some refuse the journey inward through prayer and refuse outward advice, preferring to remain

in their own ways, foreclosing the future, and remaining en-
trenched in their dilemma. Aphrodite unwittingly will be the
one who thrusts Psyche into those tasks, those transitional efforts
she must endure to be reunited with Eros. She gives Psyche a
series of tasks, hoping to make her homely. Instead, she helps
her step into a greater life and become a mature self.

Psyche's first task is to sort out a pile of seeds before
nightfall, under penalty of death. With their gifts of industrious-
ness and organization, a colony of ants comes to her aid. Robert
Johnson, in his book, *She*, suggests that the sorting here refers
not only to the menial sorting that has to be done around the
house but also to the sorting that goes on between the conscious
and the unconscious, bringing awareness of our inner feelings
and values, our introspective quest for wisdom.

This is true of all persons, male and female. In a marriage
partnership, where both have developed their own capacities,
both will have their share of sorting to do. Sorting is a task of
the gentle hero, as necessary in males as in females. Sorting is
a way of helping persons overcome stereotypes, especially those
of masculine and feminine. Sorting helps persons be equally comfortable facing the outer world and the world at home, no longer
portraying the husband as the one who goes beyond the family
interests to those of society, and the wife largely restricted to
nurturing and caring for those at home. Sorting helps both male
and female to affirm people in their humanness and ordinariness;
to provide a soft word of understanding, small gifts when least
expected, and spontaneous gestures of love; to transform even
the unexciting, difficult, mundane things into joyful and fulfilling components of life. Sorting helps us delight in the simple
activities that make human life possible. It finds joy and
sacredness in the physical world, without projecting inner gods
onto external mortals. Sorting brings us into contact with the
ants, respect for the earthly environment, and delight in the
earth's beauty taking love off the airy level of fantasy and
converting it into earthy, practical immediacy.

Psyche's second task is to go to a field across a river, get
some golden fleece from the rams pastured there, and return
before dark, under penalty of death. The wind in the reeds at
the river's edge whispers to her not to try to kill the rams for
their fleece but to wait till they leave the meadow and take the
scrapings off the bushes. The way of the gentle hero is not the

way of dangerous encounters, ecstatic meetings, tearful partings, cosmic dramas, intense entertainment. The gentle Psyche is not to be caught up in the ram's world, in competitive impersonal society where she could be bludgeoned to death. Her way is not the aggressive mounting of the charging steed, which would destroy her, but rather the way of the knight on the chess board, which moves in a subtle, unpredictable way.

Just as Penelope spent her time in weaving the tapestry and Sita dwelt in the ashram of Valmiki, so the way of Psyche is the gentle way. Both are necessary in every person, male and female, in different degrees. Some will have to go questing, hunting, winning in an aggressive fashion. Others can satisfy their needs without a power play. This is the way of the gentle hero. One may let off steam and release tension in a competitive game of volleyball; another may do it by knitting a sweater. Gandhi, for example, was effective in the struggle for independence in India while sitting at a spinning wheel in his ashram. Both the gentle way and the aggressive way are part of being human, and each person has to use both methods in a proportion that is dictated by one's biological limits and functions.

Psyche's third task is to fill a goblet of water from the river Styx, a stream guarded by dangerous monsters, with banks that will not support anyone who gets close to it. An eagle of Zeus, Eros's father, takes her goblet into the dangerous waters, fills it, and brings it back to her. Johnson suggests that this task reminds us that some things in life can just overwhelm us with their vastness, and we can appreciate them more if we take them one at a time. Sometimes we want to "grab with all the gusto we can," but other times this will not work. Sometimes we need the panoramic vision of the eagle; other times, wading in the stream is best. Sometimes we need an overview map of an entire city to get our bearings; other times we are interested only in one particular street corner.

The final task involves a descent to the underworld where Psyche must obtain a jar of beauty ointment from Persephone. For a fourth time she receives outside help, this time from a boater who gives her instructions for a successful journey. Besides paying the ferryman and tossing the bread to the dog, Cerberus, she is told to refuse to aid a dying man, assist women weaving the threads of fate, or eat anything but the simplest food in the underworld.

Why must she refuse to help others? Perhaps because in this way she can still listen to her own needs. Many people are so busy being generous with the needs of others, trying to weave the fate of others, that they have long ceased listening to their own needs. At certain times it is necessary to use the creative "no" to all the demands on our time so that our generosity can be revitalized. How often have I heard women, older than the traditional college students, say with excitement and anticipation as they begin their own college studies: "Now that I've got the kids off, I can finally do some of the things I've wanted to do for years." Why must Psyche refuse to eat food in the underworld? Perhaps so that she can escape what happened to Persephone who, in eating a pomegranate, was forced to stay in the realm of death. Psyche refuses to forge permanent ties with death.

But at the same time she does open up the beauty jar out of curiosity. In trying to put on a new face, a "mask," she makes a bad mistake. She does not receive youthful beauty, innocence, or purity but instead falls to the ground in a swoon. It is as if she is weighted down with the responsibilities of mature life and with the awareness of her own mortality. Opening the jar in spite of the taboo is a mistake, a failure, but this is also necessary for the full life. It is a reminder that some human destructiveness must be integrated into our lives for full maturity. We have to come to terms with our grievances and guilts, with our imperfections. Beauty and imperfection go together.

## Psyche's Return

Psyche has suffered the crisis of seeing her husband run away when she holds the lamp to him, and she has performed the four tasks her mother-in-law required before she and Eros could be reunited. Now, after she has visited the underworld and gone into a death swoon, Eros, who has also matured during their separation, returns to her. Her heroic task is now complete, and she joins the gods on Mount Olympus. Her salvation, her wholeness, comes as a gift of the gods. She is strengthened and healed by a combination of her struggles and Eros's cooperation. Her quest has been a struggle to come to terms with her inner world, with the world of relationships, and it is successful after her descent to Persephone's realm (a type of spiritual suicide). Her self-realization, in taking on the life of the gods, comes only after her abandonment to the unknown in the realm of death. The crowning achievement of her movement from infatuation to love, in her coming to maturity, is her reunion with Eros and their child Pleasure this produces.

No one who has been to the realm of death, that is, encountered the divine in the depths of the unconscious, can ever have a simple human life or uncomplicated relationships again. Psyche's tasks have been a gentle quest to find Eros, and her life has been a quest to find out who she is. She has become a larger self, laboriously so. Her alienation from Eros, from Aphrodite, and from her two sisters helped define her as an individual person. Now that she is reunited with Eros, however, and recognizes the divine within herself, her whole being is one of interdependent relationship. In saying yes to herself and to her limitations and failures, in accepting who Eros is and letting him be himself, she discovers her proper relationship with the unknown, achieves a union with it through her many trials, runs the full gamut of human life, and thus generates new life, Pleasure.

Moving from infatuation to love has meant suffering for Psyche, and also a death. In the land of the dead she experiences a profound change, a transformation, in her depths. Her small self consents to give up its tiny empire in order to live in the immensity of the greater universe. In living this death correctly, as paradoxical as this sounds, she completes the journey of discovery leading toward new life. The death that awaits her at the center of love is not the destruction of life but the flowering of an inner world. This death is a transformation, a death to the world and a rebirth in a realm that is bigger than life. Her small self has made a sacrifice of its narrow world, its old point of view, its old ingrained attitudes. A new set of values has come into life. Now there is evolution and change, not just a vain repetition of the old way. It may feel like impending disaster, suicide, but this delivering of the self over to a power that envelopes and possesses her is really her deliverance, her salvation, her new awareness. The sufferings of love are a privileged mode of understanding.

Letting go of her own will enhances Psyche. It is the setting aside of her final claim on her own life and the commitment of her self to the "other," the absent Eros. In this, she achieves a greater life. Accepting small deaths is her final yes to the transiency of life. Now she can laugh at life with a laughter that expresses the joy of life without, at the same time, frantically clutching it, with a laughter that embraces death as well as life. Saying yes to death, she now draws her life from Eros. She is filled with enthusiasm, and her creativity can flow. She now radiates the reality that the divine world and the personal world co-exist within her. Accepted among the immortals on Mount Olympus, she is on a new plane of existence and realizes that her physical, mundane, ordinary world has its own beauty and validity. Her humanity has its own intrinsic value.

Just as Psyche's quest is an internal one, dealing with relationships, the return is also an internal one. Her quest ends quietly with a new wisdom and equilibrium. She has not eradicated the elements of an impulse toward isolation or self-concern, but rather now she can balance the personal and the communal in a ratio appropriate to her and consistent with her commitments. With a balance that gives some things up, lets some things die, and accepts human limitations, there is a mature blending, a synthesis of accepting her past without regrets, in line with her vision for the future.

Her maturity is an effective way of adapting to the challenges of life, not by closing out the unknown, but by remaining always open to it. She eventually emerges from her experiences, which temporarily confused her, successfully integrated in an ensemble of roles. No longer is she opposed to change, but is constantly aware of the challenge to grow and the need to adapt to different demands and invitations.

The new wisdom she brings back from her quest is not her only boon for society. The result of her growth from infatuation to love is her ability to give new life, coming not for living for another, but from having something to give. Secure in her position among the gods, she recognizes her own competence and capacity for generative care.

Her heroic struggles in the four tasks developed in her a creative power she now shares with others. Triggered by her compulsion to bring light into darkness and to make beautiful what couldn't be seen, her ordeal culminates in her unleashing a creative power not only in herself but in others and in her surroundings. Her return is remarkably similar to Parsifal's when he brought happiness and fertility to the wasteland with his successful second Grail visit. Her strong inner self can now nourish and guide others and set their hearts on fire to activate necessary changes and transformations in their own lives. Healthy and whole, she recognizes that self-fulfillment demands more than turning love and marriage into just another area for personal growth, more than merely feeling good about her self. True intimacy in love and marriage is not subject merely to the whims of individualism but finds ways to manifest itself in transpersonal love in commitment.

Wholeness includes not only the power to create but the capacity to care for what is created. As she trusts her own creative power more, she can accept and encourage the uniqueness and the individual contributions of others. She can now become a genuine mentor herself and care for younger persons without her own agenda interfering, without trying to fashion others in her own image. There is a strength, an acceptance of her self as authority. Till now, authority has beeen external to her; but now, because of her change in consciousness, she internalizes this authority.

Aware of the relativity of values and goals, she can transmit to others a certain willingness and suppleness to modify the self in response to new information and to different interpersonal relationships. She can teach others the tolerance necessary for the strain that is inevitably involved in personal accommodation and compromise. She can transmit the capacity to commit the self in partnership and to abide by commitments, even though they may call for significant sacrifices and compromises.

The boon from her quest is not another trophy to hang on the wall but a gift for others, a gift for the mutual development of talents. She finds promise in others, even though they may not discern it, and draws it out by much encouraging, challenging, and criticizing. She rewards and fosters creativity by treating unusual questions, ideas, and actions with respect, and provides opportunities for others to make transitions in consciousness. She continues to invest her self, guided less by her own needs for self-preservation and self-delight, or self-worth and self-competence, and more by the demands of interdependence and a life given for others.

## Psyche's Erotic Side

Jungians have often interpreted the myth of Psyche and Eros as an example of the male's initiation into his own femininity.

The purpose of the imagery of the *anima* (the feminine side of the male) and the *animus* the masculine side of the female) is to provide a model for contrasexual development and to steer clear of those sex-role stereotypes where persons are pressured from within and without to be exclusively male or female and to feel guilty if they fail to conform. Granted, we are born into male or female bodies which shape our psychological perceptions of self and the world. Our sexual identity as men or women comprises a central part of our personality and cannot simply be ignored. Persons alienated from the other half of their humanity are to one degree or another emotionally and spiritually handicapped. There is a masculine way of nurturing, being receptive and sensitive to beauty and goodness, to cruelty and injustice; there is a feminine way to be aggressive, dominant, and analytical. Reconciliation with the contrasexual dimension of the self can revitalize a person's spirituality and make him or her whole.

The contrasexuality model helps us gain a more secure sexual identity through coming to terms with the ''other'' factor in ourselves. We become our own man when we integrate the feminine component of our personality; we become our own woman when we integrate the masculine component of our personality. Wholeness is the integration of both components in a comfortable balance. The content of the contrasexual factor differs according to personal experiences and cultural conditioning, prohibiting us from assigning fixed contents to it, for example, equating *anima* with feeling and *animus* with thinking. Those who have an overabundance of the aggressive, ambitious, and determined style of Rama, Odysseus, and Parsifal have to temper it with the gentle, caring, and generative virtues of Psyche and Sita. And vice-versa. Developing the contrasexual factor, the ''other'' side, is developing wholeness in the self through dveloping a readiness for response to the needs of others.

What happens if we consider the myth not so much as the male's initiation, but rather as an amplification of the female's initiation into her own full humanity? What does Psyche incorporate into her own self from Eros? The insipid, sentimentalized, baroque image many of us have of Eros is hardly the picture we would like to have of a god. If we let Eros be Eros, however, as Psyche learns to do, then we find that he is really quite powerful. She wants to bring Eros to consciousness. But not everything can be reduced to reason. Psyche loses Eros almost immediately when she discovers his true and magnificent divine nature. But he is still there. Although he has run home to his mother, he watches over Psyche and helps her in her trials by providing the ants, the spirit whispering in the reeds, the eagle of his father Zeus, and the tower of advice. He is thus strengthened, healed, and brought out of his childish behavior as he unobtrusively helps Psyche in each of her tasks. Her liberation and wholeness come through becoming conscious of the presence of this divine life in her and consenting to it. He too matures, becoming worthy to be her mate, reedeeming her and raising her to the level of the gods.

Though the word "erotic" has been co-opted these days by the pornography industry, there is a very positive way of talking of Psyche's erotic side, her childlikeness and godlikeness. Her quest ends in her reunion with the god Eros, who is eternal, and thus eternally young. Her recovery of the child Eros is her recovery of the divine playmate who calls her to share in his play. Playing is the key to being childlike without being childish. Playing, she emerges as younger, fresher, seeing the world through new eyes, the eyes of wonder and surprise, amazement and laughter. Living and working and loving without always asking why is the heart of erotic playfulness and celebration, the occasion to celebrate one's being in its totality, in its joys and its sufferings. Playfulness is a way of getting out of too much aggression and competitiveness, a way of resolving deep pain and division. It is the urge to relate, to join, to be in the midst of, to reach out to touch someone. It is a personal, not impersonal, wisdom that rejoices in celebration and paradoxes and serendipity and not in abstractions or theories, not in footnotes or bottom-line budgeting.

The erotic side looks at persons from the perspective of forgiving love with all the important socio-political consequences this entails. Un-self-conscious, it is the nascent realization that sexist values and patriarchal institutions must be transformed. Released from isolation and her own subjectivity, Psyche now binds all things and persons together but without reducing or merging them into one. From her perspective, the ritual phrase "male and female" has to be overturned, for all persons fit equally along the continuum of humanity. To the extent that she relates to her childlike, godlike erotic side, she is no longer overwhelmed with her own seeming inadequacy. She is at home on Mount Olympus, rejoicing in all the exhilaration that that peak experience entails.

Psyche's wholeness comes after she has befriended the divine Eros in herself, as she becomes conscious of and consents to her contrasexual side. No longer operating to her detriment, this side becomes an invaluable aid in her discovering and developing her mature self.

Incorporating the "other" brings a healthy comfort level to a marriage. There is a respect for the complementary nature of the sexes and a recognition that contributions from both sides are essential. Psyche and Eros are able to live and work with the "other" on the basis of mutual respect and friendship. They are at ease with each other in both their known side and their unknown mysterious side. The magical powers are no longer projected on the other, and the infatuation is gone. There can be a real partnership in the marriage, so intimate that they can discern some of the unknown side of the other, but not manipulate it. Acknowledging the unknown parts on their selves, each develops the spiralling self, retaining an openness to the other and a capacity for a deeper love of the other. They are able to talk together, express themselves, and listen carefully. The individual self no longer feels endangered, having developed through the struggles and the visit to the underworld, and can now be magnanimous in giving to, rather than manipulating or controlling, the other.

The reunion of Psyche and Eros is mirrored in the homecomings — human, royal, divine — of the other heroic quests. Rama and Sita, after their ordeals, join each other in the realm of the gods beyond this illusory world. Odysseus returns to Penelope after being fascinated and bewitched by the divine Calypso. Parsifal returns to Blanche Fleur when he successfully finds the Grail within himself. The mutual give-and-take that these heroes and heroines experience in the homecomings and in the development of each other's contrasexual side gives a whole new dimension to all the myths (and fairy tales) where "the hero gets the princess in the end, and they live happily ever after."

## The Gentle Quest

Psyche's quest is not one of competition but one of relationship. It is not focused on winning or on independence but on acknowledging mutuality or interdependence. The heroic quest uses the gentle approach, not an aggressive one, and strives for wholeness through complementarity. The Psyche in each of us can live in a healthy state only when it is balanced by its complement, Eros. In each of us, power without love is monstrous and brutal, and feeling without strength is wholly sentimental. The heroine's wholeness, and ours, comes through relationship and communion with the never-fully-known other, where the other refers both to other persons and to the depths of our unconscious. This wholeness is not located at some specific point in our human development but is discovered at each stage, in the relationships that are appropriate responses at each stage. Growth toward wholeness is a gradual process, a consolidation of personal resources and psychological strengths, proceeding at its own pace, sometimes the reward of aggressive pursuit, and sometimes of receptivity and readiness.

The quests of Sita, Penelope, and Blanche Fleur are also gentle. Sita finds wholeness through duty and overcoming illusions about this world; Penelope finds it staying home, knitting and unraveling; and Blanche Fleur by giving advice on how to go about the Grail quest and then waiting for Parsifal's return. Psyche performs human tasks and joins the gods, finally able to begin her marriage for real. Sita returns to her original heavenly home, to the divinity that was hers all along, after going through the illusion of this world. Penelope and Blanche Fleur remain patiently at home, waiting for their husbands to become aware of what they have known all along. Each goes about the quest in her own way, for some a new place and a new commitment, for others the original place with a reconfirmed commitment.

We are the heroes and the heroines. Like them, we are on a quest for wholeness, which is sometimes aggressive, sometimes receptive. Sometimes we thrust forward, sometimes we search within, in a ratio that is comfortable for each of us. Our struggle for the fuller self resembles the movement of a spiral in ever-expanding circles. There are thrusts outward but also returns. Although most of our lives involves struggles in the external world, it is the occasional movements inward that are the most human of all adventures. The mythic heroes and heroines are all within us, each suggesting a unique mode of self-awareness. The full range of our humanity encompasses both the aggressive and the gentle heroes, and our wholeness consists in becoming conscious of and consenting to their traits, combining them in a paradoxical unity. A harmonious union makes for effective adult living, working well and loving well, allowing for self-expression and self-transcendence. It makes us one with ourselves, one with other humans, and one with the gods and heroes.

## Review Questions

1. Describe the crisis, struggle, and return of Sita and Penelope.

2. Explain: A woman can enter the Grail Castle almost at will.

3. How does the very meaning of Psyche's name help us understand her myth?

4. What does Eros mean when he says: "Love cannot live where trust is lacking."

5. Explain: The crisis in every marriage is translating infatuation into love.

6. What meaning do you find in each of Psyche's tasks?

7. What is Psyche's erotic side?

8. Show how the quests of Sita, Penelope, and Blanche Fleur are gentle.

## Discussion Starters

1. "Imagine what a round relational model would do to our stories and ways of envisioning life. It would mean that the 'hero' would cease to mount his charger and, spear in hand, gallop off to conquer, overcome, and snatch a trophy (virgin and treasure) as a reward. Instead, to be human would mean to unfold the potential in each one within society. It would

mean protecting and developing the gifts of each in relation to others. There would be no competition because there would be no individual prize." (Jill Raitt)

2. "Personal intimacy requires me to be able to disappear from the world as an object of competition, rivalry and comparison, so as to feel my solidarity with people in their brokenness." (Henri Nouwen)

3. "We learn of our gifts from the smiles, joyful songs, and feelings of enhancement we discern in others when we act. They reveal our truest selves to us."

4. "The most distressing thing is to live an aimless life as I do. If our sufferings benefited anyone, there would be some consolation in the sacrifice." (Gustav Flaubert's Emma Bovary)

5. "The curse of fatherhood is distance, and good fathers spend their lives trying to overcome it. Perhaps the opposite is true for mothers. Don't good ones spend their lives trying, for their children's sake and their own, to leave behind the fierce nearness that begins, literally, as possession?" (Andrew Greeley)

6. "To no form of religion is woman indebted for one impulse of freedom, as all alike have taught her inferiority and subjection." (Elizabeth Cady Stanton)

7. "There is a good principle which created order, light, and man, and an evil principle which created chaos, darkness, and woman." (Pythagoras)

8. "For a man, common sense is the greatest thing in the world; for a woman, happiness is. Man is thought, and woman is intuition, and they have never mated. There is a gulf between them and it is called Fear, and what they fear is, that their strengths shall be taken from them and they may no longer be tyrants." (James Stephens)

9. "I'm not trying to prove anything as a female jockey. I do it because I enjoy it so much, and I think people should do whatever makes them happy." (Robyn Smith)

10. If you could meet one of the female heroes in the religious myths, which one would you choose? Why? What would you like to ask her?

11. What movie and TV characters today remind you of the female heroes in this chapter?

# EVIL

The hero's successful completion of adult tasks is often not the end but only the beginning of other, more expansive, struggles. These are the struggles with the "powers below," with the "prince of darkness" — the struggles against evil and death. Constructing and maintaining a meaningful world, various religious traditions tell of heroes who struggle no longer against the temptation to avoid their heroic deeds but now against the very powers of evil and death. Heroes who struggle against these greater forces are "saviors." The deeds of such hero-saviors provide a course of action that humans can imitate in their struggles to overcome, or at least to make sense of, evil and death.

In this chapter we will look at a few of the different myths in the religious cultures that have to come to grips with the forces of evil. In the next chapter we will turn our attention to hero-saviors in the face of death; and in the final chapter we will analyze the new life that comes through these struggles with evil and death, the wholeness that these saviors share as a boon with humankind.

Evil and suffering are universal human experiences. Unwarranted cruelty and pain, as well as the inevitability of death, are as much a part of our human condition as birth, growth, and pleasure. All experience natural or physical evils — pain and suffering brought by earthquakes, diseases, starvation, and floods. We have all seen moral suffering: emotional breakdowns, cruelty, alienation, and indifference. Natural and moral evils are realities both for the individual and the collective. We are all baffled to explain wars, the increasing number of violent crimes against persons, the crises of energy in the environment, or cruelty in institutionalized racism. We search vainly to find sense in napalm bombings, concentration camps, rapes, and muggings. Evil is a reality, not only in horror movies or television violence, but in the forces that seek to kill our vitality.

Evil is a mystery, not a problem, ultimately incomprehensible and insoluble. It does no good to deny that evil exists, to suppress it in our policies, our institutions, and our actions. Some try to explain it away, suggesting that it is merely banal, that individuals are incapable of telling right from wrong. But evil is not abstract and will not disappear, and no scheme can ever justify or trivialize such evils as the suffering of innocent children.

Religious cultures pose questions in their exploratory attempts to probe the mystery of evil. Why do we suffer? How do we get out of the misery and torment of existence? How can we overcome ignorance, loneliness, transitoriness, depravity? Is there a way to deal with abysmal fear, anxiety, self-centeredness? The various religious traditions differ as to which human activities and physical occurrences are to be regarded as evil. They also differ in their understanding of the status or kind of reality that evil has and develop different constellations of symbols to use in their search for meaning and hope. In all traditions, the mystery of evil and suffering is the source of human reflection and summons forth human involvement.

The starting point for myths of salvation is the recognition that evil is a reality that humans cannot ultimately control or manipulate: We suffer a real self-insufficiency in the face of human want and misery. Acknowledging the crisis, namely, that the human status is often unsatisfying, sorrowful, and unhappy, or that our situations (what we are, do, and have) are not the same as our possibilities (what we can be, do, or have). This is at the heart of the quest for salvation from suffering and evil. Once the self-insufficiency is recognized, then the savior's activity becomes meaningful. By admitting the flaw in which we all participate, the profound sense that everything is not right, we recognize the necessity of a deliverer, a savior, whose pattern of activity provides a model for others to imitate. By following the strategy of letting go of wrongly understood autonomy, of the belief that humans can solve all our problems, and of the illusion of self-enlightenment, we permit our selves to be enlightened, transformed, redeemed, or reborn. There is a kind of return to a status that can ultimately be achieved only by passing through the suffering. The ultimate reality — as always, the return to the Absolute Reality — demands purification, liberation, or redemption, and these are achieved only by letting go. Ultimate salvation from evil, suffering, and death comes only through suffering and dying, both spiritually and physically.

By studying diverse myths of evil (and, later, myths of dying) we find that there are different kinds of salvation: some in this life, some in an afterlife; some individual, some communal; some in a messianic context, some in a general cosmic context. Salvation may be happiness, knowledge, liberation, or eternal life. Or it may be a combination of these. It may be achieved by individuals after initial help (grace) from outside, or through continued mediation of a savior. In all cases, salvation occurs through the recognition, in faith or feeling or knowledge, that human power is incapable of achieving it without a savior, coupled with imitation (in lifestyle, effective rituals, actions within a given law-system or order of life) which "represents" the exemplary activity of the savior.

In this chapter we will look at the myth of the struggle of Ahura Mazda against Ahriman as a paradigm of the struggle of good against evil. After looking at other personifications of evil, we will then see how religious traditions have answered the question of *why* there is evil in the world (the "theodicy" question) and *how* it might be possible to *escape* evil (the "soteriology" question).

## Ahura Mazda vs. Ahriman

Before embarking on his career of teaching and conversion, Zoroaster (also called Zarathustra), the 7th century B.C. reformer of the Persian religion, spent seven years in a mountain cave meditating on evil in human experience. Enlightened by Good Thought and instructed in the religion of the omniscient

Lord Ahura Mazda, he resolved his problem by seeing good and evil as independent realities, having their grounding in the dualistic nature of the universe. In the *Zend-Avesta* we read of the incessant struggle of the force of life and cosmic order, Ahura Mazda (also called Ormazd) against the force of death and chaos, Ahriman (also called Angra Mainyu).

These two mark the two poles of existence. One created life, the other death; one is the master of light and truth; the other of darkness and falsehood. The real world is the result of their struggle, and all of life comes from the conflict between these two principles. From one comes wisdom, light, and truth; from the other, ignorance, darkness, and the lie. Surrounding Ahura Mazda are Good Thought, Correct Action, and Immortality; among the opposition are Evil Thought, Deceit, and Perdition. In the later derivative religion of Manichaeism, life is pictured as a struggle between the goodness of the spiritual realm and the evil of the material realm.

This polarization of life forces is reminiscent of Yin and Yang and the creation-functions of the trickster. These life forces are much more powerful, however, for they are the very lords and forces of the universe rather than merely helpers in creation. Ahura Mazda creates the world of life and warmth; but Ahriman, in his efforts to thwart the achievement of good, creates the world of death, a world so cold that even its two summer months are icy. When Ahura Mazda creates an earthly paradise where roses flourish and humming birds shine like rubies, Ahriman creates harmful and noxious insects to destroy and harass all living creatures. Ahura Mazda creates a great city for humans, green, and peaceful where they can live in prosperity; but the Dark One introduces lies and deception. When pastures are created for herds of cattle, wild beasts are then sent to destroy and maim them. Where work flourishes, sloth and poverty and misery are introduced. Against good government, tyranny and anarchy are encouraged. Ordinary folk are plunged into moral uncertainty, filled with pride and rebellious irreverence. The motley crew of the forces of Ahriman, seeking to darken the light and spoil the beauty of creation tempts humans into self-indulgence and corruption and fills them with the spirit of rage and anger, causing war and devastation.

The life of the universe is the constant struggle of these two forces. Although humans are powerless in the face of evil, they are called to help secure the final victory of Ahura Mazda by following the way of kindness, goodness, justice, and truth. If, however, they participate in murder, injustice, or lies, they give power to the forces of the evil Ahriman. All persons are free to choose which side they wish to support, and every act and thought is an expression of their allegiance. Humans have no control in the ultimate pattern; the final outcome is predetermined. After a struggle that will last for 12,000 years, the process of the world will be finished. Ahura Mazda and Ahriman will have completed their struggle for power and for the allegiance of humans, and the final outcome will occur. Ahura Mazda will ultimately triumph at the time of the final consummation. All traces of evil will be removed and the world will be regenerated.

After the death of each individual, the soul will be weighed in a balance and judged according to its deeds. The actions of all persons follow them beyond the grave, with no escape from divine retribution. Zoroastrian myths project divine rewards and punishments into an afterlife. Those whose lives accrue merits from right actions and attitudes are rewarded by Ahura Mazda after death. The wise followers of the truth cross the Separation Bridge (the bridge of Sinvat or Chinvat) to the realm of the righteous. In the house of song, they will behold the divine throne of Ahura Mazda. The foolish followers of the lie, however, will go to the place of evil thought, where they will dwell throughout the ages in darkness, misery, and suffering.

At the end of time, all souls will pass through a river of molten metal. For those who are righteous, on the side of Ahura Mazda, the journey will be like bathing in warm milk. For those who have been evil, however, the journey will be marked by intense suffering. Eventually, after this final rite of purification, they will be joined with the righteous souls to share in the reconstituted world of the pure. Thus Zoroastrianism offers salvation (healing, wholeness, overcoming evil) to all persons. Some reach it through living a righteous life on earth, others by purging their sins through suffering in an afterlife. The promise of salvation is made to all, male and female, regardless of status.

## The Devil

Since humans are forced to react to life in terms of the basic dualism of good and evil, it is not surprising that world religions have always tried to account in their myths for the presence of evil. Violence and conflict at the heart of natural rhythms of life are a natural, indeed necessary, element in explaining the unfolding process. Through their myths people have personified the evil forces of nature and of the spiritual world and sought to come to some relationship with those destructive forces that profoundly affect their lives. The personification of the forces of good struggling against the forces of evil, similar to the struggle of Ahura Mazda against Ahriman, is found in many other religions. But we have to admit that nowhere is the opposition between good and evil, light and dark, so sharply drawn as in the myths of Zoroaster.

A Mexican myth of the basic dualism, extending from Teotihuacan outside Mexico City to Chichen Itza in Yucatan, through several cultures including the Toltec, Mayan, and Aztec, is the struggle of Quetzalcoatl and Tezcatlipoca. Quetzalcoatl (the "Plumed Serpent") is the god of learning and the culture hero; Tezcatlipoca (the "Smoking Mirror") is the god of evil, wickedness, and destruction. Quetzalcoatl (and his Mayan form Kukulcan) is lord of life, who brings the gift of maize to transform the lives of humans and inspires them with values, direction, and discipline. Supposedly taking human form as a compassionate king, he is a lawgiver and civilizer, the inventor of the calendar.

On the other side of the dualism is Tezcatlipoca continually struggling against Quetzalcoatl. Though not so starkly the personification of evil as is the Persian Ahriman, Tezcatlipoca is the negative pole of energy, the ruler of the night. He is lord of the powers of darkness and the underworld, the master of half-perceptions and half-truths. Also called "He who is at the shoulder," he whispers thoughts into people's ears, inspiring them to wars and urging them to neglect worship of the gods of light and peace. As the malevolent patron god of the Aztecs for about 500 years (roughly 1000 - 1500), he is lord of sorcery and instinct. The Aztecs would sacrifice virgin youths to him as the culmination of their year-round cycle of festivities, offering fresh blood from human hearts (usually of captured warriors) in golden bowls as a gesture of thanksgiving for their victories.

In the myths of his struggle with Quetzalcoatl, Tezcatlipoca is shown to be a wayward god possessing enormous if unbridled power, and able to control much of the destiny of humans and the world. Similar to the struggles of the Evil One with Jesus and Gotama, Tezcatlipoca tries to drag down Quetzalcoatl from the spiritual world to the level of matter. He offers Quetzalcoatl some distilled tequila with the promise that the intoxicating liquor will ease his heart, banish his thoughts of death, and make him youthful again. He then causes Quetzalcoatl's daughter to fall in love with a chili vendor, creating many problems in the household. Next he lures away Quetzalcoatl's followers with vibrant music, takes the form of a warrior, and feeding on their desire for glory in battle, lures them into a stupor and begins to massacre them.

Tezcatlipoca also tempts the people to mock Quetzalcoatl by putting on a puppet show. The people are so engrossed in the material attractions and dazzling display that they actually enjoy a spectacle that degrades their god. It is as if the followers of Quetzalcoatl are in a drugged condition that gradually worsens. In the end, they eat some spoiled maize that Tezcatlipoca, disguised as an old woman, throws to them; thus, the very food given to them by their god as a sustenance fitting humans becomes their downfall.

With most of his subjects slain, Quetzalcoatl and a few faithful followers set out for Anahuac, their heaven at the center of the universe. Quetzalcoatl notices that he has become an old man and decides to leave his people. Before the devils guarding the bridge to the Other World allow him to cross over, however, they force him to leave behind all his famous craftwork (his skills of cutting gems, carving wood, and writing) and all his followers (especially his beloved dwarves and hunchbacks). Only by letting go of those things dear to him is he able to arrive in Mictlan, the land of the Dead. There he finally leaves his people, setting off on a raft of serpents.

Though it seems that Quetzalcoatl has been defeated, he has really conquered the world of material things. Tezcatlipoca remains "at the shoulder," whispering thoughts of evil and cruelty, but he will be conquered at some unknown time, for Quetzalcoatl has promised that he shall return to defeat him. Quetzalcoatl has shown that spiritual forces will triumph in the end over the only partially real world of matter. Tezcatlipoca, the force of matter, will eventually be defeated at Quetzalcoatl's return but only after enacting trials of strength.

Basic to both the Persian and Mexican dualisms is the personification of evil. The Evil One is real, not an illusion, and

drags humans down to the material level. Such personifications
of the Devil can be traced back to paleolithic caves to representations of the Horned God who represented every unexplained
good or evil phenomenon, whether pregnancy or plague alike.
In India, for example, Ravana, the ten-headed monster that
fought Rama, is the personification of evil. Given a wish by
Brahma, Ravana chose that no god or demon should have the
capacity to harm him. Brahma could not refuse the request, and
Ravana used his invulnerability to cause great misery, starting
wars on earth and slaying many warriors. Because Ravana said
that he did not need protection from humans, however, he sealed
his own doom. Vishnu has created avatars, especially Rama and
Krishna to battle and eventually conquer him.

The Hindu goddess Kali, who swaggers through the world
spreading disaster with a collection of human heads dangling
from her belt, is one of the female personifications of evil. The
goddess of destruction and life, she dances on the body of her
consort Shiva, manifesting both benevolence and malice, creativity and destructiveness. The medieval Mexicans also personify
evil as a female in Tlacolteutl, the goddess of sin and devourer
of excrement, and Ciuacoatl, who goes through the night wailing
and predicting misery and war. There are many female demons,
such as witches (so-called after the horned male god, Wicca, in
England), hags, and seductresses; but by and large the principle
of evil is generally male, and the devil is only seldom even
provided with a female consort.

Among the American Indians, there is no single figure who
opposed the Great Spirit and no devil who deliberately tries to
distort humans and drag them to evil. In their myths, life is a
constant struggle between good and evil, light and dark, and
they accept as a fact that humans combine both forces in
themselves, without having to invoke the idea of a devil to explain
why some people have a good heart and others a bad heart. Their
myths often tell of tricksters who personify the destructive side
of nature or they assign the origin of good and evil to certain
mythical figures, such as the Good and Evil twin brothers
(common among the Algonkian and Iroquois tribes), or the
Morning Star (good) and Evening Star (evil) among the Pawnee.

The ancient Greeks portray their gods as having the capacity
for both good and evil. The gods and goddesses are capable of
showering blessings upon the needy, but they can also be really

destructive. They are aloof and seldom care about human life as long as they are given proper adulation. One of their gods, a god of sexual pleasure, Pan, who is hairy and goat-like with horns and cloven hooves, has had a great iconographic influence on later representations of the devil. Devils have most often been associated with the underworld, with the realm of death. They are associated with bats, rats, flies, and snakes (seen to be immortal because they shed their skin and grow a new one) and pictured with horns (which signify fertility).

## Theodicies

Evil is a reality in the world. It cannot be explained away. This does not mean, however, that we cannot try to understand *why* there is evil and suffering. Personifications of evil may not be accurate, but at least they are an expression of what the religious traditions experience, a picture of the world in which the mixing of impulses to good and to evil are not readily explainable. The struggles of Ahura Mazda against Ahriman and Quetzalcoatl against Tezcatlipoca highlight the existence of an absolute and radical evil. In these dualisms the principle of absolute good is preserved by sacrificing its omnipotence. Myths deal with the reality of evil, with its origin and nature, and with how it can be overcome. With the notable exception of the story of human freedom in Genesis 2-3, myths do not often deal directly with *why* there is evil, the theodicy question.

A theodicy tries to explain this mystery. If the Absolute Reality is all-powerful, then it must be able to prevent evil and suffering. And if this Absolute Reality is perfectly good, then it must be willing to prevent evil. But if the Absolute Reality is both able and willing to prevent evil, why does evil exist? Why do children die of inoperable cancer? Why do innocent people suffer in prison? Why do earthquakes and tornadoes cause pain and death? Why do people lie, steal, or kill? Why do evil people prosper? All religious traditions have tried to answer these questions, and their explanations vary according to their orientation toward the Absolute Reality, their philosophical underpinnings, and the expectations of their various social groups.

The theodicy expressed in myths of dualism, by depicting the struggle of the forces of good against the forces of evil, does provide an explanation for the presence of adversity in human lives and a way of understanding the historical process. They introduce meaning into present dark moments in human history and sustain persons who attempt to lead good lives through whatever destruction and misfortune they endure, by assuring them of a perfectly happy ending.

Still, there are some difficulties with the dualistic theodicy. Indeed, by insisting on the struggle of the two hostile principles and by encouraging the division of persons into ''good guys vs. bad guys,'' it is easy for those who see themselves on the side of the forces of good to project all evil onto others and suppress conscious recognition of it in themselves. Dividing persons into mutually exclusive categories as we often do — cowboys vs. Indians, cops vs. robbers, Americans vs. Russians — might actually increase destructive behavior. It is all too easy to accuse ''the others'' of always being aggressors, of not desiring peace, of loving war for the pleasure of destruction. ''They'' are the ones who are unprincipled and unfair, who flaunt laws and customs in an open manner, who refuse to repent and are incorrigibly unfaithful. ''They'' are overbearing in demeanor, consistently setting themselves above others, taunting the weak, and acting from purely selfish motives.

With the final victory of Ahura Mazda or Quetzalcoatl assured, those who are on their side will enjoy the victory. In the great final battle in which Ahriman or Tezcatlipoca and their followers will be destroyed, evil will be completely banished and the ''good'' people will rule triumphantly forever. They are ready for the final end at any moment since the world must be destroyed in order for the principle of evil to be cured. They presume that they are not responsible for evil at all; rather, it is the devil, the counterforce of the divine will, equipped with vast and cunning powers, capable of infiltrating human experience and luring people into its wicked design. They regard themselves merely as the pawns of cosmic forces. All they can do is wait for the ultimate triumph. They will gladly participate in the final struggle, for they already know its outcome, and they will share in that victory.

The problem with this theodicy, in addition to projecting evil onto others, is a possible lack of concern for trying to improve the world, for trying to overcome the evil and suffering and injustices that are such a part of everyday experience. There is no pressure to assess historical or political factors, no need to try to improve the institutions of government. There is no possibility of compromise. With the world divided between forces, no neutral space remains.

Religious traditions have offered many other possible solutions to the theodicy problem, which in some way go against the dualist myths. We have seen in the Adam and Eve myth that evil is one of the consequences of the human freedom that comes as a gift from the Absolute Reality. That is, the human possibility for creativity, truth, love, personality, and divine-human dialogue also implies the possibility of falsehood, error, and sin. A far higher level of goodness is attainable only through an open world in which development through choice and suffering is possible. The human capacity for goodness has not yet achieved maturity, and so humans freely bring on their own violence, and their own suffering. The freedom that divinizes humans also reveals their degradation. Suffering, then, is often the result of the misuse of human free will.

There are also difficulties with this theodicy solution. Why is suffering so great? How do we explain those evils that are not the result of human choices, such as cancer or earthquakes? Wouldn't it be better to have a world in which there is human happiness without suffering, than a world where human happiness is so often precluded because of human freedom?

Another attempt to explain why there is evil, which has been common in the Christian philosophical tradition but not in myths, insists that evil does not have any independent reality. Evil is merely the privation of good. It is the accidental lack of perfection in the universe, the inevitable result of the creative process. This solution suggests that the Absolute Reality is in no way responsible for evil since evil isn't a reality. Evil is merely something missing, something that ought to be there but isn't; it is a real deficiency, but not a reality. Humans then have to take individual initiative to bring out the good that should be there, relying on the activity of God who forgives humans and provides the power (grace) needed for fulfillment in life. This solution does not seem particularly powerful or appealing when innocent people suffer or when human despair strikes, nor does it coincide closely with psychological reality.

There are other theodicies, too. Evil exists, for example, to serve some good. Evil and suffering provide an opportunity for enhancement, for the general welfare of society, for the enrichment, of personal human consciousness. Evil might provide the challenges necessary for growth into maturity. Thus, evil is not unfortunate, but the hardship from which future growth will come. Incongruities and disharmonies in human experience are not intrinsically evil, but rather a kind of subordinate good whose real value is not recognized until the future is taken into consideration. There are benefits of evil. A dam might stop water, yet it supplies electric current. A gardener has to prune a tree to obtain more fruit. Evil is the necessary by-product of growth. In the process of growth and development lie the possibilities of many failures.

Examples of human attempts to explain evil could be multiplied. When all is said however, evil is a mystery, forever shrouded from human understanding. Rational theodicies are never satisfying. all attempts to explain why the righteous suffer and the wicked flourish ultimately fall short. They evade the existential reality of suffering, of rape, murder, napalm. In fact, some theodicies actually cause more suffering. The theodicy of predestination, for example, where success and wealth were signs of attained salvation, actually led to the persecution of those who weren't saved (according to their system). This meant the execution of thousands of people who were considered to be witches. The irony is that their very theodicy to explain evil actually brought more destruction and suffering.

Such a tragic episode in human history should not make us feel that we should not at least attempt to answer the theodicy question. Though many instances of suffering — the horror of concentration camps such as Auschwitz, for example — may stump all human explanations, we must continually ask why there is evil. To evade the question would diminish our human stature. The proper question to ask in such instances, however, is not where is God when such evil occurs, but rather where are the humans who could prevent such outrages.

## Soteriologies

Zoroaster's solution to the thorny problem of theodicy pushes the rewards and punishments into an afterlife, thus giving meaning to the apparently meaningless suffering of the righteous. So, too, in the Mexican myth of Quetzalcoatl, the two principles of good and evil struggle until some indefinite time when good will eventually triumph and the righteous will be rewarded. In both cases, human participation in the conflict is quite limited. Their only real choice seems to be to try to lead lives that will put them on the side of good when the end comes in the final cosmic battle. The visible suffering during their lives seems justified or rectified by their future invisible reward — a way of compensating later for what they have to suffer now. While acknowledging the reality of evil, there is nothing they can do to alleviate or eliminate it.

Other religious traditions do offer not only an explanation for suffering but also prescribe courses of action to avoid future misfortunes. Their particular resolution of evil depends in part on how they portray evil. Myths that deal with the resolution of evil and suffering are called "soteriological" myths or soteriologies. They incorporate different elements: They offer a strategy or method for overcoming evil, and they provide a description of the final state after evil has been overcome. A full soteriology follows the pattern we have adumbrated in earlier chapters: There is *a crisis* (the reality of evil and suffering); *a struggle* (both what the religious culture's savior does to overcome evil and suffering and what individuals within the tradition can do, usually in imitation of the savior); and finally, *a return* (the solution to the problem of evil and suffering, and the reunion with the Absolute Reality).

One great and universal wish of humankind expressed in all religions is how to overcome the crisis of evil, how to pass beyond the self in its human condition. Our tragic human flaws are universal, whether isolation, or alienation, or fear of failure, or boredom, or natural disasters, or suffering of all sorts. Soteriologies offer various paths (or strategies, or rituals, or ethics) that call for imitation of the exemplary pattern of the hero–savior to overcome these crises. Some of these strategies are discussed in this chapter. The tragic consequences of those who do not successfully carry out the strategy during their lives (for example, hell, the underworld), will be discussed in the next chapter, on death. The successful return (to the kingdom of God, Nirvana, Golden Age, Utopia, as well as the feelings of peace, freedom, joy, enlightenment which may be anticipated here and now) will be part of the subject matter in the final chapter, on resurrection.

Not all soteriologies are positive, nor are they all religious. The ancient Greeks have a tragic soteriology. Evil is due to fate, due to the capricious activity of the gods and goddesses. They are jealous of humans and cannot endure any greatness but their own. Heroic greatness consisted in awareness of their plight and provisional refusal and combat against it, but in the end, there is final submission to it. In spite of their refusal to be defeated by evil, the Greeks have to acknowledge that they can never gain a final victory. There is little hope of removing this tragic burden, though they might hope to come to terms with it either in an Apollonian, calm, resigned fashion, or a Dionysian, ecstatic, orgiastic style.

The modern, scientific, rational world view ignores the power of evil by denying the existence of gods and demons. War, exploitation, crime, and psychological illness, for example, can be overcome by strategies such as "one more war to end all wars," a different political system, more education, or correct psychological conditioning. Violence and evil can be alleviated by channeling energy and enthusiasm into socially acceptable outlets by controlling awareness of violence in the news media, by isolating violent members of society in jails, or by displacing violence through identification with non-violent heroes. It is as if any evil can be eliminated by appointing a committee. There is no need of a savior in this soteriology, much less a need to imitate a savior, because its devotees don't feel they need one. They are masters of their own fate, and technology and science have given them the opportunity to control and direct their own future.

By way of critique of this soteriology, we might point out that technology has provided humans with increased ability to manipulate, dominate, and destroy, but it has not supplied any dependable assurance that suffering and evil can be destroyed nor any overarching meaning in the face of continued suffering. The realities of evil and suffering remain; in fact, the emergence of vast and terrifying nuclear arsenals intensifies rather than alleviates feelings of dread and uncertainty concerning the meaning and duration of human existence.

Within the religious traditions, the appropriate soteriological strategy varies considerably. Different types of activity or purposeful non-activity can lead people away from present evil conditions and toward the desired goal, the fuller religious self, or the return to the Absolute Reality. Moral discipline and ethical activity as well as participation in the life of the religious community are always encouraged. Gaining knowledge (which might help in overcoming ignorance and restoring cosmic harmony) and practicing meditation (types of Yoga, Zen, and mystical prayer, for example) are common. So, too, are rituals (prayers, penance, sacrifices, perhaps the repetition of the *Qur'an* to overcome separation from Allah's love) and imitating a savior (perhaps Rama and Krishna, the avatars within Hinduism, or the Bodhisattva within Mahayana Buddhism, or Jesus within the Christian tradition.

In dualism, salvation occurs by aligning the self with the principle of Good. In many of the philosophical theodicies, it is by acceptance of redemption or forgiveness as a gift of the Absolute Reality. For the spiralling religious self, the strategy is to let go of the small self and to say yes to the gods–heroes–saviors within.

Among the world religions there are two major types of soteriology, two different but perhaps ultimately complementary ways of hoping to experience a final resolution to the mystery of evil and suffering. The Western resolution, begun in Zoroastrianism and continued into Judaism and Christianity, sees the defeat, redemption, or transformation of evil in a messianic kingdom. There is no rational explanation of evil but neither is there acceptance of it. Evil is a genuine, unexplainable mystery. In the Christian formulation, salvation occurs through discipleship, that is, imitation of the savior, Jesus. It is possible to experience the reality of this salvation here and now and not only in an afterlife or at the end of the cosmic battle.

The other resolution is found in the Eastern — Hindu, Taoist, and Buddhist — traditions. Evil, which is due to ignorance or craving, is overcome in the ultimate or hidden reconciliation of the opposites, the Yin and Yang. In the Buddhist formulation, salvation or enlightenment occurs through following the Eightfold Path and imitation of the compassion of the savior, Buddha. The solution in both these soteriologies is the expending of the small self and the attainment of the full religious self through reunion with Absolute Reality.

## The Answer to Job

With the exile of so many of Jerusalem's leading citizens to Babylon in the 6th century B.C. Jewish faith in continuing national existence was shaken, and individuals became more conscious of their own personal status and destiny. With this dawning individual self-consciousness, there came the agonizing theodicy question, the question of Yahweh's justice to the individual. This problem is most poignantly expressed in the Book of Job. Why does the just and righteous person suffer and the wicked person prosper? The traditional theodicy was simply that all suffering is the result of our own actions, a punishment for something we have done wrong. This theodicy is the one that the author rejects through the complaints and questions of Job.

Satan is presented as a member of the celestial court, with the function of opposing and harming humans. He roams the world as God's messenger, functioning as a chief prosecutor to afflict the faithful and test their virtue. As the result of a wager with Yahweh, Satan inflicts severe misfortunes on Job, who loses his children, wealth, property, and endures severe bodily agony. Yet, Job refuses to renounce his faith. His three friends take the traditional theodicy position, that is, that suffering comes because Job has done something evil. They cannot understand his protests of innocence. Job's suffering is intensified because they are quite unable to understand suffering apart from the traditional notions of evil. Still, Job maintains his innocence and wishes to take Yahweh to court to prove it. He wants a law-and-order reply.

When it is obvious that his three friends cannot persuade him to admit his guilt, a brash youngster, Elihu, tries to impress his wisdom on the elders by suggesting that the purpose of suffering is to be a deterrent. Perhaps others who see Job suffering will be persuaded not to do evil for fear of similar consequences. Suffering, says Elihu, is a trial by which Yahweh ensures the loyalty of his people, as well as a spiritual training for maturity and strength.

Yahweh finally comes to Job. He rejects the positions of Job's friends and Elihu and gives Job an answer that is totally unexpected. Speaking from a whirlwind, Yahweh reminds Job of their respective positions. He rehearses the beauty, majesty, and mystery of creation. Job is silenced with this show of power and wisdom, and his direct personal experience of Yahweh shatters his human arrogance. Confronted by the numinous majesty of Yahweh, he submits to the will of Yahweh, to the mystery of suffering: "Now my eyes see thee: therefore I despise myself and repent in dust and ashes." At this, Yahweh removes Job's suffering and doubles his family and possessions.

Job doesn't understand his suffering, but he is able to bear it. He concludes by saying that he has seen the Absolute Reality through his suffering. As his ancestors Jacob and Moses before him, who both experienced Yahweh in the barren, lonely desert in the midst of much suffering, Job experiences joy through suffering. Yet suffering is Yahweh's responsibility, and it is absolutely and forever unfathomable by human reason. Thus Job gets no real answer.

The possibility of retribution in the next world — the soteriological factor — does not appear in Jewish Scriptures till later, in the Book of Daniel. Here we see, very briefly, that if the righteous suffer on earth despite their goodness and fidelity to the law, they will be compensated in an afterlife. The "pious" people know that in the afterlife people will be punished in proportion to their evil deeds, and that all the power, wealth, and authority gained in this life will matter nothing in the world to come, where only fidelity to the divine will counts. This solution to evil plays only a very small part in the Jewish myths, however.

The belief in the resurrection of the dead, which was never universal among the Jews, probably came from Zoroastrianism. From them the Jews also developed their belief that God will act on their behalf by sending a deliverer, similar to Ahura Mazda's final destruction of Ahriman, who will conduct a cosmic war between the forces of good and evil in the struggle before a new age can begin. This savior, this Messiah, is a messenger of Yahweh, a descendant of the royal family of David who will destroy the power of the Jewish enemies on the Day of the Lord. He will be a political ruler with special powers for this function; he will be the personification of wise observance of the Law, and he will inaugurate the messianic age, an era of peace, justice, mercy, and prosperity. He will restore the Golden Age the Jews hoped for, in vain, under their Greek, Roman, and other foreign rulers. The human role or strategy is to follow the laws of the Torah, that is, total obedience to their covenant with the one God.

Christianity, which grew out of Judaism, inherited a modified dualism. In the biblical myths, the devil (Satan, the

"Adversary") has power and attributes similar to Ahura Mazda. His ultimate end, too, will be similar, for Satan and his powers will be defeated through the savior, Jesus Christ. Jesus, the Messiah, by his life of loving, caring, forgiving, and serving will inaugurate a new kingdom in place of Satan's hold over humans. A kingdom of goodness, light, and spirit will be forever established. This, in a few words, is the Christian soteriology as found in its Scriptures. Evil is a reality in the world, and it can be overcome by imitation of the self-expending life of the savior, Jesus.

Later Christian views of the devil, while they show the devil of the New Testament to be one stage of a developing concept, sometimes obscure the reality of evil. Over the centuries Christianity came to identify the devil with fallen angels or with the serpent of Genesis or with Lucifer and asked questions about his domain, hell: Where is it? What is it like? Is it everlasting? A complex theology of possession and exorcisms developed, and the devil came to be associated with the antichrist and with non-believers. These theologies sometimes obscured the simple New Testament story of the reality of evil and the saving activity of Jesus.

Jesus, the God-man, is an archetypal paradigm of the savior figure. For Christians, he is the Messiah, sent from God, who brings a new insight and a new way of doing things in the human struggle against evil and death. For Christians, Jesus is the savior because he is the one who fulfills the messianic promises of God's salvation, God's "shalom," through his compassionate acts of healing and his self-expending suffering. For his heroic–salvific activity, God has raised him to a new life. He sets the example for all Christians to follow: He is the way, the truth, and the life.

In the Christian Scriptures, especially the gospels, there is no attempt to develop a theodicy to explain the mystery of evil. In fact, demonic possession is one of the most common means Satan uses to obstruct the reign of God. Jesus exorcizes demons by the power of the spirit and cures diseases sent by them. Thus he makes war upon the kingdom of Satan and thereby makes known to his followers that a new age has dawned: "If I drive out demons by the power of God, it is because the kingdom of God is come among you." Jesus interprets his healing ministry as a means of setting persons free from demonic compulsions and opening them to the possibility of a restored life in relation to God. Not an all-powerful superman nor a powerless victim, Jesus also overcomes evil by his suffering, which was the result not of compliance but of resistance and fearless confrontation of corrupt political and evil religious authorities.

In contrast to the reign of the devil who brings war, famine, sickness, and death, the reign of Jesus consists in making peace, feeding the hungry, curing the sick, and raising the dead. In spite of war, he brings peace and harmony with reality at the deepest level; in spite of famine, he brings sustenance through serving others; in spite of sickness, he brings the wholeness of no longer working at cross-purposes with God; in spite of death, he brings the gift of eternal life through relating to God as a loving Father.

Jesus is the "word" (that is, symbol or manifestation) of God, doing humanly what God is doing. He makes God's doings understandable to Christians and enables them to go and do likewise. This is the Christian soteriology in a word, the way to overcome suffering, evil, and death. In the Christian tradition, Jesus is the means of access to the divine and also the one who does what God is doing by giving his very life for others. The God-man thus identifies with those who are oppressed, who suffer, who are peacemakers. He is self-expanding — taking on divinity, the full religious self — because he is self-expending. He gives his life to share his insight with others, revealing to humans who God is and what they can become — the more abundant life of the whole self, the spiralling self.

In any soteriology, we recall, persons can "overcome" evil by imitating the saving activity of the heroic savior. This activity is spelled out in different ways in the Christian Scriptures. In his letters, Paul claims that the followers of Jesus are freed from sin, death, and the law. They are saved in spite of themselves and only have to open themselves in faith to accept divine grace. The demonic principalities and powers are real, yes, but God delivers humans from that power. Humans are thus liberated to live in the midst of evil possibilities without being so obsessed in the effort to transcend their situation that they destroy themselves and their world. Even if demonic powers can destroy life, they cannot destroy the meaning of life.

In the synoptic gospels, humans are called to work for the eventual transformation of the world, to co-create a community full of the Spirit who will overcome the devil's reign. Following the political pragmatism of Jesus, they are to settle down to the task of gradually humanizing the world rather than trying to reshape the world through cataclysmic efforts. active imitation of Jesus does not mean naive glorification of suffering nor tolerant acceptance of evil but rather challenging evil situations and conditions, and protesting against enslaving suffering. This becomes real through feeding the hungry and clothing the naked (in Matthew); through loving, caring, and forgiving others (in Luke); or through suffering service of others (in Mark). In the Gospel of John, discipleship consists in living from an eschatological perspective: Christians overcome death, darkness, and the merely material world as they move toward the life, light, and truth which are already present in the community.

Active imitation of the Christian savior is expressed through compassion. Compassion is the capacity for deep concern, the moral outrage in the face of injustices. Compassion is sympathy that has invaded the body, striving for peace as a way of life, the peace that comes as a gift from Jesus' suffering. It is relieving the actual pain of others through justice-making and through a keen awareness of the interdependence of all living things. Compassion means becoming divine, or rather, remembering and recovering one's divine origins as "image and likeness" of God. Compassion is expanding the self, taking on the divine, the full religious self, by expending the self in serving, caring, loving, and forgiving others. Compassionate love is the fullness, the enhancement, of life. "Greater love than this no one has, than to give up his life for his friends." This is the Christian answer to Job.

## The Compassionate Buddha

The other theodicy and soteriology in the major religious traditions is developed in the teachings and life of Gotama, the Buddha. We have seen that Gotama achieves his adult task, his Enlightenment, "Buddhahood," in discovering the Truth of the Middle Way. No longer living in the hell of wavering between luxury and asceticism, he spends his next forty-five years in a public ministry, sharing this insight with others. He is a savior, enlightening others to overcome evil and suffering and offering them a way of life through compassion by which they, too, can escape their human predicament.

Gotama goes beyond the classical Hindu position which pinpoints the cause of evil in ignorance. In the Hindu *Vedas* and *Upanishads,* people are said to be under the sway of Maya, that is, under the illusion that material things are ultimately real. Humans live in ignorance, lacking awareness that Atman (the individual soul or life-force) is really identical with Brahman (the cosmic life-force, the Absolute Reality). Further, evil comes from Karma (the indisputable law of cause and effect that governs everything in the universe) and Samsara (the wheel of rebirth that humans must endure).

Individuals have no one to blame for their misfortunes except themselves, and they are rewarded or punished in successive incarnations, according to the degree they performed their duties in prior lives. For the Hindus, Moksha (liberation) is the way out of suffering, the deliverance from Maya, Karma, and Samsara. Moksha can be achieved through different types of Yoga — the Yoga of knowledge, of devotion, of good works, and of contemplation. Yoga is the way of "yoking" Atman and Brahman. Yoga re-orients individuals so that the illusion of selfhood is dissipated, ignorance is overcome, and spiritual release (Moksha) from suffering is achieved.

Gotama's insight is that Moksha cannot be taught but only experienced. No amount of teaching or learning can overcome illusion and suffering. He explains this in his *Parable of the Arrow:* A man was shot with a poisoned arrow. When others wanted to pull it out and tend the wound, the victim refused them, until he knew who shot the arrow, what kind of arrow was used, and what kind of poison was in it. Before all this could be learned, of course, he died of the poison. This is similar, Gotama said, to those who want to know everything about Atman and Brahman before they will do anything about their own suffering and misery. Gotama's own theodicy and soteriology are very simply expressed, not in heavy philosophical language, but in the Four Noble Truths.

The First Noble Truth is that the whole of human lives, insofar as we are tied to Samsara, is suffering. All of life is suffering even if we are reluctant to admit it. We forget that some things, while pleasant, may involve the sufferings of others. (Who thinks, for example, of the feelings of the turkey at Thanksgiving?) Some things, while pleasant, are tied up with anxiety because we are afraid to lose them. (The owner of an expensive sailboat worries that someone will steal it or run into it.) Some things, while pleasant, bind us to further conditions that cause suffering. (We eat and drink so much that we get sick.) All pleasures are fleeting, and we can only enjoy them for a moment.

The Second Truth is that suffering is due to craving, to attachment, to desire. Suffering is due to whatever makes us act as individuals, with the illusion that we have an independent self. The body, feelings, perceptions, impulses, emotions, and acts of consciousness all make us think we have an independent self and make us cling to the illusion that Atman is separate from Brahman. If this explains why there is suffering, then how can it be overcome?

The Third Truth states that suffering is resolved by disengaging from the wheel of Samsara and Karma, that is, by abolishing desire. This does not mean getting rid of all desire, for a person should desire the end of suffering.

The Fourth Truth tells us how to get rid of desire, by following the Middle Way between luxury and asceticism. This leads to Nirvana, the extinction of the hellish illusion of an independent self. The Middle Way does not lead to the destruction of the world nor the self, but rather the destruction of the illusion that there is an independent self. What remains is Atman, which is really Brahman. It is the removal of the self from the process of perception so that the subject becomes one with the object and with all objects; there is a return to the One, to Absolute Reality. Nirvana is the extinction of pain and suffering, and thus, of the burden of existence. Nirvana is the cessation of Maya, of clinging and craving, the end to the rounds of Karma and Samsara.

In Theravada (early) Buddhism, Nirvana is achieved through following the Eightfold Path (proper views and intentions; proper speech, conduct, and livelihood; proper effort, mindfulness, and concentration). Mahayana (later) Buddhism spells out this proper mindfulness and concentration in Zen, a technique of meditation. Mahayana Buddhism is much more universal in scope than Theravada, especially in the notion of the Bodhisattva. Gotama was the primary Bodhisattva, that is, one who is on the brink of achieving Nirvana but pauses out of compassion to help others in their quest for release from suffering.

Mahayana Buddhism is primarily a religion of salvation through compassion (*karuna*). It is an expression of universal release, rather than individual salvation through rising above the world by a reclusive monastic existence. Mahayana Buddhists strive to be bodhisattvas, not by bearing the suffering of others, nor having pity on them, but by actions that reveal the goodness that dwells in their hearts. They strive to share a goodness that transcends the existentiality and particularity of the personal self and brings others to wholeness.

Gotama is the archetypal bodhisattva, the paradigm of the savior figure, who brings compassion to the community. He is the model for other Buddhists to imitate as they strive for that true and absolute consciousness which is beyond the polarities of male and female, nature and culture, a consciousness liberated from suffering through awareness of union with Absolute Reality.

## Appropriating the Shadow

Whether the devil exists as an independent reality is secondary to our real and direct experience of evil. If we do not acknowledge the powers and principalities of evil, they will continue to disrupt our lives, leaving us frustrated and frightened. And yet, we cannot attribute all evil to outside forces. This would excuse us from examining our own personal responsibility for vice, for unjust societies, for the harm we bring to others. Both the recognition of the basic existence of evil and the strong efforts to overcome it and integrate it are necessary for our social and intellectual lives, but most especially for the development of our full religious selves.

When we admit the independent reality of evil both, within our selves and outside, we have moved beyond the hero–villain stage. There is a liberation, a burden removed, as we no longer feel we have to strive to become perfect or to think that evils can be corrected by such measures as adjusting education, penal laws, or welfare arrangements. On this part of the journey toward wholeness, we join the savior and come to recognize what Jung has called our "shadow" side, all those parts of our selves we have repressed. We befriend the dark side of ourselves, our deepest feelings and recesses, whether of pleasure or pain.

It is a shattering experience to admit that the shadow, the aspect of our personality we are ashamed of or will not recognize because it is unacceptable to our conscious personality, is an archetype in us. It consists of the repressed feelings in our unconscious, which often make us project our repressed hostilities on others. The shadow is our instinctual, irrational side that hides itself in an infinite variety of seemingly virtuous behaviors. It dominates us to the degree that we are unaware of its sly and everlasting presence, that we do not recognize and appropriate it, that we are lulled into believing that "perfection" consists of refusing to admit this evil within us.

Our refusal to admit the shadow is particularly harmful when we project it on others, either personally or collectively. This gives us an excuse for evil behavior toward others, for example, to make war on an enemy because we project evil onto them rather than our selves. Such projection has led to the execution of witches, to the wholesale slaughter of the Jews in the Holocaust, to much of the hostility between Americans (the "good guys") and the Russians (the "bad guys").

Once the shadow is admitted and accepted as a reality, it can be transformed into a positive source of energy for the personality. It contains the potential for greater growth for the unlived side of the self as we come to recognize that there is a balance of opposites in life and in our selves. Healing, or the wholeness of the self, comes not in overcoming evil, but in self-realization, that is, in the forgiveness of the shadow in the self. It is an opening up, a letting go, a recognition and consent to the demonic within the self. Acknowledging the demonic goes further, for it means forgiving others too. My healing is not complete without bringing healing to others and sharing compassion with them, for how can I have inner freedom without external peace?

Bringing healing to others is a rich soteriological solution to the problem of evil. Evil is overcome through commitment to attain human justice and social righteousness. It does not come through overreliance on technological solutions or the rationalization of violence in the struggle with the demonic. Wholeness comes through compassionate love, in spite of the reality of evil and amid the unceasing suffering of the world.

## Review Questions

1.  What is the difference between a hero and a savior?

2.  Explain: Suffering and evil are a mystery, not a problem.

3. Explain: The myth of Ahura Mazda and Ahriman is basically dualistic.

4. Is it really necessary to believe in the existence of a personal devil?

5. What is a theodicy? Which major theodicies are discussed in this chapter? Can you think of any others?

6. What is a soteriological myth?

7. What is the answer to Job?

8. Summarize the teachings of the Four Noble Truths of the Buddha.

9. What does it mean to appropriate the shadow?

## Discussion Starters

1. "There are two equal and opposite errors into which our race can fall about the devils. One is to disbelieve in their existence. The other is to believe, and to feel an excessive an unhealthy interest in them. They themselves are equally pleased by both errors, and hail a materialist or a magician with the same delight." (C. S. Lewis)

2. "One reason we create gods is that we want to believe the world is ruled by benevolent powers; but when these powers don't eliminate suffering, tragedy, and death, we evoke devils and monsters to absorb the blame for evil."

3. Create a myth to explain why evil exists. In your myth, is there an eventual end to evil? If so, how?

4. What is your reaction to this prayer? "Saint Michael the Archangel, defend us in battle. Be our protection against the wiles and snares of the devil. Restrain him, O God, we humbly beseech thee. And do thou, O Prince of the Heavenly Host, by the power of God, cast into hell Satan and all the other evil spirits who prowl about the world seeking the destruction of souls. Amen."

5. "Go(o)d and (D)evil depend on each other like concave and convex. The same instinct that personifies good into God transforms evil into Devil."

6. "Christians range themselves with God in his suffering: that is what distinguishes them from the heathen . . . Man must live a 'worldly' life and so participate in the suffering of God." (Bonhoeffer)

7. "The price of hating other human beings is loving oneself less." (Eldridge Cleaver)

8. "We are advocates of the abolition of war; we do not want war, but war can only be abolished through war; and in order to get rid of the gun, it is necessary to take up the gun." (Mao Tse-tung)

9. "A little rebellion now and then is a good thing, and as necessary in the political world as storms in the physical." (Thomas Jefferson)

10. What movie and TV characters today remind you of the saviors in this chapter?

11. If you could meet one of the saviors in myths of evil, which one would you choose? Why? What would you like to ask him?

# DEATH

Although death is the natural rhythm of created reality and an essential part of our humanity, it seems an unjustifiable violation of our selves. We do not merely know we are going to die, we dread it. Death, which is more than just the inevitable event at the end of life, is somehow always pathological, requiring some expression of sorrow, even though the deceased might have enjoyed a full life and faced only a grim existence if dying were prolonged.

With death, a sense of futility overwhelms us with unprecedented force. What do we gain for all our toil? Qoheleth asks: "What is the use of all our wisdom? Our fate is the same as the beast's: We both spring from dirt, and to dirt we shall both return." The thought of dissolution violates our sense of self, our sense of justice, and our sense of meaning. Like the other great crises of human life, death is the catalyst for wide-ranging responses: vibrant emotions, obsessive fears, intensive self-questioning, giant swings from ornate ritual to quiet meditation.

Some people try to camouflage the reality of death. They portray it as a temporary separation, a movement into a liminal status. They routinely shelter children from the dying, thinking they are protecting them from harm. Death is as much a part of life as birth; yet birth is a cause for celebration, while death is a dreaded and unspeakable issue to be avoided by every means possible. Perhaps these people find death so frightening because it is inevitable and unpredictable. Recently, however, dozens of books on hospices, bereavement, and on death and dying are signs that most of us do not totally evade, ignore, or deny death, or treat it as another disease to be conquered. In many of these books, which seem almost a reaction against a former cultural taboo, death is interpreted as a vital stage in human growth and development, as a rite of passage in which both the living and the dead acquire a new identity.

Religious traditions have all addressed the mystery of death, posing the same questions that have baffled us throughout human history. Why do we have to die? Why do we die when we do? What happens after we die? Are there ways that we should live that will better prepare us for death and the possibility of life after death, or is this the only life we'll have? How can we be happy and at peace, knowing that we will have to die? Does our answer change if we deny an afterlife? How are our status in life, our problems and joys, related to how we will die? Asking such questions as these are part of the mystery of being human. Seeking to understand death can be a highly creative force. The questions are not just questions of good and evil but also of growth and enlightenment, of the fuller self we can become during life.

Myths in the religious traditions foster maturity in recognizing the reality of death (Gilgamesh), and they help reduce anxiety in the face of death by asserting the origin or causes of death (Balder), describing the journey to the land of the dead (Orpheus), and finding significance in death (Jesus). Heroes in these religious myths who face the mystery of death for all of us are saviors. The savior descends into the underworld where he is an explorer in the realm of death itself. He faces in depth the mystery that we humans fear so much. The savior is our human hope of overcoming death and understanding its meaning.

Though death is a necessary reality, we need not *really* die. The hero–savior faces death and (often) dies for us. Because the savior has faced the unknown, we can now share the mystery. The savior is a paradigm of dying to the small self so that we can be raised up to a larger self. In the myths of the savior, life is part of a much larger existence that transcends the life span of the small self — a new life either through the continuance of individual consciousness, or through participation in a greater transpersonal life. The span of years on earth is but a moment in a continuum. Death may be a disjunction, but not a termination.

## Gilgamesh

The *Epic of Gilgamesh* is a powerful myth about nature and culture, the value of human achievements and their limitations, friendship and love, separation and sorrow, life and death. The chief text from the Library of Ashurbanipal of Nineveh dates to the 7th century B.C., and is itself the result of more than a thousand years of transmission and textual expansion. The masterpiece of Babylonian (Iraq) literature, it concerns Gilgamesh ("He who discovered the source," or "He who saw all"), who was perhaps a real king of the land of Sumer, reigning over the city of Uruk. He is the main hero for a series of marvelous adventures, centering especially around his grief for the death of his best friend, Enkidu.

The inhabitants of Uruk complain to the gods that Gilgamesh is despotic, oppressive, and headstrong. Because he causes so much consternation, they beseech the gods to create another man to fight him, and thus curb his misuse of power and redirect his energies and interests. The gods answer by sending Enkidu, a hairy hunter who has grown up in the desert, living with and protected by wild beasts. Their first encounter is a violent wrestling match, a test of strength and endurance. The battle ends in a draw. Honor is satisfied on both sides, and the two become inseparable friends. They now direct their energies to adventures that promise to bring meaning to life and immortality through fame.

Seeking out the demon Humbaba in a mountain of cedars perhaps in Lebanon or Syria, they slay it and destroy the forest. The goddess Ishtar is so impressed that she invites Gilgamesh to be her lover and promises him power, chariots, treasures, and honor. He rebuffs her roughly, accusing her of being inconstant and reserving a wretched fate for her lovers (the shepherd boy, Tammuz, and her gardener) when they cease to please her. At this, Ishtar smoulders with rage, complains to the gods, and insists that a bull be sent from heaven in reprisal. If she doesn't get her way, she will descend to the land of the dead to have her sister, Ereshkigal, queen of the underworld, release the dead spirits to circulate among the living.

So she gets her wish. A divine bull comes down, and its very breath slays hundreds of people. Enkidu succeeds, however, in seizing the bull's tail and Gilgamesh delivers the death-blow. Enkidu hurls the bull's thigh in Ishtar's face. The two victorious warriors are welcomed by the cheering crowd. Gilgamesh exclaims, "We're heroes; killing monsters isn't so tough." But Enkidu is somber: "Killing isn't free; we shall pay for it."

Meanwhile the gods have gone into council, and charges are preferred: The divine cedar forest has been violated, Humbaba killed, Ishtar twice insulted, and the celestial bull slain. They call for Enkidu's death: "Number two must go." Enkidu learns in a dream of his impending death. A feathered, batlike demon will smother him and take him off to the underworld. He will skulk around in the darkness, eating dust and clay. Enkidu bemoans his fate. He will not die as a hero in battle or on the hunt but as the pathetic victim of an illness. His illness lingers for two weeks, during which he grows weaker and weaker, wasting away before the eyes of Gilgamesh.

Gilgamesh at first rejects the reality of death, refusing to bury the body for a week, until maggots begin to swarm over it. Mad with frenzy, he lets his hair grow long and flees throughout the land, trying to escape his fears: "When I die, will I not be like Enkidu?" He wants everyone else in Uruk to mourn. How else can he endure today and tomorrow and the next? Where can he discover the secret of how to escape his own inevitable fate? Finally, driven to battle against death itself, he resolves to visit Utnapishtim who, with his wife, was the only human to survive the deluge and receive from the gods the gift of immortality.

To reach Utnapishtim, Gilgamesh must undertake a dangerous journey to the mountains at the end of the world where he meets terrifying scorpion-men who guard the entrance to the underworld. After trying to dissuade him, they obligingly indicate the route and allow him to pass through a dark tunnel where he must struggle for many hours. Coming to a glorious garden where trees are hung with jewels, he meets the sun god who tells him: "Stay a while and enjoy this garden of delights. The eternal life you seek you will never find. Make every day a day of rejoicing, for man is powerless against death."

But Gilgamesh will not be diverted and proceeds on his way presently meeting Siduri, a barmaid. She thinks he is a tramp and orders the doors barred. Only after he reassures her that he is so disheveled because of his laborious travels does she reluctantly welcome him. Her advice is the same: "You'll never find eternal life, for when the gods created man they gave him death, and kept immortality for themselves. Make merry day and night; make every day a day of joy; dance, play, wear dazzling clothes, refresh yourself with water; let your wife rejoice in your bosom. For this is the fate of man."

Gilgamesh won't be swerved, and is given directions to Sursanabi, Utnapishtim's boatman. Sursanabi, too, tries to talk Gilgamesh out of his quest but finally agrees to ferry him across the Sea of Death. There is one condition though. He must never touch the waters of death. Once the poles are dipped into the water, they must be discarded. When the poles run out, Gilgamesh is forced to tear off his shirt and use it as a sail.

Gilgamesh finally arrives. Utnapishtim points out that nothing lasts forever. Contracts are only for a term; age-long feuds die out; rivers rise and swell but subside; when the butterfly leaves the cocoon, it lives but a day. Death comes by divine decree, and no one has any choice but to accept it. Still Gilgamesh isn't satisfied since Utnapishtim himself has escaped death: "Tell me your secret, how you made yourself like the gods." Utnapishtim tells the story of the flood and the ark and how the gods rewarded him and his wife with immortality.

When Gilgamesh hears this tale, he knows his quest has been in vain. The old man has no secret formula to give him, no hidden knowledge. The scorpion-men, the sun god, the barmaid, and the boatman were all right: He won't find immortality. Still, he refuses to yield. So Utnapishtim challenges him to a test — to overcome sleep for six nights and seven days. Utnapishtim tells his wife: "This man who seeks to live forever cannot even go without sleep. When he awakes he will deny that he was sleeping, so give him proof. Bake a loaf of bread every day and place it next to him. They will get more moldy every day, and then he can see from the state of the loaves how long he has slept." Sure enough, when Gilgamesh does wake up, he tries to pretend he never slept. But the loaves are proof. He now knows he won't find immortality.

As Gilgamesh prepares for the return home, Utnapishtim's wife tells her husband not to send him away empty-handed but to give him a parting gift for his effort and pains. So Utnapishtim tells him: "Here's a secret. At the bottom of the sea is a plant. If you come into possession of it, you can, by tasting it, regain your youth again." Gilgamesh quickly makes plans to acquire the plant (called "Graybeard-grows-young"), not caring that it pricks him. He decides not to use it for himself right away but to carry it back to the old people of Uruk. This will be some reward for his pains. After again crossing the perilous waters with Sursanabi, he decides to cool off in a spring. He sets the plant aside while he swims, and a snake, attracted by its fragrance, devours it and flees into the sea. When Gilgamesh sees that the plant has passed from his hands, he weeps: "All my labor is a waste. I toiled in far lands to obtain the boon of new life — for a serpent . . . . For myself I have gained nothing." Resigned at last to the fate of all humans, he returns to Uruk. Still haunted by the fear of death, he calls up the shade of Enkidu who goes on to describe the mournful condition of those who are everlastingly imprisoned in the somber kingdom of death.

Gilgamesh's quest for immortality ends with this vision. His quest has been a typical heroic quest. His crisis comes with the death of his beloved friend, Enkidu; the struggle is in overcoming all the obstacles in his search for immortality; the return is the realization that there is no (physical) way of overcoming death. Death is inevitable. He is destined for the same terrible fate as Enkidu. This picture of gloom is typical of Sumerian and Babylonian thought. Humans live a brief span in the service of the gods; when that time is completed, they go to the land-of-no-return.

## Balder and Loki

Gilgamesh's myth tells us dramatically that death is a reality of life. There is no possibility of coming back from the grave. Even when we admit the reality of death, however, we still ask why there has to be death, or what is the cause of death. Many myths attribute the cause of death to a punishment, a mistake, or an agreement. The most fundamental cause of death in myths, however, is due to the dualistic nature of the world. Death is part of the rhythm of the cosmos, a balancing principle along with life itself. The Norse myth of Loki and Balder gives us a tragic picture of this dualism, in a way more pessimistic than the Iranian myth of Ahura Mazda that we studied in the last chapter. Unlike Ahura Mazda, who will eventually have the better of the cosmic duel, the Norse world of gods and humans crashes to a gloomy end in the apocalyptic "Twilight of the Gods," Ragnarok. This story is masterfully told in the 13th century Icelandic *Prose Edda*.

Balder is of the inhabitants of Asgard, the home of Odin and his attendant gods. He is a radiant youth beloved by all, the god of light. Son of the god Odin and the goddess Frigga, Balder's tragic death is brought about by the malice of Loki, who is a typical trickster–shadow figure, the antithesis of all that the society valued. Loki has the Protean gift of changing shape; at times he resembles a shaman, at times a mischievous fool in Odin's court. Time and again, by his folly and scheming, he renders Asgard vulnerable to the plotting or assaults of its enemies.

Troubled by a dream of his death and presentiments of evil, Balder explains his disquietude to the other Aesir, the other gods. Since the death of Balder would be like the going out of the sun, they make every effort to forestall his death. His mother, Frigga, goes around the world extracting a promise from every living creature not to hurt Balder. Since Balder is well loved, they all willingly promise. The gods make merry by throwing stones and spears at Balder and watching them all turn aside harmlessly. They are secure in the knowledge that nothing can harm Balder. But shadows are deepening over Asgard, and Odin has an intimation that the last great battle is surely coming, when the gods themselves will be destroyed. He rides out to Niflheim, the home of Hela, to reassure himself. But when Odin asks why gold and shining rings are hanging all around, Hela says that they are done for Balder's coming. Odin then learns that Hoder will strike the fatal blow against his brother Balder and rides sadly homeward.

Meanwhile Loki is jealous of Balder and the others playing with him and attempts to find a way to destroy him. Approaching

Frigga in the disguise of an old woman, Loki asks her why all the other gods are throwing things at Balder. She replies that they are throwing spears and stones to prove the success of the pledges not to harm him. She has extracted a pledge from every thing on earth except a tiny shrub of mistletoe that she thought was too young and weak to take an oath. That is the information that Loki is looking for. Quickly resuming his shape, he goes east of Valhalla to find mistletoe. Returning, he finds the blind Hoder and asks why he isn't throwing at Balder. When Loki volunteers to guide his aim, Hoder throws the mistletoe at Balder. It pierces his breast, and he falls dead in a pool of blood. The light of the universe has gone out.

The Aesir weep bitterly at the loss of their beloved companion. Odin is sad, for he knows that peace and light have fled from Asgard forever. Hoder, after consulting with Frigga, persuades Hermod, the swiftest of the gods, to go to Hela to ask if she might allow Balder to return. Meanwhile the gods prepare Balder's funeral with sorrowful hearts, carrying his body aboard his ship. Nanna, his faithful wife, is overcome, and her body is laid beside Balder's on the funeral pyre. Thor raises his hammer and the pyre is given its ritual consecration. The boat floats out to sea as the flames leap higher and higher. The scene is gloomy and desolate. Summer is ended and winter is waiting at the doors.

Hermod rides down dark and perilous roads for nine days, crossing a bridge roofed with burning gold, and arrives at the barred gates of Hela. His horse leaps the gates and he enters the kingdom of the dead and spends the night with Balder before approaching Hela. Hela is not without pity. She will permit Balder to return to Asgard on one condition: If everything on earth and in Valhalla (the place of bliss for fallen Norse warriors) will weep for Balder, she will release him. If however, one single being refuses to weep, if one eye remains dry, then she will be obliged to keep him with her. Hermod hurries back to the Aesir, joyful. Messengers are sent out and soon the sound of weeping is heard throughout the world.

Everyone weeps — except for Loki. When Hermod begs him to weep, Loki replies: "Neither during his life nor after his death has Balder rendered me service. Let Hela keep what is hers." Loki has found a way of making sure that Balder will never return. The shadows thus deepen over all things, and the day of Retribution — Ragnarok — fast approaches. The final doom is signalled. There will be war upon war; wolves will devour sun and moon; earthquakes will break up solid earth. Nothing will be left in the end. The final fire will consume the whole world in the downfall of the gods.

## Etiologies of Death

This Norse myth is typical of many myths where death is due to a Great Destroyer, a dualistic principle of evil, a capricious trickster. In other myths many different causes have been given, all of them seeing death as an intruder, a humiliating outrage. Death may be due to an enemy, a magical hostile act, or the jealousy of the gods who wish to drive humans from the earth. Death may not have been intended by the Absolute Reality, but its coming cannot be reversed; or it may be the occasion to give people a much needed rest, after which they will be restored to life in a new form.

Let us look briefly at the four most common types of myth that deal with the cause of death. In addition to attributing it to the principle of dualism, as we have just seen, myths often find death's origin in a punishment, a mistake, or an agreement.

To ascribe death to a principle of evil or a trickster is to consider it as a part of the natural world, of the rhythm of the cosmos. We saw this not only in the Loki-Balder myth but also in the role of the serpent-trickster in Genesis 2-3.

Among the Caddo Indians, Coyote plays the trickster role. Famine threatens the people. There are so many people that there is not enough food for all. Coyote declares that death must be allowed to take away the old ones. He orders a hole cut into the sky to take away the dead, with the stipulation that they may return when there is again plenty of food to eat. The best warrior shoots an arrow that sticks in the sky and then shoots other arrows into it, forming a ladder to the hole in the sky. After all the old people climb up the ladder, Coyote pulls the arrows out of the sky. The people exclaim: "See what Coyote has done! Now our loved ones can never return from the land of the dead." From then on, Coyote has been lonely and howls at night with his nose pointed toward the sky where the chain of arrows used to connect the heavens and the earth.

A second group of explanations of the origin or cause of death center around punishment for failures. We saw this theme in the disobedience of Adam and Eve and the curiosity of Pandora. An Australian myth tells of women who are forbidden to go near a certain hollow tree where there is a bees' nest filled with honey. When a woman chops into the tree one day to get at the honey, a huge bat — the spirit of death — flies out into the world. Among the Cherokee Indians, the daughter of the Sun is bitten by a snake and dies. Sun tells humans to take a box and go where the spirit of his daughter is and bring it back to her body. They are forbidden to open the box with the spirit in it until they have arrived where her body lies. Impelled by curiosity, however, they open it, contrary to the divine injunction, and the spirit of life escapes. The fate of humans is thus decided. All must die.

Death as a mistake is a third common theme. Among the Hottentots, it is a message that gets twisted. The moon sends the louse to promise immortality with this message: "As I die and dying live, so you also shall die and dying live." The hare overtakes the louse on its way and promises to deliver the message. He forgets it however, and it comes out garbled: "As I die and dying perish, so shall you too." The moon in anger strikes the hare on its lip, and it has been split ever since.

In parts of Polynesia they tell of how all old people used to change their skins when they grow old and so renew their youth. One day, one mother makes the mistake of being seen by her child when she is changing skin. The child cries when he cannot recognize his "new" mother. The mother feels so sorry for her child that she puts her old skin back on again and later dies, as do all other people thereafter.

The fourth kind of myth considers death as the result of an agreement. Perhaps the most famous is that told among the Blackfeet, Arapahoe, and other North American Indian religious traditions. Old Man and Old Woman ponder whether humans should die for four days and then come back to life, or whether they should die and remain dead. Old Man says: "I know how to decide. I will throw a buffalo chip into the river. If it floats, humans will die for four days and then come back to life. If it sinks, humans will die forever." They agree. Old Man throws the buffalo chip into the water and it sinks. Sometime later they have a daughter, and she dies while still very young. Old Woman says: "I have changed my mind about death. I think they should come back to life. I want my daughter back." But Old Man replies: "It's too late. We have already decided. Let's not change our minds."

Another famous myth is told among tribes in Malaysia. In the beginning, people do not die, but they grow thin with the waning of the moon and fat again when it waxes. The population increases so alarmingly, however, that a son of First Man asks his father what they should do. First Man says to let things go on this way but his brother intervenes: "No, let people be like the banana tree, which dies as soon as it produces fruit." When they submit their problem and disagreement to the Lord of the Underworld, he decides on death. From then on, instead of renewing their youth like the moon, people die like the banana trees.

## Descent to the Underworld

Because humans continue to suffer and die with regularity and inevitability, many myths deal with the process of dying, the journey to the abode of death. Gilgamesh went through the dark tunnel and crossed the perilous Ocean of Death. Hermod rode for nine days down dark, perilous roads over a river bridge, and his horse jumped the barred gates of Hel — that dreary place where the food was bad and the company dull. In these myths the hero makes a perilous passage of descent to the underworld where he finds himself an explorer in the realm of death and, thus, faces in depth what humans fear so much. Retrieval of a loved one is the most common theme of these journeys to the underworld (Orpheus), but there are also other motifs, including preparation for that journey (the Tibetan *Bardo Thodol*), and the passage of judgment (the Zoroastrian Bridge of Chinvat).

The Orpheus theme — journey for retrieval of a loved one — is present not only in the Gilgamesh and Balder myths but also in a Japanese version where Izanagi searches for Izanami after she has died giving birth to fire, as well as in dozens of North American Indian myths (where, in some cases of shamanic flight, the search is actually successful). Orpheus, a most wonderful musician, the son of the Greek Muse Calliope, boldly follows his young wife, Eurydice, who has died from a serpent's bite. He hopes to win her back from the underworld with the power and charm of his music. He wins his way past Charon, the ferry-man of the dead, past Cerberus, the hell-hound who guards the gates of Hades, past the judges of the dead and even melts the hearts of the Furies. Hades, ruler of the underworld, grants him permission to take Eurydice back to the land of the living on one condition: Orpheus must not look back until both he and his beloved stand in the light of day. With all of Hades holding their breath in hope, the pair make their dangerous way back to the upper world. Stepping finally into the light, Orpheus turns joyfully back to see if Eurydice is safe. She is still in the shadows, however, and Hades's taboo has been violated. Lost to Orpheus forever, Eurydice murmurs her farewell and returns to the under-world. Orpheus wanders the earth in sorrow and finally rejoins her.

A second theme in myths of the journey to the land of the dead centers around the preparations for the journey. This theme finds a parallel in the stories told by many people from their own experiences. Raymond Moody, in *Life After Life,* has provided accounts of people who were dying but lived to tell about it. As they describe it, there was an eerie sound in their ears. They moved quickly through a long tunnel at a distance from their body. Friends and others came to meet them and a Being of Light appeared. After their life was evaluated, they approached some kind of border or barrier. Though they wished to remain due to their feelings of intense joy, love, and peace, they finally had to leave to be reunited with their physical body. With these accounts in mind, we see myths as warnings and preparations for a journey after death from a different perspective. Practices of burying people with gifts, special clothes, a Masonic apron, a favorite toy, perhaps with a cross or Bible in their hands no longer seem totally inappropriate. Ritual prayers to help the departed make the journey or take on a new cogency. Thus in an Aztec prayer, the dead person is warned of the dangers along the way back to the skeleton god Tzontemoc ("He of the Falling Hair") and is provided with water, an identity card, and a little dog (killed and cremated for this purpose) for safe passage.

A classic text of the preparation for the journey is the *Bardo Thodol,* the Tibetan Book of the Dead from the Tantric branch of Mahayana Buddhism, dating back to the Eighth Century A.D. The book offers instructions to guide a dying person into the intermediate state of "bardo," the time between death and the return to a new body. The text recognizes that the great majority will shrink from being absorbed into the Clear Light of Absolute Reality. They will continue to exist with their individual Atman, subject to the powers of Karma and Samsara, which reassert themselves. The soul will then encounter a series of good and evil powers, benevolent and wrathful gods. The dying person is warned that these visions are all illusions, mere projections of the subjective mind into its post-mortem world.

In contrast to the Western religious traditions where individuals have to face the harsh reality and finality of death, the Eastern religions face the overwhelming possibility of having to be born again. Thus they encourage the soul to struggle during the intermediate state and not to lose power or be seduced by these images. For if it considers these projections to be real, then the soul is still unliberated, and the pull of the cycle of birth and rebirth will be so strong that it will draw that soul increasingly toward its next birth.

A third theme in myths of the journey to the land of the dead describes the judgment that culminates the journey. In some myths there is no judgment, for the same fate is reserved for all. When Enkidu looks about in the gloom in his nightmarish dreams, he realizes that princes and temple personnel alike are now slaves to the gods of the House of Dust. The Hel (that is, "concealed cave") that Hermod visits is also a place where high and low alike endure the same fate. Some other myths may provide an improved version of earthly life — maybe a "Happy Hunting Ground" — where a "good life" in and of itself brings no reward.

In most religious traditions, however, there is some kind of judgment, perhaps at the crossing of a perilous bridge that determines the future existence of the dead. The Chinvat Bridge in the Zoroastrian tradition, for example, is so steep that the wicked cannot keep their footing and plunge into an abyss. The bridge projects from the mountain peak of judgment, and on this bridge the soul's final destiny is decided. Such bridges, whether as thin as a needle, as sharp as a razor's edge, made of spikes or fire, are symbols of a dangerous boundary but also of special opportunity. Protected by a gatekeeper, or a pack of wild dogs, by grotesque guardians or some other destructive power, these bridges are a type of threshold for a difficult rite of passage the soul must undergo before it can pass into a new zone of experience. Happiness after death is determined by how a person crosses this threshold.

But what determines how a dead person will cross? Perhaps it is social rank. In Peru, for example, the mansions of the Sun are reserved for the Incas and their nobles. In the Congo, the rich fare the best, for the grandeur of the funeral determines their state in the afterlife. Sometimes the fate is determined not by rank, but by the nature of the death. The Aztecs, for example, all make a perilous journey under the earth, passing over nine rivers. Most arrive in Mictlan, the place of the Dead, but a select few go to the House of the Sun. Places are reserved for those who have fallen in battle, been sacrificial victims, or who have died in childbirth. They are privileged to a continued existence of pure joy, accompanying the sun on its daily course, or becoming hummingbirds to suck honey. Another select group, the devotees of the rain god Tlaloc, and those who die through drowning, lightning, or dropsy, live with no drought, famine, or war somewhere beneath the waters.

In most myths, however, fate on the journey of judgment is determined by one's moral conduct in life. Many North American Indian religious traditions describe this journey. Among the Choctaw, persons must travel Death Trail after they die. They come to a deep and rapid stream with steep rugged hills on each side. The Death Trail leads over the stream, and the only bridge is a very slippery pine log. Six persons on the far side of the bridge have rocks in their hands and throw them at the dead as they try to cross. Those who have been evil try to dodge the stones but fall off while the good spirits are able to walk over safely and enter a Happy Hunting Ground where there is always feasting and dancing, and many buffalo. Among the Gallinomero of California, good souls voyage to the Happy Westen Land beyond the Big Water, but those whose lives have been evil go to an island in the Bitter Waters, an island barren and desolate, covered only with brine-spattered stones. Here they live as always, with no food but the broken stones, and no drink but the salt water. The Assiniboin tell of the dead migrating toward the south where the climate is mild, the game abundant, and the rivers stocked with fish. Those whose lives are evil, however, will have to dwell in perpetual snow and ice and in the complete deprivation of all things.

A Chinese picture of this journey is particularly vivid. Three bridges lead to the Gate of Demons that guards the town of the ten Yama Kings. One bridge is gold — for the gods; another is silver — for virtuous persons who will either journey to the Land of Extreme Felicity or to the dwelling place of the Immortals, or else go straight to the tenth Yama King for reassignment in another existence. The third bridge — for undeserving and criminal souls — is several miles long, with no rails. Many fall into the waters rushing beneath where they are preyed upon by bronze snakes and iron dogs that bite them and tear them to pieces. Eventually they, too, are handed over for judgment. A register is consulted to see if the nine Yama kings should torture them some more. If so, the souls might be cut into little pieces, plunged into a cauldron of boiling oil, sawed in half, have their tongues cut out, or compelled to swallow gold and silver. After their appropriate sufferings and punishments, these souls also go before the tenth Yama King who decides in which form they will be reborn.

Division into separate realms of judgment where the righteous are rewarded and the evil punished is a gradual change in the history of the major religious traditions. The Sheol of the ancient Hebrews, for example, a place where the dead lead a pale, shadowy existence, is combined with Gehenna to produce an underworld place of torment. The shadowy Greek Hades gradually merges with the more sinister Tartarus, and the torments, reserved for only a few, are extended to all the unjust.

Fire, with its qualities of tempering or annihilating, extends back to the third millennium B.C. in Egypt, where the evil are tossed into fiery lakes or pits that reduce them instantly to ashes. Other cultures later elaborate their version of the fiery pit, culminating in the excessive images of hell in the medieval Christian tradition, which portray the horrors of purgatory and hell beyond the mind's endurance.

What about hell in the Christian tradition? The early church Fathers interpret the darkness, weeping, gnashing of teeth, and fire as metaphors for the menacing possibility that persons may completely miss the meaning of life. Hell is not to be understood as a physical place, they suggest, but as exclusion from fellowship with the living God. Hell is a way of saying that persons have the power to shut themselves off from reunion with Absolute Reality, from God's fellowship. Images of hell do not supply information about the hereafter but are intended to bring persons here and now to absolute seriousness regarding God's offer of eternal life and need for conversion in present life. Those who don't take the warnings seriously about the possibility of eternal refusal are judging themselves here and now.

On the apocalyptic Last Day, the judgment of the present time will be revealed. Tempering the harsh statements about eternal damnation are expressions of hope of universal mercy. This universalism would regard all humans as ultimately returning to reunion with the Absolute Reality from the very outset, but it does not do justice to the seriousness of life, to the importance of free decisions, or the weight of individual responsibility.

Hell is the mode of existence of those who are self-satisfied, who barricade the self from others, who have nothing more and desire nothing more than they are themselves. It is the revolt against love, becoming totally self-enclosed. If hell is endless, it is not so because it is created by the absolute Reality but rather by those whose decisive choice is against love.

## Victim and Victor

The hero who undergoes great suffering and struggles to get to the Land of the Dead and then emerges with a new consciousness after his rite of passage is a savior in the sense that he heals our fears of death and provides us with the realization that death cannot be overcome (physically), but must be undergone before we can achieve wholeness. Gilgamesh does not save us from dying, but he points beyond himself (as also Balder and Orpheus) to the unknown, acting out the life of all of us, revealing the way each of us must travel. In one sense, Gilgamesh's frantic search for immortality fails when he loses the plant that could have rejuvenated him; but in another sense he succeeds, for he awakens consciousness of human mortality. Gilgamesh's quest is successful insofar as he learns that death is one of the rhythms of life. Though death is a reality, it is but a moment to be lived through, a turning point, another rite of passage in life, similar to birth, puberty, and marriage. The boon he leaves us is the realization that there is no way of preventing death, but it is still possible to make it a part of life.

The hero who faces death for the sake of the community is thus a savior because he brings significance to death.

Ordinarily, however, savior refers to a hero who brings meaning to death precisely because he dies by some violent means — hanging, or dismemberment, or piercing with mistletoe. Thus the ancient Babylonian kings are ritually killed as part of the Akitu Festival in order to allow a new order to come in. In Polynesia, the heroine Hainuwele is ritually killed and from her body springs life-giving crops and plants. It is in this context that the central event of Christianity — the person, ministry, death, and resurrection of Jesus — are best understood. Jesus, too, is a savior, not in taking death away but in taking away its sting and in giving hope of a new life after death, a life of reunion with God, the Absolute Reality.

Jesus dies and "descends into hell"; that is, he dies and journeys to the World of the Dead. Whether this descent is considered the final suffering after death or as a triumphal journey, Christians have always found in it an act of salvation for the sake of all humanity. The saving act of Jesus — the victim as victor — is described in a variety of ways in the Christian Scriptures. The meaning of the cross and death of Jesus can be summarized in three statements:

1. There is no resurrection without death. For Christians to say that "Jesus saves us from death" does not mean that they will not die; rather, it means that death does not have absolute dominion over them. Jesus, too, had to die. The Messiah must suffer to come into his glory (Mark). Death is the hour of Jesus' glorification, and the event necessary for sending the Spirit (John). The death of Jesus does not find its meaning as a tragic miscarriage of justice but rather as the inevitable consequence of Jesus' lifestyle. He is faithful till the end in the total giving of himself (Luke). Dying with Christ, Christians rise with Christ (Romans), and the power of death is abolished (First Corinthians). Jesus' parting gift is his own peace, a peace the world cannot give, a peace that banishes fear (John). By his death, Jesus takes away all the power of evil, renders the demonic powerless (Matthew), and sets free those held in slavery by the fear of death (Hebrews).

2. The scapegoat brings satisfaction. The scapegoat was a live goat over whose head all the sins of the children of Israel were confessed and which was sent into the wilderness symbolically to bear their sin on the Day of Atonement. Many Christians consider Jesus, the Lamb of God who takes away the sins of the

world (John), to be a scapegoat bearing the blame of others, whose sacrifice brings a reconciliation betwen God and humans. Jesus is the sacrifice that eliminates the need for any other sacrifice (Hebrews), the one who brings redemption, justification, sanctification, and new access to God (Paul). His death is an atonement, the "at-one-ment" with God, whereby nothing can separate Christians from the love of God, "neither death, nor life, nor angels, nor principalities, nor height, nor depth, nor anything else in all creation" (Romans).

3. The cross reveals a new relationship with God. For Christians, Jesus is the God-man, who is self-giving love. No longer is God to be considered an aloof being who rewards good and punishes evil, but rather as a passionate presence to all of human life. God, in the suffering and death of the God-man Jesus, is present in the loneliness of human suffering and death. This does not mean that God dies — such a statement doesn't make sense in the context of Absolute Reality — but rather that there is a divine sensitivity. The Christian God is a God of compassion, and the death of the God-man on the cross makes Good Friday not a day of frustration but a day of fidelity, for humans are not forsaken even in the hour of death.

## Overcoming Fear of Death and Aging

Death preoccupies people, frightens them, and makes them invent fantasies to help cope with its inevitability. The saviors help us overcome this fear of death by bringing significance to it, enabling us to see it as part of the inevitable rhythm of life. Indeed, it is no longer the blandness of Utnapishtim's immortality that attracts us but the expectation of death that shapes our daily purposes, sharpens our zest for each moment, and inspires our noblest and most brilliant works. Siduri the barmaid's advice is worth heeding: "Make merry day and night; make every day a day of joy; dance, play, and refresh yourself." Qoheleth recognizes this truth also: "It is well for a person to eat and drink and enjoy all the fruits of his labor under the sun during the limited days of the life that God gives him for this is his lot." Gotama, the compassionate Buddha, expresses it in a parable:

> There was once a man who was crossing a field and met
> a tiger. He ran to a great cliff and caught hold of a root

and swung over the side of the cliff. But at the bottom of the cliff was another tiger. Soon two little mice came along and began to gnaw on the vine. The man looked in terror at the tiger below. But then he saw a strawberry vine. He picked the strawberry and ate it. How delicious it was.

No savior has faced the mystery of death and brought back a more liberating message.

Facing death can be a growth experience for people, the chance to learn something they have never learned before. But this growth does not have to wait until the last moments of life. Those who have overcome the fear of death recognize the consent to the deaths we die every day. Here we are not referring to negative death — as the absence of relationships, as powerlessness, or apathy, or mental paralysis, as insensibility of exhaustion — but to positive death, as the letting go of the small self. Only living persons can die, but it is also true that only dying persons can really live. Zen Buddhists express this in a paradox: "Those who die before they die, do not die when they die." The saviors bring meaning to our lives by helping us reconcile ourselves with death. Because we are really able to die, we are really able to live. Now every single moment of every day is transformed because the pervasive fear of death is removed. We are taken up by beautiful things just by walking, chatting, breathing, eating, and having friends. Death is not catastrophic or destructive but one of the most constructive and positive elements of life. This is true whether we are talking about terminal illness, aging, or letting go of the self.

For those steeped in the mythic tradition, death comes not as a dreaded stranger but as an expected companion. Not all have the benefit of myths, however, and their struggle to deal with death in a wholesome way is much more difficult. Both the hospice movement and the insights of Elisabeth Kubler-Ross in her book *On Death and Dying* have brought solace and reconciliation to many with terminal illnesses. Their recognition that dying patients go through several distinct stages on their way to death, as time permits, has helped many cope with their own mortality.

When terminally ill patients become aware of their critical state, their initial reaction is 1) denial, or disbelief. Why me, they ask in shock? Such denial is healthy and enables them to go on with their daily lives and to mobilize their defenses. It

cannot go on till the end, however, because some reality of life
will keep them from burying their head in the sand. 2) Anger
and irritation follow, and envy directed at everyone. Resent-
ment is harbored against healthy people and blame is directed
at others for not paying attention to earlier complaints. 3) Next,
bargaining brings a temporary, superficial truce, merely putting
a later deadline on the inevitable. This stage is a good time for
unfinished business, for doing whatever deprives them of a sense
of peace, usually in their relationships with others. 4) The depression that follows comes in two parts: reactive depression, where
there is a mourning of all the little losses — job, energy, appetite
— that entail becoming dependent rather than self-sustaining;
and preparatory grief — a silent stage where the dying person
doesn't want to be cheered up and wants to see only one or two
people, more concerned with what lies ahead rather than behind.
5) Finally, there is acceptance of the inevitability of death. There
is a detachment from all ties and a peaceful and serene submission to what cannot be changed. The struggle is over. Hope,
which has been a constant thread through all the stages, disappears, and death is near.

Eventually the struggle against the inevitability of death is
over for all of us. Particularly blessed are those who have gone
through this struggle and overcome death before their deathbed. This is especially true of those many aging persons who
seem to understand the Zen paradox "Those who die before they
die, do not die when they die" better than most. They seem
to know what many of us only glimpse from research rather than
experience: Aging is a time for growth, with its own gifts and
insights. The times when aging persons who have such gifts and
insights share them with us are graced moments.

With age, options decrease and choices diminish rather than
expand. As with every stage of life, there are particular crises,
perhaps problems regarding retirement from a life-long job,
moving to a different community, or even the death of a spouse.
Still, aging is not necessarily only a time for that steady decline
which ends in death; it can also be a time for growth, a time
with its own advantages. Those who have learned to age gracefully have made time a friend, not an enemy. They still celebrate
their birthdays rather than dread them. "The crown of old people
is ripe experience," Qoheleth tells us, and their experience, when
shared, can give courage to others. Indeed, like the saviors in

myths of evil and death, they can serve as a model for the rest of us who will someday face the inconveniences of accumulated years. They have a legacy to leave, not just heirlooms but their reminiscences; not just wills or inheritances but their inner wisdom. Freed from preoccupation with the self's mortality, they are now freed to give the self for and to others.

Those who grow old with dignity live with the grain, not against it. They have learned to compensate, making dozens of right decisions each day. Willing to compromise, they are less willing to believe that the world can be changed tomorrow and their patience lightens unavoidable burdens. Old divisions of background, occupation, success, and social roles have softened, fuzzed through the spectrum of age. Their strong sense of community provides them with companionship and relieves them of the notion that they are indispensable. They have allowed ambition, competition, and outer responsibilities to drop away at the right times. For them, to lack things gracefully is a prayer worth praying; to grow obsolete gracefully is a challenge worth accepting.

They possess the gift of seriousness. They no longer tend to harp on the trivial and do not blame their misfortunes on circumstances or conditions. Decisions of the spirit are of primary importance for them — not what happens to them, but how they feel about what happens. Perhaps it is a touch of nostalgia or senility, but they remember early things very vividly and forget things that happened yesterday. More likely, this is because they are remembering the things that are vital, the events that have acquired an enormously enhanced meaning in the whole of their lives. Centering everything on their religious self, they experience life as a circle instead of as a straight line and savor it both horizontally and vertically, in its breadth and depth.

Moments are precious. They don't feel compelled to make every second count, as if it could be their last. Conversely, moments — glances, sounds, touches, tiny rituals — are complete in themselves. Life is not a preparation for tomorrow, nor a remembrance of yesterday, where somehow today gets lost in the shuffle. Because they have made the crucial discovery that humans have zero control over the quantity of life still at their disposal but considerable control over the quality of time, they can invest each present moment with zest, excitement, and fulfillment.

## Letting Go

Death is not the end, the saviors tell us, because the religious self survives. The transcendent dimension present in our experiences remains. We reap in death what we have sown in life. And if what ultimately matters is the religious self that we are becoming, then all of life is a preparation for dying. Our lives are successful insofar as we can let go of the narrow self and open our selves in vulnerability to our depths. Dying to the small self is something we do continuously, not just at the end of our physical lives. Undertaking the search for the depths of the religious self is the ultimate goal of growth and will make us able to face the final end with peace and joy, knowing we have lived well.

The archetypal descent of Orpheus, or Gilgamesh, or Hermod, or Jesus into the depths of the underworld is a journey none of us can avoid, for only after we have undertaken it can the religious self be manifested. Our descent into hell is the experience of impotence and despair in which our small self dies so that the larger religious self might come to life. Our descent from our conscious side into the depths of our unconscious side is a descent to retrieve our Eurydice side, our Enkidu side, yes, even our Loki side. The victorious saviors help us in the descent, the discovery, and the return — omitting nothing, sacrificing none of the strangeness, making no compromises. Just as we have seen in the previous chapter that the saviors beckon us to incorporate the shadow from the unknown mysterious depths of our unconscious, so now they invite us to incorporate our mortality into our consciousness and to consent to it. They help us find wholeness at the center by dying to the small self. "If it dies, it bears much fruit." In the process of spiritual growth of the individual, the small self dies to make room for a new center of being, the religious self. The fruit is an integrity of life, a balance of good and evil, spirit and flesh, light and dark, life and death.

Giving up the self to the unknown means enduring suffering, but it must happen in order for wholeness to occur. For Christians, the symbol of this ultimate letting go is the cross. The way of the cross is a journey to death, the struggle of the small self to the bitter end. Mortification, the death of the small self, does not mean leaving behind one kind of being for another.

The small self refers to the imaginary importance we give ourselves, the facades that cover our person. Only what has a merely illusory existence can be discarded without loss to the whole. It is this fantasy that must disappear. Dying on the cross, daily, is giving up the ego-illusions, freeing the self from worshipping itself. Total emptiness admits the Absolute Reality in power. Only in total giving can the fullness come, the life of limitless abundance. When death is no longer feared, then nothing blocks the capacity for self-realization any longer, and we can then be unique and special selves.

We have suggested that Gilgamesh's descent to the depths of the underworld is ultimately successful because he brings us back the awareness that although we die, there is something — the larger self — that survives. His journey is successful in another sense, too. Rather than using the plant of immortality to make himself a young king with absolute power, Gilgamesh wants to feed it first to the old folks of Uruk. He conquers death — and his small self — when the welfare of others starts concerning him as much as his own. Accepting the inevitability of his own death, he can now move beyond his regard for the small self into more rewarding and saving pursuits.

We, too, are successful in our descent into the depths of the self when we become conscious of and consent to the saviors within us, when we take on their strength. Their strength saves not only the self, but others. For those persons who do not fear death, who have become skilled in letting go, death has no dominion over them, no sting, and they can be instruments of healing. To lose one's life is to be detached from it and committed instead to loving and caring relationships, to the happiness of others.

Letting go of the self — "emptiness" in the Eastern traditions, "mortification" in the Western — means compassion. The religious self expands, paradoxically, through expending itself for others. Compassionate love is the unqualified expending of the self. Greater love than this no one has, than to give up one's self for others. Loving compassion brings a vulnerability that binds people together, not a vulnerability of fear, but of those who care. Loving compassion is the fullness of life, and when life is full, death is overcome.

# Review Questions

1. How do myths of death help people overcome their fear of death?

2. What are the different types of myth which deal with the origin of death in the world?

3. What is the purpose of the savior's descent to the underworld?

4. In myths of a last judgment after death, what are some different means for determining whether a person will go to hell or heaven?

5. What was the meaning of hell in the early Christian church fathers?

6. "The crown of old people is ripe experience." What lessons can we learn from those who have entered their golden years?

7. What is "dying to the small self"?

# Discussion Starters

1. You have been asked to write the libretto for a new opera version of the Epic of Gilgamesh. Having briefly introduced the story, you go on to assert that "though the story ends in despair, the journey may still be considered successful." Elaborate on your assertion.

2. What would you like your best friend to say about you at your funeral if you were to die tomorrow? What would you like to see for an epitaph on your tombstone if you were to die fifty years from now? What epitaph would you most fear to find on your tombstone?

3. "Whoever has lived long enough to find out what life is knows how deep a debt of gratitude we owe to Adam, the first great benefactor of our race. He brought death into the world." (Mark Twain)

4. "One's vision of time is always expanding, from the child's vision of the moment to the youth's vision of the lifetime to the man's vision of the great time. While one's vision of time is expanding, though, one seems to be losing one's hold on eternity. One loses first the timelessness of the child, then the inexhaustible time of the youth. One ends with the mortal existence of the man." (John S. Dunne)

5. "A man may be born, but in order to be born he must first die, and in order to die, he must first awake . . . . When a man awakes, he can die; when he does he can be born." (Gurdjieff)

6. "Death is the supreme festival on the road to freedom." (Bonhoeffer)

7. "Children's play ends with the universal resurrection of the dead. Adult's play ends with universal burial. Whereas the resurrection is the paradigm of the world of children, the world of adults creates the cross." (Ruben Alves)

8. "There are well-known insects which die in the moment of fecundation. So it is with all joy; life's supreme and richest moment of pleasure is coupled with death." (Kierkegaard)

9. What movie and TV characters today remind you of the saviors in this chapter?

10. If you could meet one of the saviors in myths of death, which one would you choose? Why? What would you like to ask him?

# ESCHATOLOGY

Religions almost universally have developed myths that point to some sort of life after death, perhaps in a heaven or Nirvana, in one life or several, soon after death or at the end of the world. In contrast to the finality of death, these myths hold out the hope for a new life and a new world. In their symbolic presentations of the ultimate human destiny, classic mythologies echo the human will to conquer death. Myths that deal with the end, either of individuals or of humanity collectively, and myths that portray the possibility of new life and a new world, are eschatological myths. Such myths bring the future into the present and anticipate the end of the world.

In the myths of saviors we have seen already, the saviors help people become aware of and consent to the mysteries of evil and death. Eschatological myths are also myths of saviors. In them the saving activity continues. Saviors are those who overcome death and take on a new life as the culmination of their process of self-realization. This new life may be impersonal (Osiris accompanying the daily movement of the sun and Persephone reappearing each year as part of springtime fertility) or personal (Jesus in the resurrection). With the savior's new life, perhaps after a violent death or a descent to the world of the dead, the defeat of death is finalized. The savior is taken out of the cycle of life and, no longer limited to the local and material, assumes a cosmic role.

Our primary interest is in those eschatological myths that stress the role humans can play regarding their future life. These myths actuate persons in their lives and point to a new world that can somehow be affected by present human behavior. The new life is not something merely added to human history but a quality of life that begins in the present life. The future is antici-pated in the present and somehow grows out of it, both through ritual participation and everyday activities. For those integrating the myths into their own lives, this is the culmination of their process of self-realization, the movement toward wholeness, from the small self to the religious self.

In this final chapter we are going to study some of the myths of resurrection (or reincarnation, or rebirth) of saviors. We will ask how it is possible to participate ritually in this life and also look at various mythic descriptions of this new life. Finally, we will investigate what implications this new life may have in helping release the divine potential that vibrates in the core of each person.

## Isis and Osiris

The myth of the return to life of Osiris is narrated in the Pyramid Texts of the Egyptian *Book of the Dead*. These texts incor-porate hymns, prayers, and incantations for an afterlife that were inscribed on the walls of burial chambers of kings, dating as far back as 2600 B.C. The story, which also exists in a version from Plutarch, provides a complex of psychological forces and social relationships: the love and justice of Osiris; the conjugal fidelity and material tenderness of his wife-sister Isis; the filial piety of Horus. It is a fierce protest of the human spirit against death's apparent victory and love's seeming defeat. It holds out hope for the final triumph of justice over wickedness, of life over death, in another world.

At first a primitive fertility god who teaches agricultural skills, Osiris is associated with regenerative and life forces. Over the centuries he passes from being a god of the dead to a god of the living, becoming equal to and gradually surpassing Ra, the sun god. He is a savior who achieves immortality, offering the same victory over the grave to his loyal Egyptian worshippers. Isis is the Great Mother, a goddess of many names. She is benevolent, teaching women to grind corn, weave linen, and domesticate men regarding marriage. Out of compassion, she teaches the divine secrets for curing illness and disease. To those who live under her protection, she extends their lives beyond death. She too is a savior, indeed even more so than Osiris whom she brings back to life.

After Osiris has gone about the world bringing humans the boons of agriculture and civilization, he returns laden with gifts. His success makes his brother, Set, jealous. Devising an evil plan to kill Osiris, Set prepares a festive banquet, and offers a richly decorated casket as a gift to anyone whose body will fit it perfectly. Many try it, but they are too short, too stout, or too lean. When Osiris is finally persuaded to lie in the coffin, Set and seventy-two fellow conspirators spring forward, fasten the lid, and solder it with lead. That night they dump the casket into the Nile and it floats away. As Set usurps Osiris's throne, land and law are in disorder; corruption, drought, famine, and disease rock the realm. The desert encroaches upon the once green and fertile land, destroying the crops in the Nile valley. The destructive and desiccating powers that stand as a constant threat to Egyptian life and civilization hold sway.

Isis is desolate. She flees to the swamps to mourn her husband, cutting off her hair and tearing her robes to shreds. After much wailing, she sets out to locate Osiris's body. She learns that the wooden chest has floated ashore in Syria where the trunk of a quickly growing tree has completely encircled it. In the meantime the Syrian king has taken the tree down and used it as the central pillar in his royal palace. How is Isis going to get her hands on the casket? She decides to disguise her true nature until she can find a way to acquire the tree. She befriends the queen, Ishtar, and asks her for a job as a nurse-maid. As luck would have it, there is a child that needs nursing, and she takes the position. She rears the child by giving it her finger instead of a breast to suck and by secretly placing the child like a log in the palace fire each night, hoping in this way to feed the child with immortality and burn away the mortal elements of its body. One night the queen unexpectedly sees what Isis is doing and, thinking that her child is being burned to death, instinctively grabs it from the fire. The child is thus robbed of immortality and Isis's cover is blown. She has to reveal her identity to explain her actions. The royal couple, satisfied with her explanation, give her the tree trunk that contains the coffin of Osiris. Returning to Egypt, Isis opens it and throws herself in rapturous love upon the dead Osiris. She has to conceal the body among the marshes until her son, Horus, can regain his father Osiris's throne. Osiris's resurrection is impossible until Horus can avenge him.

One night while Isis is away, Set, in serpent form, slides through the marshes and discovers the hidden body by the light of the full moon. Raging with anger, and wishing to destroy Osiris forever, he cuts the body into fourteen pieces and carries each piece to a different part of Egypt. Isis has to begin her search all over again. Enlisting the aid of her sister Nephthys, she gradually recovers the parts of the body, reassembling it with the art of embalming. She locates all the pieces except one, the phallus, which has been devoured by a crab. Modeling a clay penis, she makes the body whole, transforms herself into a large bird and attempts to animate the corpse by beating her wings.

The body is whole, but it is lifeless. The sun god Ra takes pity on Isis for her continued lamenting and sorrow and sends Anubis, the Lord of the Mummy-Wrappings to help embalm and bury Osiris. This jackal-headed god, with his skills of mummification, effects the proper preservation of the body. When Anubis has performed his secret rites, Osiris comes back to life again, but as king of the underworld, the realm of the dead. Osiris proclaims: "I have been knitted together; made whole and complete, I have renewed my youth; I am Osiris, the Lord of Eternity." This death and resurrection of Osiris is repeated each year in Egypt as the Nile River yearly dwindles and then swells again to flood stage, spreading its fertilizing mud over the fields. Osiris returns each year bringing luxuriant crops and vegetation. Indeed, it is repeated each day, for Osiris patrols the cosmos in his sun chariot. The sun ascends from the darkness so that humans and nature may continue to live, once again to join with what has become separated and lost in the darkness.

Osiris is now the judge of the world of the dead, but more than this, he binds the world together by his authority. In him life and order triumph over death and chaos. Evil is forced to serve good. Horus struggles to avenge his murder and to restore cosmic order by dethroning Set and placing the royal crown on his own head. Horus and Set are locked in perennial combat — each day in the struggle of light against dark, and each year in the combat of fertility against drought. By continually over-coming the implacable adversary of life and vegetation, Horus restores and provides again the blessings of new life and growth that Osiris once brought to humanity.

## Demeter and Persephone

In the Isis–Osiris myth, Osiris is a savior because he is the one who is resuscitated, the one who rules the land of the dead. Still, we must really recognize the efforts of Isis to bring him to new life. In her crisis of losing her husband, her struggle against the forces of evil, and her return with the boon of mummification, we easily recognize that she, too, is a savior. Her role is much more than merely wailing at the scene of death or at the tomb, for she offers her devotees a share in the life she brings to Osiris.

The Greek myth of Demeter and Persephone, which reflects certain Egyptian influences, does highlight the female savior-role in raising another to life. The daughter, Persephone, is a savior-figure because she returns to life periodically each year. But her mother, Demeter, is even more a savior, for it is she who undergoes the crisis of losing her daughter ultimately to death, struggles against the forces of Hades to bring her back to life again, and returns with a boon (a ritual) for her Greek devotees.

It is Demeter's role, more than Persephone's, that instills the Greeks with the courage to overcome their fear of death. Her story inspires them with the knowledge and awareness that, even though gods and goddesses may die, they return to life. It is the rituals of Demeter, the Eleusinian mysteries, that the Greeks participated in, hoping thereby to share in immortality.

As we learn in a Homeric hymn to Demeter, Persephone wanders off by herself one day while playing with her youthful companions in the meadows. Fascinated by the intoxicating scent of the narcissus flower, she bends down to pick one. At that moment the earth opens and Hades, the Lord of the Dead, appears with chariot and horses. He quickly seizes her in spite of her cries of protest and carries her back to the underworld, witnessed only by Helios, the sun, and the goddess Hecate who has heard Persephone's cry.

Bitter sorrow seizes Demeter's heart as she becomes aware of Persephone's disappearance. Hopeless and disconsolate, she flies like a bird over land and sea, ranging the land for nine days looking for clues. Meanwhile Persephone is in Hades's underworld where she sits on a golden throne surrounded by treasures. She is not ill-treated, but she is sad, not taking to Hades who has fallen in love with her and is determined to have her as his wife. On the tenth day of her search, Demeter learns from Hecate that Persephone has been ravished away. The two women go to Helios to force him to tell them what has happened and who is responsible.

Upon learning the particulars, Demeter is furious and demands that Zeus force Hades to release her daughter. Zeus, who has been a party to his brother Hades's kidnapping, urges Demeter to cease lamenting as this is, indeed, a good marriage for her daughter. Once more, Demeter begins her lamenting. Since Demeter is the goddess of grain and agriculture, the earth gradually becomes sterile, a vast lifeless wasteland. Eventually her sorrows bring her to Eleusis, a small town not far from Athens. Sitting by the Maiden's Well, with the countenance of a sad old woman, she meets the daughters of the king who take her to the palace. Refusing all food and drink, she manages a small cheerful smile only at the buffoonery and jokes of an old woman of the court.

Then, in a series of episodes reminiscent of Isis, she serves as nurse, and is discovered attempting to make the royal child immortal by laying it on a fire while the parents sleep. Again the maternal instinct and desire to have the child live forever! To explain her actions, Demeter reveals herself in her true divine majesty and beauty. She then orders a temple to be built at Eleusis, where her worshippers can celebrate her rituals. She remains in the palace, still in sorrow.

Slowly the leaves on trees turn brown and fall off; no new seeds sprout; all vegetation dies. The earth is in sorrow at the loss of Persephone. Demeter sits for a whole year, meditating in her sorrow and refusing to bring any new life to the world until she is once more beside her beloved daughter. Prayers of the people ascend to Mount Olympus, but the gods are helpless.

Zeus implores Demeter without success, then all the gods in turn. Demeter has won, and Zeus reluctantly sends Hermes to tell Hades to release Persephone from the realm of death. Hades is reluctant to let her go, but since she has been homesick and has refused to eat or even come near him, he agrees. Before sending her back to earth, however, he tempts her to eat a few pomegranate seeds. In her joy and haste, Persephone takes the fruit and eats it. Now the pomegranate is a symbol of marriage and the effect of eating it is to render the union of wife and man indissoluble. Persephone, in blissful ignorance, has ensured her return to the underworld. Stepping into Hermes's golden chariot, she returns to the world of light where she embraces her mother with great emotion. In the mother and child reunion they talk of their sadness and their hopes. Then Demeter asks her: "Surely, daughter, you didn't eat anything during your imprisonment. For if you have not eaten anything, you can live with me on Olympus. But if you have, then you must return to the depths of the earth." Persephone woefully admits that she has tasted the fateful pomegranate. What sorrow. Demeter has to lose her daughter again. If only she hadn't eaten!

How can the dilemma be resolved? Is the world to be forever without fertile vegetation while Demeter weeps for her daughter? There has to be a compromise. After some bargaining, Demeter reluctantly agrees to allow Persephone to live part of the year with her husband in the realm of the dead and the rest of the year above ground with her. Before returning to her place on Mount Olympus, Demeter teaches the people of Eleusis her divine science, bestows on them the gifts of the grain of corn and the art of harnessing oxen, and gives them instructions on how her rituals — the Eleusinian mysteries — are to be celebrated.

When darkness comes with the approach of winter, Persephone once more descends to her husband. The flowers are hidden in the bowels of the earth with her, sleeping their winter sleep. Each spring the earth puts on a mantle of a thousand flowers to greet her return. Persephone springs to life and brings with her all the plants that humans and animals depend on for their sustenance.

## The Paschal Mystery of Jesus

Osiris returns to new life daily in the sun chariot and annually in the flooding Nile. Persephone comes again in the blossoming of the earth each spring. Both are saviors insofar as they overcome death. They periodically return to the human world, bringing new life with them. Isis and Demeter are saviors, too, in the crucial role they play in making new life after death possible for Osiris and Persephone. Both the Egyptian and Greek eschatological myths help their devotees consent to the mystery of death by pointing to a new life after death — a new life which is periodic and impersonal.

In the Christian eschatological myths of the savior, Jesus, totally different dimensions are brought to this new life. The death of Jesus — his gift of self for others — becomes meaningful precisely because he is raised up and given a victorious new life by Yahweh. The complex of myths that deal with Jesus' apotheosis — that is, his death, resurrection, ascension-exaltation, and gift of the life-giving Spirit — is called the "Paschal Mystery." The myths of this Paschal Mystery do not stress that Jesus' new life is an indefinite extension or perpetuation of his earthly life in another realm, with no essential differences. Nor is this new life the simple resuscitation of a corpse, a return to mere terrestrial existence. The new life is not reincarnation in another body. Unlike the Egyptian and Greek savior myths, the new life is not mere immortality, where the spirit or soul imprisoned in the body during life escapes at death to continue its existence. The proclamation of new life is more than a firm conviction that his cause goes on, remaining linked historically with his name while he no longer exists as, for example, architects live on in their buildings, or Mozart and Beethoven are revived when their symphonies are performed.

What do the myths of the Paschal Mystery proclaim then? The resurrection is historical. Jesus is a real human, and his resurrection a real event. His resurrection entails the gift of new life to the whole person. The physical body sown in death is raised up a glorified body, a body both continuous and discontinuous with the earthly body. His individual existence is retained, not discarded or absorbed into the sun chariot or spring flowers, with their cyclic comings and goings. His human destiny is not dissolved into nothingness, rather it is transformed and fulfilled. His death and resurrection are cosmological in extent: He opens up the possibility of new life after death to all humans, not just a handful of devotees.

The four gospels each narrate various elements of the Paschal Mystery. They portray Jesus' death by violent means, similar to the deaths of Osiris and Persephone. They recount the sudden joyous turn as the disciples discover the empty tomb. They spell out the announcement of the resurrection, amplify the community's experiences of the risen Jesus (on a mountain in Galilee, at a meal in Jerusalem) and describe Jesus' great commission to his apostles to baptize and teach others the good news about the kingdom of God, to preach forgiveness and bring them his Spirit. They narrate the ascension — his visible leave-taking — as he is lifted up on a cloud and passes to heavenly existence, his exaltation in glory with the Father. Finally, they describe how the risen Christ gives the assembled disciples his Spirit to be the dynamic and effective mode of his presence among them when he is no longer manifest. The narratives of the Paschal Mystery proclaim the good news: Jesus lives with God, and more, he is the breath, the dynamism, still present in the Christian community.

Though the meaning of the Paschal Mystery of Jesus in the gospel accounts is consistent, the diversity in the appearance stories is puzzling. Indeed, there are insurmountable discrepancies as each author embellishes his narrative with particular details and episodes. The gospel narratives are products of varying traditions and composition, and it would be foolhardy to try to harmonize them. Only Draconian twisting could reconcile, for example, how many women came to the empty tomb, or who greets these women with the announcement of the resurrection, or what message and mission is given to these witnesses at the empty tomb, or their reaction to that message. The great commission Jesus leaves with his apostles in his initial encounter is variously fixed in Jerusalem or in Galilee, and its content differs with the evangelists. Each gospel writer has a story not found in the others: a substantial bribe offer, a meeting with two disciples returning home, a case of mistaken identity, a new power to handle snakes and drink deadly poisons.

In spite of these divergences, the consistent message of the gospel writers is overwhelming. The apostles and disciples encounter the risen Jesus. They cannot remain quiet, for the world and its history is now transformed. The frightened group, on the verge of fleeing back home in despair after betraying, denying, and failing their master, suddenly become confident and convinced of Jesus' presence. Such a revolutionary transformation cannot be explained by a vision or hallucination, nor merely by an empty tomb. What induces them to proclaim with a degree of challenge and cogency that Jesus is alive is their conviction of his continued presence. Their experience of his love and power is a type of conversion process, compelling them to preach with new confidence, despite the scandal of his persecution and violent death.

A new language — the Paschal Mystery — is needed to explain this real presence, and stories are told to express the different modes of this presence. Jesus is present, for example, in the celebration of the eucharistic meal. Two of the disciples are returning home to Emmaus. Jesus joins them and explains the Scriptures to them, how he had to suffer to be exalted in glory. They ask him to join them in a meal at the end of their day's journey. He stays with them, takes bread and says the blessing. At last their eyes are opened. They quickly return to Jerusalem to share with the others their joy at recognizing Jesus in the explanation of the Scriptures and the breaking of the bread.

Jesus is present also in touching the lives of others. Mary Magdalene at first fails to recognize Jesus when she visits the tomb, mistaking him for a gardener. When Jesus reveals his identity, he tells her not to cling to his mere physical presence any longer. Sent to tell the other disciples that Jesus is ascending, Mary is commissioned to witness to his presence from now on in an non-physical way.

Jesus is present in faith. Thomas, not present when the others encounter the risen Jesus, refuses to believe until he can see and feel Jesus. A week later Jesus extends his peace to Thomas and declares: "Blessed are those who have never seen me and yet have found faith." That is, happy are those who accept the good news without insisting on factual evidence of his presence.

Jesus is present in forgiveness. Peter is asked three times if he loves Jesus, and three times he is forgiven for denying Jesus. His rehabilitation to discipleship by being forgiven is the basis of his authority in the early community. He can extend to others the same forgiveness that he has received from the risen Jesus.

The presence of Jesus — expressed in, but not limited to the eucharist, touching lives, faith, and forgiveness — is the central meaning of the Paschal Mystery. This presence has other consequences for Christians in relation to Jesus, God, and their own lives. First, Jesus' miracles and parables are seen from a new perspective, for his activity has been validated by God. His new life is the authentication of his claim of authority and of doing God's will in his service of the poor and the oppressed. Secondly, in the resurrection, they also see God's activity as concluding one era and inaugurating another, a new world where new possibilities and a new relationship to God are now open. Death is not the end, for the definitive rule of God has begun. Finally, the Paschal Mystery has world-changing consequences for their own activity. The giving of the Spirit is not just the enthusiasm of a religious movement; the ascension is not just a leave-taking. Rather they are the incentive to the apostles to journey to the ends of the earth, to take up Jesus' mission of proclaiming salvation, that is, the good news of humanity's possible return to union with Absolute Reality.

## Ritual Participation in New Life

The myths of Isis–Osiris and Demeter–Persephone are of principal interest to us because of the rituals associated with them. Religious cults in honor of Osiris in Egypt and Demeter in Greece were called "mystery religions." In them worshippers performed secret rituals that enabled them to enter collectively into the exemplary patterns of their saviors. Reenacting the myths enabled them to identify with their gods in the struggle against the forces of evil and death and to share in their victorious new life. Constant ritual repetition of the myths heightened their emotions and tightened their bonds with their saviors who were their teachers and guides on the paths to the afterlife.

Egyptians in the mystery religion of Osiris acquired and participated in the promise of their own immortality in two different rituals. One ritual, practiced throughout their lives, was a temple service commemorating the death and rebirth of Osiris by passing an image of the god through the skin of a sacrificed animal. Various prayers, ceremonies, wearing of amulets, and repetition of formulas reenacted not only the death of Osiris, but also the wandering, grief, and joy of Isis. Devotees believed that they would thus become counterparts of Osiris and eventually be transformed on the day of their own deaths. An emotional ecstasy gripped the worshippers as they held a public procession of Osiris's phallus, the very emblem of his life-giving power. Performing this ritual was their guarantee that their earthly existence had eternal significance.

The other ritual, performed at funeral services, was the rite of mummification. In repeating the rites of Anubis over their dead, they paralleled the reconstitution of Osiris's body. Just as Osiris overcame death and was mummy-wrapped, so the beloved dead would in their own mummification transcend death and achieve immortality. Originally only the dead pharaohs or kings were allowed this mummification, but the royal mortuary ritual was gradually democratized under the principle that everyone has an immortal soul. As part of this funeral ritual, participants also ate wheat, barley, and bees, and retold the story of the "eye of Horus." Horus had his eye poked out in his struggle with Set. Snatching it back, he reverently approached Osiris, opened his lips, and fed him the eye. Since the eye was the part of the body that contained the soul, Osiris thus took on its life-giving power, and the strength of the eye flowed through his limbs.

The Eleusinian mysteries were the most famed and honored of all the Grecian mystery cults. These solemn festivals in honor of Demeter were a ritual celebration and commemoration of the frightful disappearance and the springtime return of youthful, carefree Persephone. Thousands of worshippers were drawn to the Eleusianian festivals for centuries for the promise of blessed immortality. In their dramas they symbolized the soul's condition, its long wanderings through many lives, followed by gradual purification and eventual reunion with spirit. Those who had been initiated into the secret rituals of Demeter were promised a privileged fate after death. "Blessed are they who have beheld these holy acts." They bound themselves with this promise: "I swear to give up my life for the salvation of my brothers, who constitute the whole of humankind, and if called upon, to die in the defense of truth." They originally believed that those who did not participate in the mysteries were doomed to the gloomy darkness of Hades, but the blessed afterlife was gradually opened to the Athenians and then the whole of Greece.

The ritual began with the bringing of sacred objects from the small city of Eleusis into Athens, a ceremonial purification in the sea at Athens, and then the return to Eleusis, with songs along the way. Sacrifices were then made to the gods, together with a torchlight dance. A period of fasting followed, symbolic of Demeter's nine days of wandering and grief. In the central ritual that followed, there was a sacramental feast and dancing in honor of Demeter, the Earth Mother. The devotees drank from a circular sacramental cup and ate cereal cakes from sacred vessels. Partaking of this drink and food, they shared in the divine life of the goddesses Demeter and Persephone. The mysteries symbolized the promise of victory of life over death, recalled the promise of the fruitfulness of the earth, and expressed the truth that immortality can be realized only through the sacrifice of what is most precious.

Christians also have their rituals in which they share in the activity and life of their savior. In baptism they are initiated into the community of those who share in the death and resurrection of Christ:

> By baptism we were buried with Christ, and lay dead, in order that, as Christ was raised from the dead in the splendor of the Father, so also we might set our feet upon the new path of life. For if we have become incorporate with him in a death like his, we shall also be one with him in a resurrection like his (Romans 6).

The most powerful celebration of the savior's Paschal Mystery, however, is in the liturgical drama of the eucharist, that is, "Thanksgiving" or the Lord's Supper. This Christian ritual par excellence may be performed daily. In it the Christian's hope for life after death is expressed most intimately: What has happened to Jesus can now happen to any and all humans. The eucharist affirms the resurrection in the midst of death. The reality of evil and death is not minimized, but transformed. Joy in the new divine life predominates. As failure is encompassed by triumph, disaster is surrounded by victory; and the cross is swallowed up in the resurrection.

In the ritual of the eucharist, Christians are called into communion with each other. As a preparation to celebrate worthily the sacred mysteries of the death and resurrection of Jesus, they mutually express their unworthiness and their sorrow for sin. They hear again the good news of their reunion with the one, which has been achieved in the Paschal Mystery of Jesus, and are called to respond to this good news by the gift of their selves. They then celebrate the wholeness of life by participating in a family meal. This ritual is the Christian eschatological ritual, for it recalls the past, celebrates the present, and anticipates the future.

## Life After Death

So far we have studied eschatological myths in which saviors overcome death, and glanced at eschatological rituals in which the saviors' devotees may share in the new life. Now we examine eschatological myths that describe the abode of the new life after death.

The heaven in both the Egyptian and Greek myths was temporary, consistent with their principle of the transmigration of souls. Heaven was more or less a stage or step that the soul had to pass through in order to be gradually purified before going on to higher stages of existence and eventual reunion with the spirit-world.

In the Egyptian myths, there are conflicting descriptions of what awaits the individuals after death. The spirits of the dead were pictured as living in the Duat, that is, in caverns or chambers representing the twelve hours of the night. Here, helpless, they remained in complete darkness except for the one hour the sun spent with them in its nightly journey. At that hour, the sun god Ra brought light, food, air, and knowledge. Each night they awaited Ra to welcome him with joy and wailed again when he passed on. As for the initiates of the Osirian mysteries, those who were mummified were armed with spells and talismans to escape the dangers they confronted after death. Those who passed the judgment when their hearts were weighed against the feather of truth were led by Horus to the throne of Osiris in whose company they associated with their friends, ate of the finest fowl, and enjoyed incense. The spirits could roam about freely as long as their mummified bodies remained intact and they were sustained by regular funereal offerings. Later, the belief developed that an incorruptible body would germinate from the earthly body even if it were not mummified.

In Greek myths, the afterlife was transferred to the heavens, the upper regions of the sky. Instructed in the proper passwords, the initiates could elude the planetary demons of the middle space between earth and heavens, and soar to the superior heavens. There they lived in bliss with the gods and fellow-initiates.

Other myths spoke of a paradisal good place, a fragment of this world that remained inviolate. Out over the Atlantic Ocean behind a barrier of water, at the world's end, lay the Isles of the Blessed and the Elysian Fields. According to Homer, living was easy there. No snow fell, no strong winds blew, and there was never any rain. Occasionally referred to as the Garden of the Hesperides, in which a tree bore golden apples of immortality, or the Land of the Hyperboreans, where the inhabitants spent their time banqueting and dancing in the sunshine, this realm was only for a chosen few. The immortals there were beautiful and vigorous, but also shallow and frivolous, for their passions were only minimally engaged. As for ordinary persons after death, they were dismissed as shades, with no personal immortality.

As a place of joy and peace, the afterlife is the counter-image of the hells we saw in the last chapter. Descriptions of the afterlife as the definitive eschatological destination are a valuable mythical tool. They help people discover their destiny, interpret their present, and provide a vision of the future that operates as a self-fulfilling prophecy.

The myths tell of a definite place, another world somehow part of the universe. It is a blessed and happy place where there is a good climate, no sickness or sorrow, and no hard work. Persons live in familiarity with the gods, delighting in divine companionship. The myths envision this other world as a place similar to what they know, but with specific improvements, especially a lack of the usual ills. There is comfort, safety, and happiness for the dead loved ones, plenty to eat, time to dance, sing, and glorify the gods. For those from cold climates, heaven is light and warm; for those from parched lands, it contains flowery oases, shade, and fountains. Hunting peoples seek a Happy Hunting Ground; farming peoples imagine that the earth will produce abundantly and spontaneously from its fertile soil. Viking warriors seek a feast in the heroes' halls of Valhalla after dying bravely in battle; the Jews hope for a family reunion in Abraham's bosom. Muslims look forward to a graded series of paradises as depicted in the *Qur'an,* all filled with sensual delights suited to male Arab tastes. Those who have lived in total submission (Islam) to Allah live in a sort of splendid oasis, wearing silken robes, lying on couches, with unlimited fruit, wine, and harems.

This type of heaven is also depicted in Eastern religion, in particular in the Mahayana Buddhism that developed in medieval China. In keeping with the Hindu–Buddhist view of the cyclic nature of the universe and the principle of karmic reincarnation, this heaven is temporary, similar to those in Egypt and Greece. Some dead spirits go to K'un lun Mountain far away from their land at the center of the earth. Here, there is an endless series of amusements and banquets and magnificent gardens in which grows the Peach Tree of Immortality.

Others who call on the Amitabha Buddha at the hour of death have their souls cleansed before they are allowed to mingle with the inhabitants of the Land of Extreme Felicity in the West. Here, where they are separated from humans by an infinity of worlds, there are trees whose branches are formed of precious stones, lakes flowering with lotuses, and river banks paved with precious stones. Everything they hear — the delightful songs of birds, the music of the wind in the trees — reminds them of the three refuges: the Buddha, the Law, and the Community. These celestial realms are mere consolation prizes, appealing to those who are not ready for Nirvana, which is the total release from the bondage of personality or from the illusion of an individual self.

Of the many Christian depictions of the new afterlife two have been very influential over the centuries in providing images of heaven and eternal life. These are the apocalyptic vision elaborated especially in the final book of the Christian Scriptures, the Book of Revelation, and the medieval version elaborated in the Paradiso, the final portion of Dante's *The Divine Comedy*.

Apocalyptic myths are a type of eschatological myth related to dualism in their radical disjunction between good and evil, light and dark, angels and demons. They are popular in times of persecution, using symbolic language to comfort believers and encourage them to transcend their present unhappy situation. Apocalyptic (uncovering or revealing) myths suggest that God, the Absolute Reality, has revealed the secrets of the imminent tragic end of the world to his believers. Since continued life is of no importance, they should be able to remain faithful even in their difficult situation and link themselves to a new world that exists apart from their suffering. By joining with the forces of good in the coming great struggle with evil, they will be among the blessed who survive in the afterlife.

The Book of Revelation uses apocalyptic language to envision a new age ushered in by a cosmic cataclysm, which is the culmination of the divine plan. It is steeped in symbolic imagery: plagues, the darkening of the sun and moon, the shaking of the powers of heaven, monsters of chaos, the wrathful destruction of the evil beast. The end of the present world will be heralded by wars, earthquakes, famines, death. Fearful terrors will be set loose upon the world. Jesus, the victorious martyr and slain Lamb, who in his resurrection has triumphed over death, is the warrior who will overcome the antichrist in the final battle. Those who forsake Christianity will be tortured with fire and brimstone, and the smoke of their torment will ascend forever and ever.

Those who have shared in the victory over the beast shall live in a new heaven and a new earth, depicted as the New Jerusalem descending out of heaven from God. This holy city will have the radiance of a priceless jewel. Its streets will be paved with pure gold, like translucent glass; its foundation walls will be adorned with jewels of every kind. The city will not require either sun or moon to illuminate it because God's glory is its light, and the Lamb is its lamp. The river of the water of life will flow from the thrones of God and the Lamb, down the city streets, a free gift to the thirsty. On either side of this flowing water will stand the tree of life, which will produce twelve crops a year, a different one for each month. The victorious faithful will share in the wedding supper of the Lamb. They shall be the bride, clothed in the shining linen garment of their righteous deeds. In this new Jerusalem, God will dwell with humans, and they shall be his people. God will wipe away every tear from their eyes, and death shall be no more, neither will there be mourning nor crying nor pain anymore, for the old order has passed away (Revelation 21).

Dante's masterpiece, *The Divine Comedy*, elaborates another version of the afterlife that still influences many Christians' vision of heaven. The symbolism is so rich that it has sparked many different allegorical, moral, and spiritual interpretations since he wrote it in A.D. 1300. He sets his vision of the other world in the autobiographical context of a journey through the circles of hell, up the mountain of purgatory, and through the spheres of the heavens until the vision of God is attained in paradise.

In the midst of his life, Dante awakens to find himself lost in a dark wood, where the right road is wholly lost and gone.

How is he going to journey through life in such a way as to enter into paradise? Climbing a desert slope to get his bearings, he finds that beasts block his way and he has to retreat to the plain. Virgil, the Roman poet, offers to show him the way.

The way to paradise is not direct, but has to detour through hell and purgatory. The way down is the only way up. The Inferno — hell — is a vast abyss in the center of the earth, divided into nine elaborately structured circles arranged as a downward-pointing cone through which he makes his descent. The circles are a comprehensive museum of human aberrations, containing those who have separated themselves from others in some perversion of love. Having abandoned all hope, they scream in isolation. Purgatory contains nine terraces, gradually ascending a high mountain. There the souls are gradually being cleansed and healed from the seven deadly sins. To pass through purgatory, Dante has to climb the mountain. At first, the steps up the winding path are very wearisome, but they become less tiring as he ascends.

In Eden, which is the earthly paradise at the top of Mount Purgatory, Virgil leaves Dante, allowing him to wander at will until he finds his beloved, Beatrice. Beatrice ("Bearer of Happiness") agrees to accompany him through the heavens of paradise only after he has imbibed of the waters of forgetfulness to take away all memories of his wrongdoings. The heavens in paradise are constituted according to the Ptolemaic system. They include the moon, sun, known planets, fixed stars, a ninth heaven where Dante first glimpses the divine essence and listens to the chorus of angels, and finally, the tenth heaven, the Empyrean. To enter these regions of eternal blessedness, Dante is cross-examined by Peter on the meaning of the three virtues of faith, hope, and charity. As they move from one heaven to the next, Beatrice introduces him to martyrs, warriors, crusaders, founders of religious orders — the entire church militant and church triumphant.

At last, Dante is ready for the Empyrean at the final summit of paradise. How can he describe this tenth heaven, this "foretaste of the great supper of the Blessed Lamb?" How can he share the happiness that awaits the Christian at the end of life? The images he uses — light, the sea, a white rose, and the center — recall visions from the Book of Revelation. They have remained with Christians over the centuries and influenced their representations of the afterlife.

Light of ever-increasing intensity enshrouds the blessed in their bodily form as Dante moves from heaven to heaven. The brightness of the garment of light is proportionate to the fervency of love in each one. In the lower circles of heaven, this light is reflected as through a mirror. Dante is dazzled by it to the verge of blindness, since it is all the brighter in contrast to the dark air he has traversed. As he nears the Empyrean, the light appears in the form of a river which issues spárks that drop on all sides into blossoms, like rubies set in gold. The light in the Empyrean is so keen and so intense that it is impossible for him to turn away from it.

The sea that threatened to swallow Dante at the beginning of his journey has also undergone a transformation. The sea is the whole of creation, the sea of creatures who are impelled by love, as so many ships or rivers destined to different ports or goals. The sea is both the beginning and the end. Just as all waters come from the sea by evaporation and return to the sea by many rivers that flow into it, so all creatures return to God as their proper resting place. The sea instills a deep peace of the spirit at the still point of the Empyrean, a peace that surpasses passion, tension, and conflict: "And his will is our peace. It is the sea to which all moves."

A white rose stands at the center of the sea of light, with its petals unfolding all around. In this ultimate vision, the blessed appear to be part of this white rose, reflected in the calm sea, looking up at God. Ultimate unity with God is revealed in the rose, the flower of countless leaves. Beatrice draws him into the yellow of this eternal rose. "Behold," she says, "how great the assembly of the white robes. See our city, how wide its circuit. How vast is the spread of this rose in its outermost leaves." As petals of the rose, the blessed are no longer flames, or lights, or jewels, but clearly seen in their human forms, a token antic- ipation of resurrection of the body. Their individual identity remains and finds its wholeness in relation to the rose. They dwell in the bliss of the rose. There is movement to the center, from the many to the one, and back from the one to the many. In the rose the complex interdependency of all things is manifested, the whole of creation is woven together. Gazing on the rose garden, Dante is prepared for his final rapturous vision of God.

At the center of his vision is a single point. Here, Dante sees the whole universe "bound with love into a single volume."

Gazing at this still point, he realizes that the words of Beatrice, who has now left him, take on meaning: "The nature of the universe that holds the center quiet and moves all the rest around it begins here as from its starting point. On that point the heavens and all nature are dependent." Dante momentarily experiences the truth that nature, humanity, and God are as one. For an instant he is aware of the love which is the center, the joy, of the universe. His will and desire are turned by love: "Instinct and intellect balanced equally; as in a wheel whose motion nothing jars; by the love that moves the sun and the other stars."

## Heaven and Eternal Life

The central purpose of eschatological myths has never been to encourage people to hold onto images of heaven or eternal life for their own sake. These symbolic images of space and time were never meant to be taken literally, as genuine pictures of some ultimate future. Their function is rather to bring peace and tranquility, to encourage people to take the present seriously, to integrate inevitable death into a meaningful life, to act out of a conviction of hope both for their selves and for the world.

Heaven and eternal life will not feature disembodied souls floating through the skies, up there, over there, outside, above, or beyond this world. The future will not consist merely of the resuscitation of decomposed bodies which will then be the instrument of the souls' enjoyment of perpetual bliss. The final golden age will not be a return to the beginning as if nothing had changed, with a restoration of innocence and peaceful simplicity. Time will not be everlasting, continuing in a purely linear fashion, the endless prolongation of this life's happier moments. There will not be a total rift between this world and heaven and eternal life, as if this life had no connection with what is to come.

This does not mean, however, that myths of heaven and eternal life are stories lacking any clear rational support; rather, they are attempts to deal with the limits of human hope. Still, because so many have taken the elaborate details in the myths literally, this positive function is all but forgotten. Apocalyptic myths are particularly vulnerable here. Throughout the centuries, groups have calculated in vain the exact date of the impending end and have identified the beast with every tyrant in history. They are convinced that the general destruction of the world implies they can have minimal involvement in their history and that their lives will have no impact on their afterlife. The result is that many people dismiss myths of the afterlife as childish illusions, wishful projections, or irresponsible refusals to face human life in all its dark moments. They consider myths of the future to be of the same ilk as fortune-telling, tea-leaf reading, lunatic visions, astrological horoscopes, and science fiction.

How can the hope underlying eschatological myths be more properly emphasized? The Egyptian and Greek myths are not much help. True, they do bring the afterlife into the present in their ritual celebration of the mysteries. Yet they ultimately project fatalism. Transmigration and immortality of the soul detract from the importance of human involvement here and now. The savior roles of Isis–Osiris and Demeter–Persephone are ultimately limited.

Medieval myths are also deficient. Pure Land Buddhism's Land of Felicity in the West completely undermines the doctrine of timeless and spaceless Nirvana, and Dante's Paradise is ultimately a prolongation of earthly life in a physical place out in space. These versions of the afterlife are more a revealing index of their own societal values and changing interests than authentic extensions of the simple truths expounded by Gotama and Jesus. In the final analysis, the most direct and profound expressions of the hope that undergirds the eschatological myths are in the discourses that the saviors Gotama and Jesus address to their followers.

After a public ministry of some forty-five years, Gotama ate some bad meat, became ill, and eventually died. In his farewell discourse to his followers, he made the savior's vow — that the least of those who set out on the path to release would at last prevail and achieve Nirvana. After his body lay in state for several days, it ignited spontaneously on a magnificent funeral pyre. His body was entirely consumed, leaving only what seemed to be a heap of pearls. Thus during his final human life, Gotama achieved his apotheosis: He shattered for himself the bounds of the last threshold of illusion. He was the Buddha, the Awakened and Enlightened One.

What was the Nirvana he promised? Gotama was reluctant to talk about it and warned against trying to ascertain its meaning by collecting disconnected quotations. His followers should not desire to study what Nirvana is, but to experience it. A blossoming flower in spring is Nirvana; a falling leaf in autumn is Nirvana. Having achieved Nirvana is like a deer living in a forest who might lie down in a heap of snares but is not caught in it. It is like a deer roaming the forest slopes who walks confidently, stands confidently, sleeps confidently. Nirvana is not personal happiness, but total release from the bondage of personality. Nirvana is not life in some celestial realm; this is only a consolation prize, and temporary. Nirvana occurs only after the last death, with no further reincarnations. Yet paradoxically — and this is the very heart of his teaching in the Four Noble Truths — Nirvana is attainable in this life, at this moment, in every aspect of life.

Nirvana means "blown out" or "extinguished." This is not to be understood purely and wholly negatively, however, as pure and simple nothingness. Nirvana is the extinction of the independent self and of the burden of existence. It refers to a changed state of mind, the state of "no mind," the "snuffing out" of the grasping or desire for individual existence. It is non-attachment to the small self and the removal of the self from the process of perception so that subject becomes one with object. Nirvana is the realization of deep identity with Absolute Reality, the dissolution of a state of alienation by a return to unity with the One.

In his parables, Jesus does not use the metaphors of mystical body or the apocalyptic city of the heavenly Jerusalem. In plain and direct language he proclaims the kingdom of heaven (the "reign of God") as a messianic banquet, a wedding feast, a harvest. He stresses the corporate nature of salvation, where people let go of the small self and "become as little children." In his farewell discourse in John's Gospel, when the time has come to enter into his glory (another symbol for heaven and eternal life), his parting message is one of peace, such as the world cannot give. Wanting to set their troubled hearts at rest, he tells his apostles he is leaving to prepare a place for them in the many dwelling places of his Father's house. About to return to the One, to his unity with the Absolute Reality, he prays that they might all be one, as he and the Father are one.

In Jesus' message, death is not destruction; life is changed, not ended. There is a new life in a new world, beyond space and time, something definitively new, personal, and interdependent. He wants his followers to take the present seriously as well as aspire for the future. Human life can never be regarded as trivial. Heaven and eternal life are a homecoming, the successful completion of a pilgrimage or an ordeal. Belief in the afterlife does not sedate human life nor lead to immobility. It does not deny the bitterness of the genuinely tragic, much less disguise or sugarcoat it. The afterlife is peace — the peace that comes after a struggle, a peace that is present all the time once it has been discovered. It is an experience that can continually be recaptured, here and now, and never go stale. The Christian afterlife is not an ending or a perishing, but a consummation. The individual person finds the larger self by losing the small self in the reality of God. In the reunion with God, the Absolute Reality, the finite self is transformed by divine strength, power, and love.

The meeting point of the two saviors, Gotama and Jesus, is the common hope they hold out for all humans. In both there is the promise of peace and tranquility, of refreshment and release from tension through return to the One, or reunion with Absolute Reality. There is no question of entry into some place or time after death. Heaven is not at the far edges of space, and eternal life indicates a quality of life, not the quantitative continuation of one unending event after another.

Indeed, the heart of their message is that it is possible to experience and realize the kingdom of God or Nirvana here and now, at each moment of letting go. Not only during the graced moments of rituals can persons share the reunion with the One and be encompassed by the fullness of life, but at each moment, even in the midst of this world marked by death.

The religious journey to the afterlife is not a pilgrimage to a place or to the future. Because the "end" is not a specific place or time, all symbolization is ultimately deficient. Yet our very humanity demands that we continue to picture it. With this in mind, we might perhaps best represent the end in the context of the spiralling religious self as the encircled point.

The goal of all our religious striving is the still point at the center of the spiral, where the beginning and end are one. Jesus' "kingdom of God within" and Gotama's "Jewel at the center of the Lotus" are the point at the center, embracing what embraces it. The small self that "con-centrates" on the center and recognizes the wholeness that comes through reunion with this center is no longer "off-center." The center of the spiral is tantalizingly close, yet hard to find, for it is beyond the opposition of inside and outside, of spiritual and material. To experience the center is to experience the point common to all, and thus to see and feel the unity and wholeness of the universe despite its diversity and tensions. In the center, senses and psyche, reason and faith, are all integrated. All polarities are transcended and all opposites reconciled in return to the center. In comparison, everything else is trivial.

## Final Salvation

Myths of saviors express a message of hope: Experiences of the final human destiny can be present at any moment of our lives. Apart from ritual anticipations, what are the manifestations of this salvation? Where can this experience of universal peace, infinite love, and overflowing joy be found in our day-to-day living?

Salvation is the freedom from fear of death and the liberation to enjoy this life. We accept the pleasures that come along, aware that our merely human ideals (life, liberty, pursuit of happiness) are only shadows of wholeness. With no longer anything to lose, we are not afraid to take risks, and we can love life before death. Recognizing and consenting to our mortality — not having world enough or time — we are spurred to achievement. In the hope of moving toward fulfillment, we neither flee the world nor preoccupy ourselves with "saving the soul." There is no fatalistic resignation in face of basic human anxieties, no despair nor cynicism in the face of evil.

Salvation is the freedom from the obsession of striving for some utopia or perfect harmonious social order on earth. We don't have to rely solely on human effort or ingenuity, on constant advances in technology and science to bring us satisfaction. We are not compelled to try to predict the future by statistical extrapolation or computer prognosis, nor despair in the face of occasional technological or scientific breakdowns. Traditions and authorities are provisional, and precepts and prohibitions are relative, ultimately giving way to the perfect freedom beyond law and morality, anchored in Absolute Reality.

Salvation is made present when persons do what the saviors
are doing, whether bringing others life (as did Isis and Demeter)
or serving them with compassion (as did Jesus and Gotama).
The resurrection and apotheosis of the saviors is the initial
impetus to transform the world, working to mend broken relationships and to acknowledge forgiveness. The saviors extend
hope for the collective future of all humans, and call for corporate rather than individual salvation. Salvation is realized in
taking up the cause of life wherever it is injured, desecrated,
destroyed, and in identifying with the weak, the sick, the poor,
and the underprivileged. Salvation is manifested in attesting in
very practical ways to the new quality of life that has broken
the universal rule of death, perhaps by advocating housing for
the elderly, voicing opposition to the arms race, finding alternatives to prisons, supporting the poor in their struggles to
raise their families. The saviors' call to compassion is a call
to personal involvement, not merely shuffling along with the
crowd.

Salvation is the passion for life in all its fullness, the awareness that there is some continuity between our history and our
eschatological end. It is the life-giving transformation and fulfillment of humanity in all its dimensions — individual and social,
spiritual and corporal. In vigilant and hopeful expectation, we
are able to live our lives to the hilt here and now, to romp with joy
through the whole length and breadth of the human adventure.
When that happens, the life that had seemed momentary is found
to be momentous, and the present that seems to be no time at
all is found to be eternal.

# Review Questions

1. What is an eschatological myth?

2. What was the purpose of Egyptian mummification? Why
   do you think the process was eventually discarded?

3. Why are Isis and Demeter rightly called saviors?

4. What events constitute the Christian Paschal Mystery?

5. What are the eschatological dimensions of the Christian ritual of the Eucharist?

6. What are the dangers of taking apocalyptic myths literally?

7. Explain the mythical significance of the first and last lines of Dante's *Comedy:* "In the middle of the way of life/I woke to find myself in a dark wood/where the right road was wholly lost and gone . . . . Instinct and intellect balanced equally/as in a wheel whose motion nothing jars/by the love that moves the sun and the other stars."

8. Explain Dante's images of heaven and eternal life.

9. What is the major function of images of heaven and eternal life?

10. What is the meeting point of the teaching of Buddha and Jesus regarding the nature of the afterlife?

# Discussion Starters

1. "A map of the world that does not include Utopia is not even worth looking at." (Lewis Mumford)

2. "Every man, every woman, carries in heart and mind the image of the ideal place, the right place, the one true home, known or unknown, actual or visionary." How would you describe your ideal home? In what kind of community would it be set?

3. "There is an inmost center in us where Truth abides in fullness." (Mohandas Gandhi)

4. "At the still point of the turning world . . . . Where past and future are gathered. Neither movement from nor towards, neither ascent nor decline. Except for the point, the still point, there would be no dance, and there is only the dance." (T.S. Eliot) What is the still point?

5. "We always imagine eternity as something beyond our conception, something vast. Why must it be vast? Instead of

all that, what if it is one little room, like a bathhouse in the country, black and grimy and spiders in every corner, and that's all eternity is?'' (Dostoevsky)

6. "Salvation's much too big a word for me. I don't aim so high. I'm concerned with man's health; and for me his health comes first." (Albert Camus)

7. "Wonder why we try so hard/wonder why we try at all/you wonder why the world is turning around/when in the end it won't matter at all." (Moody Blues)

8. "If the world is a mystery to be savored, and used responsibly but never explained, then time is the filter through which humans perceive the mystery of being, and now is a strange gift that will never come again." (Sam Keen)

9. "If it be granted that we say Yes to a single moment, then in so doing we have said Yes not only to ourselves, but to all existence." (Nietzsche)

10. "Really it makes no difference whether you think the end of the world will come in a thousand years or five million years, whether you think time will have an end or that the world is eternal; there is still a need to speak humanly of a life's importance in relation to it — a need in the moment of existence to belong, to be related to a beginning and to an end. People die only because they cannot join the beginning and the end."

# EPILOGUE

Developing our full human selves is the task of a lifetime. The continuous attempt to recognize and release our human potential is the best condition for keeping our lives from becoming stale and aimless. To reach human maturity and wholeness, we must consent to growth and action in our changing perceptions of ourselves. Even more crucial, however, we must develop our religious dimension, since humans are essentially oriented to mystery. Thus the study of religion, insofar as it aids our understanding of our religious dimension, is an important and, indeed, indispensable element for our well-being.

The study of religion is a legitimate intellectual inquiry, as important as the development of moral and ethical discrimination and the attainment of professional and technical skills. Indeed, religious truths are not only a portion of our self-awareness, but the very condition of that awareness. Myths, which help constitute the foundation of human cultures, point to that sense of mystery that is conveyed only in religion. Myths bring genuine religious questions to the surface, helping us to get in touch with life's meaning and purpose. They are stories from religious traditions that help us focus on our own lives, constantly referring us to the central symbols of the full life in the context of Absolute Reality.

Myths are stories that create a world for persons to inhabit and be comfortable with. They affect both communal and individual life patterns. As communal literature, they make it possible for entire cultures to live amid cosmic and sociological tensions and pressures. Through their archetypes, they communicate what is true for all persons everywhere. At the same time, they help individuals comprehend their human purposes and their human limitations. Opening up alternative dimensions of being fully human, they provide identity to individuals lost in the vastness of the universe and bring hope to those overcome by the meaninglessness of their own existence.

Myths have a life-affirming quality. They do not confine or restrict human behavior, nor limit human imagination, nor hinder human adventuring into new realms or exploring new concepts. They emphasize individual self-acceptance, give us a basis of judgment, and free us from worrying about what others think we should be.

The interrelationship of myths and self-awareness is dynamic: being open to one encourages openness to the other. Self-awareness becomes more effective the more we fully appreciate the mythic dimension of our lives, both by recognizing and becoming conscious of archetypal themes, and by consenting to and appropriating these themes in our lives. Incorporating the exemplary patterns of the mythic gods, heroes, and saviors in our lives, we activate both the manifest and latent possibilities of wholeness in ourselves. We carry on in our familiar worlds with a clearer vision of the human dignity and divine possibilities inherent in each of us. Myths play an important role as we actively grow from the small self to the full religious self.

The stories of gods, heroes, and saviors in myths vibrate with life. They are a relief from the dry and abstract argumentation sometimes found in theology and religious philosophy. Whereas theological and religious speculation sometimes make the doctrines of different religions appear to be contradictory, the proper study and appreciation of myths tends toward a synthesis, toward some kind of ultimate unity of all religions. The proper study of myths presupposes, of course, that we avoid many dangers, not only of insufficiency in scope, unity, or depth, but also of false contrasts between them.

The responsible study of myths also requires that we clearly respect the fundamental differences in the religious traditions while going deeply into mutually illuminating similarities. Still, the truths expressed in the religious myths are so powerful that they illuminate each other rather than precipitate mutual annihilation. Penetrating into the depths of other religions ultimately gives a fresh and specific cogency to our own traditions and makes them lively in thought, devotion, and action.

The myths of gods, heroes, and saviors all form parts of a single commentary on the religious self: We have met them, and they are us. As we become conscious of and consent to them at the core of our selves, they help us realize, "make real," and anticipate our ultimate return to the One, to Absolute Reality. They lead us to wholeness by revealing universal themes within particular situations.

Myths of the *gods* help us come to terms with mystery and give us the impulse to rediscover the unity of being. They underscore our roles as co-creators, with the responsibility of stewardship of the cosmos. They provide us with a holistic vision that enables us to put order in chaos, to find a place for anarchy and license.

Myths of the *heroes* spell out the exemplary patterns that give glamor to our ordinary lives. In their confrontation with evil monsters, heroes dare us to leave the security of the commonplace and entertain the challenge of unusual surprises. Their quest helps us live with the paradoxes of life, prove the self in the prime of life, and bring a boon to the others in our community. Insofar as their quest is gentle, they show us the importance of human relationships and help us confront the psychic energies in the depths of our unconscious.

Myths of the *saviors* bridge the mysterious and the lucid, the familiar and the strange. They enable us to struggle with evil, admit the flaws in our selves, and bring healing to others. They prepare us for overcoming death by revealing what lies beyond death and providing the model of letting go of the small self.

Seeking to find the whole self is a journey, a spiralling pilgrimage from error to truth, from darkness to life, from alienation to communion. This journey cannot be plotted steadily along a rising curve if it is to allow for true freedom of response. Trying to find a particular way that suits our individual personality, we learn very quickly that there are bound to be mistakes, for there are always risks involved, always the element of the unknown. Yet the risks must be taken, the mistakes endured, and the unknown acknowledged if we are not to become rigidified, truncated, one-dimensional selves. Uncritical acceptance of whatever life brings, refusal to push with determination in any direction, or the denial of hidden parts of the self would all lead to imbalance and an unfinished personality. The personal crises that inevitably accompany the maturation processes become more manageable as we are conscious of and consent to the archetypal mythic figures.

Myths help us experiment with the variety of persons we can be by showing us the whole gamut of human experience. There is not just one way, one truth, or one life, but many routes to wholeness and personal fulfillment. By drawing us out of our small selves, myths help us recognize and be at home with what is "other" or "different." Ranging from the bottom of hell to the heights of paradise, they help us experience peace in war, life in death, light in darkness, joy in suffering, resurrection in the cross. This is the valuable process of overcoming polarities, the experience of ultimate wholeness, not in some future life but here and now. It is living at the still point where everything matters. Myths help us exist without lurking in insecurity, without always being worried about evaluations, or judgments, or rewards and punishments. They enable us to rejoice here and now in our being and our becoming.

Myths energize the spiralling circles of self-awareness. They either expand the self to enclose the wholeness of the universe, or they expend the self to vibrate with the still point at the center. They help us become progressively more joyful as we are inspired to a life that is both higher and deeper, a life of growing awareness of the presence-yet-absence of the divine. They help us successfully traverse the confusing terrain of our lives as we constantly move back and forth in experiencing the polarities, recognize new possibilities, and decide to emphasize those that bear most personal promise. Myths help the process of wholeness, of dying and rising where the small self is gradually replaced by the sophisticated self engrossed in religion's mysteries.

Myths help us achieve that wholeness which is the integration of all aspects of our being and the union with Absolute Reality. Wholeness is the awareness of the Oneness of the gods, heroes, and saviors who are both inside and outside of us. Better, wholeness is the awareness that there is no longer any inside or outside. Once this wholeness is achieved, it seeks to find expression in our daily lives. Its manifestations are evident in many ways or paths of religion. Wholeness may follow the middle way between asceticism and luxury, or the way of the cross and resurrection. It can be discerned in the way of rhythm and orderly nature, or the way of the gentle quest. It might follow the way of knowledge, effecting insight into Absolute Reality as the transcendent wisdom that encompasses all, or the way of meditation and deliberate withdrawal from all ordinary conscious life that keeps one from experiencing affinity with Absolute Reality.

Throughout this book I have continually alluded to two particularly powerful ways of religious wholeness. One is the way of ritual, of participation in those ceremonial actions that represent the experience of the superabundance of reality and the great moments of the exemplary pattern. The other is the way of compassion, an ethic of healing and forgiveness, of service and charity at all levels, focused upon bringing both individual and social conduct into conformity with Absolute Reality as cosmic righteousness.

There are many expressions of religious wholeness, none of them at odds with the others. They all make present the Absolute Reality that transcends this world, yet manifests itself in this world, thereby sanctifying the world and making it real. The gods, heroes, and saviors in myths all point to this Absolute Reality within us. Recognizing and consenting to their message, we find that all things are part of each other, balanced in harmony. That's the challenge and the legacy of myths. More than that, it is the source of the inexhaustible enthusiasm and incredible excitement of being alive.

# BIBLIOGRAPHY ———————————————

In addition to the books mentioned for each chapter in the following pages, I list here those sources that I used more extensively in writing this book.

Alexander, Hartley Burr. *The World's Rim.* Lincoln, Nebraska: University of Nebraska Press, 1967. Insight into the life and mind of North American Indians as expressed through the myths and rituals of the human life-cycle.

Burland, Cottie. *Myths of Life and Death.* New York: Crown, 1974. Traces myths through the triple paths of human life, seasons of the year, and cosmic directions.

*Encyclopedia of World Mythology.* New York: Galahad Books, 1975. Myths of the world, presented both by cultures and mythic themes.

Gray, Louis Herbert, ed. *Mythology of All Races.* New York: Cooper Square Publishers, 1964. Comprehensive collection of myths and commentary by competent scholars from all quarters of the earth and all ages. 13 volumes.

Lowry, Shirley Park. *Familiar Mysteries: The Truth in Myth.* New York: Oxford University Press, 1982. Recurring patterns and symbols in world myths. Strong Campbell influence.

*New Larousse Encyclopedia of Mythology.* New York: Hamlyn Publishing Group, 1974. Reference work. Myths of the entire world presented by cultures.

*Parabola.* A periodical published quarterly by the Society for the Study of Myth and Tradition.

Stanford, Barbara. *Myths and Modern Man.* New York: Simon & Schuster, Washington Square Press, 1972. Thematic groupings of myths of creation, perfection and death.

1    MYTH AND SELF-AWARENESS

Bausch, William J. *Storytelling: Imagination and Faith.* Mystic, Conn.: Twenty-Third Publications, 1984. The power of stories to capture and pass on from one generation to the next the wisdom, imagination, and faith of a people.

Keen, Sam. *The Passionate Life: Stages of Loving.* New York: Harper & Row, 1983. Self-awareness in developing the capacity to love.

Robertson, James O. *American Myth, American Reality.* New York: Hill & Wang, 1980. The truths behind the American myths.

Tilley, Terrence W. *Story Theology.* Wilmington, Del.: Michael Glazier, 1985. The dancing of metaphor, the learning of stories, and the living of truth.

Wiggins, James, ed. *Religion as Story*. New York: Harper & Row, 1975. Narratives as entry into the human condition.

2    MYTH AND RELIGION

Campbell, Joseph. *Myths to Live By*. New York: Bantam Books, Viking Press, 1972. The vital link of humans to their myths and the way in which myths can extend human potential.

Clift, Wallace. *Jung and Christianity*. New York: Crossroad, 1982. Commentaries on the stages of life and the functions of myth.

Eliade, Mircea. *Myth and Reality*. New York: Harper & Row, 1975. Representative work on the structures of myth and what they reveal.

Jung, C. G., ed. *Man and His Symbols*. Garden City, N.Y.: Doubleday, 1964. The process of individuation in the language of symbols and archetypes.

Sexson, Michael W. "Myth: The Way We Were or The Way We Are?" in T. William Hall, ed. *Introduction to the Study of Religion*. New York: Harper & Row, 1978. The arguments for and against the validity of myths.

Watts, Alan. *The Two Hands of God*. New York: Collier, Macmillan, 1963. Myths of polarity which reveal the mystical unity that binds opposite forces together.

3    CREATION

Bolen, Jean Shinoda. *Goddesses in Every Woman*. New York: Harper & Row, 1984. Finding the Greek goddesses in everyday life.

Downing, Christine. *The Goddess: Mythological Images of the Feminine*. New York: Crossroad, 1981. Greek myths that concretize and particularize what is authentically feminine.

Larue, Gerald. *Ancient Myths and Modern Man*. Englewood Cliffs, N.J.: Prentice-Hall, 1975. Cosmological and eschatological myths of the ancient Near East.

O'Brien, Joan and Wilfred Major. *In the Beginning: Creation Myths From Ancient Mesopotamia, Israel, and Greece*. Chico, Cal.: Scholars Press, 1982. The capacity of creation myths to reveal distinctive traits of specific cultures.

Van Over, Raymond, ed. *Sun Songs: Creation Myths from Around the World*. New York: Mentor Book, New American Library, 1980. Basic themes of creation myths; discussion of various theories and interpretations of myth.

4    THE SEPARATION

Fox, Matthew. *Original Blessing: A Primer in Creation Spirituality*. Santa Fe, N.M.: Bear & Company, 1983. Away from the fall/redemption theology toward a holistic approach.

Howes, Elizabeth B. and Sheila Moon. *Man the Choicemaker*. Philadelphia: Westminster Press, 1973. Jungian interpretation of the human condition, especially in the context of the Garden of Eden.

Kenik, Helen. "Toward a Biblical Basis for Creation Theology" in Matthew Fox, ed. *Western Spirituality: Historical Roots, Ecumenical Routes*. Notre Dame, Ind.: Claretian Press, 1979. Creation-centered spirituality: the essence of human dignity and relationships.

L'Heureux, Conrad. *In and Out of Paradise.* Ramsey, N.J.: Paulist Press, 1983. Creation themes with special emphasis on the meaning of the Adam and Eve story.

Ricoeur, Paul. *The Symbolism of Evil.* New York: Harper & Row, 1958. Myths of the beginning and the end: the structure of the Adamic myth and the eschatological vision of history.

Sproul, Barbara. *Primal Myths: Creating the World.* New York: Harper & Row, 1979. Wide-ranging collection of world cosmologies. A good source book for myths of separation.

Vawter, Bruce. *On Genesis: A New Reading.* Garden City, N.Y.: Doubleday, 1977. Survey of recent scholarly interest in the Jewish myths.

## 5   Tricksters

Cox, Harvey. *Feast of Fools: A Theological Essay on Festivity and Fantasy.* Cambridge: Harvard University Press, 1969. Clowns catching a glimpse of another world impinging on this one, upsetting its rules and practices.

Gill, Sam. *Native American Religions.* Belmont, Cal.: Wadsworth Press, 1982. Tricksters and clowns and their functions in religious ceremonials.

Hultkrantz, Ake. *The Religions of the American Indians.* Berkeley, Cal.: University of California Press, 1979. The evolution from the culture hero to the trickster in the context of Indian cosmogonic myths.

Hyers, Conrad. *The Comic Vision and the Christian Faith.* New York: Pilgrim Press, 1981. Tricksters and clowns and the arbitrariness of life.

MacGlashen, Alan. *Savage and Beautiful Country.* Boston: Houghton Mifflin, 1967. Jungian treatment of tricksters, clowns, and carnivals with examples drawn from the British tradition.

## 6   The Hero's Childhood

Brown, Raymond. *The Birth of the Messiah.* Exhaustive commentary and summary of recent scholarship on the infancy narratives of Matthew and Luke.

Campbell, Joseph. *The Hero With a Thousand Faces.* Princeton, N.J.: Princeton University Press, 1968. The monomyth elaborated. Adventures and transformations of the hero.

Coomaraswamy, Ananda. *Buddha and the Gospel of Buddhism.* New York: Harper & Row, 1964. Consideration of the Buddhist myths and systems in relation to Hindu and Christian mysticism.

Leeming, David. *Mythology: The Voyage of the Hero.* New York: J. B. Lippincott Co., 1973. Anthology from world mythologies. Coincides with the various stages of the monomyth of Campbell.

Rank, Otto. *The Myth of the Birth of the Hero and Other Writings.* New York: Vintage Books, 1959. Freudian approach to the major themes in the hero's birth.

## 7   The Vision Quest

Cunningham, Lawrence S. *The Catholic Heritage.* New York: Crossroad, 1983. Contains a survey of pilgrimages throughout religious history.

Dunne, John S. *The Way of All the Earth.* New York: Macmillan, 1972. The spiritual adventure of passing over to the religious experience of Gotama, Muhammed, and others and back again with new insights.

Jewett, Robert. *The Captain America Complex: The Dilemma of Zealous Nationalism.* Santa Fe, N.M.: Bear & Company, 1984. The temptations of Jesus to be a heroic Messiah without a struggle.

Larsen, Stephen. *The Shaman's Doorway.* New York, Harper & Row, 1976. Shows how the shaman's vision can expand our own awareness.

Turner, Victor. *The Forest of Symbols.* Ithaca, N.Y.: Cornell University Press, 1967. Study of the characteristics and experiences of those "betwixt and between" the stages of life.

Van Gennep, Arnold. *Rites of Passage.* Chicago: University of Chicago Press, 1960. The classic text on the liminal period in rites of passage.

## 8   THE HEROIC TASK

Fowler, James W. *Becoming Adult, Becoming Christian.* New York: Harper & Row, 1984. Narrative structures fitted and shaped into the master story of a rich, unique religious tradition.

Johnson, Robert. *He.* New York: Harper & Row, 1977. Jungian psychological concepts used to understand masculine psychology based on Parsifal's search for the Grail.

Lord, George DeForest. *Trials of the Self: Heroic Ideals In the Epic Tradition.* Hamden, Conn.: Archon Books, Shoestring Press, 1983. Odysseus and his quest from a Jungian perspective.

O'Collins, Gerald. *The Second Journey.* Ramsey, N.J.: Paulist Press, 1978. Difficulties faced during the adult years of life.

Thompson, Helen. *Journey Toward Wholeness.* Ramsey, N.J.: Paulist Press, 1982. Jungian model of adult spiritual growth.

Whitehead, Evelyn and James Whitehead. *Christian Life Patterns: The Psychological Challenges and Religious Invitations of Adult Life.* New York: Doubleday, 1979. The journey through life and its responsibilities.

## 9   THE GENTLE HERO

Christ, Carol P. *Diving Deep and Surfacing.* Boston: Beacon Press, 1980. Images of transformation that inform women's quest for identity.

Harding, M. Esther. *Woman's Mysteries Ancient and Modern.* New York: Harper & Row, 1976. A psychological interpretation of the feminine principle as portrayed in myth, story, and dreams.

Johnson, Robert. *She.* New York: Harper & Row, 1977. Jungian psychological concepts used to understand feminine psychology based on the myth of Psyche and Eros.

Ulanov, Ann. *Receiving Woman.* Philadelphia: Westminster Press, 1981. Studies the opportunities for all women to find their own particular style and skills.

Washbourn, Penelope. *Becoming Woman.* New York: Harper & Row, 1977. The quest for wholeness in female experience.

## 10   EVIL

Davis, Stephen T. ed. *Encountering Evil: Live Options in Theodicy.* Atlanta: John Knox Press, 1981. Five attempts to explain why there is evil in the world. With valuable critiques.

Kelsey, Morton. *Myth, History, and Faith.* Ramsey, N.J.: Paulist Press, 1974. The remythologizing of Christianity using a Jungian framework.

Russell, Jeffrey Burton. *The Devil.* Ithaca, N.Y.: Cornell University Press, 1977. History of the concept of the devil in Eastern and Western religions up to primitive Christianity.

Sanford, John. *Evil: The Shadow Side of Reality.* New York: Crossroad, 1981. Jungian approach to the problem of evil in myths.

Woods, William. *A History of the Devil.* New York: G. P. Putnam's Sons, 1974. The devil as the key to understanding human fears as they shape the world.

## 11    DEATH

Aries, Philippe. *The Hour of Our Death.* New York: Alfred A. Knopf, 1981. Meditation on changing attitudes in the West toward death from earliest Christianity up to the present.

Dunne, John S. *Time and Myth.* Notre Dame, Ind.: University of Notre Dame Press, 1973. Human confrontation with the inevitability of death in the cultural, personal, and religious spheres.

Henderson, Joseph L. and Maud Oakes. *The Wisdom of the Serpent.* New York: Collier Books, 1971. Myths of death, rebirth, and resurrection from a Jungian perspective. Initiation as spiritual education and psychic liberation.

Hick, John. *Death and Eternal Life.* San Francisco: Harper & Row, 1980. Encyclopedic collage of the insights on the afterlife as found in the world's major religions.

Shea, John. *Stories of God: An Unauthorized Biography.* Chicago: Thomas More Press, 1978. Perspectives on the meaning of the death of Jesus.

## 12    ESCHATOLOGY

Haughton, Rosemary. *Tales from Eternity.* New York: Seabury Press, 1973. The world of fairy tales and the spiritual search to live happily ever after.

Head, Joseph and S. L. Cranston, eds. *Reincarnation: The Phoenix Fire Mystery.* New York: Julian Press, 1977. A compilation of texts from East and West on death and rebirth, spanning the centuries.

Kelsey, Morton. *Resurrection: Release from Oppression.* Ramsey, N.J.: Paulist Press, 1985. Jungian approach to evil, death, resurrection. Section on Dante.

Luke, Helen. *Dark Wood to White Rose.* Pecos, N.M.: Dove Publications, 1975. Jungian psychology in context of Dante's *Divine Comedy.*

Sanford, John. *The Kingdom Within.* Ramsey, N.J.: Paulist Press, 1980. Biblical images of the Kingdom from a Jungian perspective.

Watts, Alan. *Myth and Ritual in Christianity.* Boston: Beacon Press, 1968. Universal character of symbols in myths and ceremonies of Holy Week signifying the inner meaning of life.

# INDEX

Gilgamesh, 46, 117
  commentary on myth of, 238-255
  myth of, 235-238
Good and evil, 74-77
Gotama. *See* Buddha
Graduation, 134
Greek myth, 45, 46, 50, 52, 56, 57, 73-74,
    91-92, 116, 119, 165, 168, 171-176,
    187-189, 214-215, 220, 243-244, 262-264
Gregory of Nyssa, 150

Hajj, 153
Hanuman, 162, 164, 167
Happy fault, 85-86, 107
Heaven, 277-281. *See also* Afterlife
Hebrew myth. *See* Jewish myth
Hell, 247-248
  in Dante, 275
Heracles, 117, 165, 170
Hermod, 240, 243, 245
Hero. *See also* Heroic quest
  as archetype, 32, 180-181
  childhood, 110-131
  origins, 115-120
  temptations, 141-143
  vision quest, 134-156
Heroic quest, 110-112
  as task, 159-181
  as gentle, 202-204
  as monomyth, 164-167
  as rite of passage, 167-171
Hesiod *Theogony*, 45, 50
Hindu myth, 27, 44, 45, 46, 47, 48, 57, 75,
    82, 85, 97, 119, 160-164, 214, 217
Holy Grail, myth of Parsifal and, 176-180
  commentary on myth of Parsifal and,
    178-180
Holy Week ritual, 85-86
Homer *Odyssey*, 171-176
Homeric hymn, 264
Horus, 259-262, 269, 271
Humans. *See also* Wholeness
  and creativity, 58-60, 82
  and freedom, 77-81, 83, 84
  and relationships, 83-84
  characteristics of, 81-84
  creation of, 47-50

*I Ching*, 40, 42, 49, 58
India. *See* Hindu myth
Indonesian myth, 48
Indra, 82
Infatuation, 189-193, 197
Initiation, 129-130, 136
Irish myth, 118
Ishtar, 235-236

Isis, 56
  commentary on myth of Osiris and, 262-282
  myth of Osiris and, 259-262
Izanagi and Izanami, 49

Jamaican myth, 48
Japanese myth, 46, 49, 243
Jesus. *See* Christ
Jewish myth, 45, 46, 47, 48, 49, 50, 56, 64-66,
    97, 117, 118, 221-223
*Job, Book of,* 221-223
Johnson, Robert, 194, 195
Jung, C.G., 22, 35, 80
  approach to myth of, 30-34
  archetypes, 31-33
  collective unconscious, 31
  criticism of, 34
  individuation, 33

Kali, 51, 53, 57, 97, 214
Knowledge of good and evil, 74-77
Krishna, 12, 51, 118, 119
Kubler-Ross, Elisabeth, *On Death and Dying,*
    251-252

Lent, ritual of, 154-155
Levi-Strauss, Claude, 21
Loki, myth of Balder and, 238-241
Lotus Sutra, 19

*Mahabharata,* 160
Mahayana Buddhism, 53, 85, 112, 228-229,
    244, 273, 278
Malaysian myth, 243
Malcolm X, 153
Marduk, 44
Marriage, 189-193
Mary, mother of Jesus, 55, 97, 104, 121,
    122, 124, 126
Maui, 118
  commentary on myths of, 91, 107
  myths of, 89-92
Mayan myth, 45
Mecca, 152-153
Mithras, 123
Monomyth, 164-167
Monsters, 127-129
Moody, Raymond, *Life After Life,* 244
Moses, 117, 121, 141-142, 166
Mother goddesses, 55-57
  functions of, 56-57
Muhammed, 18, 141
Muslim, 141, 272
Mystery religions, 268-271
Myth
  and Absolute Reality, 18-19
  approaches to, 21-34